SECURITY FOR COSTS IN INTERNATIONAL ARBITRATION

LLOYD'S ARBITRATION LAW LIBRARY
Series Editors: Robert Merkin KC and Hakeem Seriki

LLOYD'S ARBITRATION LAW LIBRARY

Arbitration Practice and Procedure
Interlocutory and Hearing Problems
Third Edition
Mark Cato, Julian Critchlow and Robert Merkin

Rules of Evidence in International Arbitration
An Annotated Guide
Nathan D. O'Malley

Injunctive Relief and International Arbitration
Hakeem Seriki

Singapore Arbitration Legislation
Annotated
Second Edition
Robert Merkin and Johanna Hjalmarsson

The Practice of International Commercial Arbitration
A Handbook for Hong Kong Arbitrators
Anselmo Reyes

Transnational Construction Arbitration
Key Themes in the Resolution of Construction Disputes
Edited by Renato Nazzini

Rules of Evidence in International Arbitration
An Annotated Guide
Second Edition
Nathan D. O'Malley

Merkin and Flannery on the Arbitration Act 1996
Sixth Edition
Robert Merkin and Louis Flannery

International Investment Dispute Awards
Facilitating Enforcement
Esra Yildiz Üstün

Arbitration Clauses and Third Parties
Asli Arda

Security for Costs in International Arbitration
Cameron Ford

For more information about this series, please visit: www.routledge.com/Lloyds-Arbitration-Law-Library/book-series/LALL

SECURITY FOR COSTS IN INTERNATIONAL ARBITRATION

CAMERON FORD

informa law
from Routledge

First published 2025
by Informa Law from Routledge
4 Park Square, Milton Park, Abingdon, Oxon OX14 4RN

and by Informa Law from Routledge
605 Third Avenue, New York, NY 10158

Informa Law from Routledge is an imprint of the Taylor & Francis Group, an informa business

British Library Cataloguing-in-Publication Data
A catalogue record for this book is available from the British Library

Library of Congress Cataloging-in-Publication Data
Names: Ford, Cameron (Lawyer), author.
Title: Security for costs in international arbitration / Cameron Ford.
Description: Abingdon, Oxon [UK] ; New York, NY : Routledge, 2025. | Series: Lloyd's arbitration law library | Includes bibliographical references and index.
Identifiers: LCCN 2024029624 (print) | LCCN 2024029625 (ebook) | ISBN 9781032766805 (hardback) | ISBN 9781032766881 (paperback) | ISBN 9781003479628 (ebook)
Subjects: LCSH: Arbitration (International law) | Arbitration and award. | International commercial arbitration. | Security for costs. | Investments, Foreign (International law)
Classification: LCC K2400 .F65 2025 (print) | LCC K2400 (ebook) | DDC 347/.09—dc23/eng/20240626
LC record available at https://lccn.loc.gov/2024029624
LC ebook record available at https://lccn.loc.gov/2024029625

ISBN: 978-1-032-76680-5 (hbk)
ISBN: 978-1-032-76688-1 (pbk)
ISBN: 978-1-003-47962-8 (ebk)

DOI: 10.4324/9781003479628

Typeset in Times New Roman
by Apex CoVantage, LLC

For Product Safety Concerns and Information please contact our EU representative:
GPSR@taylorandfrancis.com
Taylor & Francis Verlag GmbH, Kaufingerstraße 24, 80331 München, Germany

CONTENTS

Acknowledgements ix
Foreword xi
Table of Cases xiii
Table of Legislation xxvii

CHAPTER 1 INTRODUCTION TO THE CONTROVERSY 1
Introduction 1
The significance of security for costs 2
The controversy 2
The arguments 4
Annexure 1A: Arbitral legislation provisions relating to security for costs or interim measures 6
Annexure 1B: Arbitral rules relating to security for costs or interim measures 9

CHAPTER 2 THE EVOLUTION AND NATURE OF SECURITY FOR COSTS 11
The historical background and evolution of security for costs 11
The juridical bases of the facility 15
Prevention of abuse of process 15
Creditor protection 16
Clausula rebus sic stantibus 18
Contrary to the historical basis 20
Logical fallacy 20
Civil law basis for common law remedy, and replacing a universal basis with a limited basis 20
Substantive law basis for procedural remedy 21
Arbitral procedure governed by *lex arbitri* 22
Marginalises traditional discretionary considerations 22
Undermines utility of the facility 22
Excludes other deserving situations 23
The nature of the discretion 23
The consequences of an order for security for costs 24
Consequences of an application 24
Usual outcomes of an application 25
Consequences of an order 25
Maintaining access to justice 26

CHAPTER 3 POWER AND PROOF 28
Power 28
(1) Agreement of the parties 28
(2) *Lex arbitri* 29
(3) Institutional rules 31
(4) Case management powers 31
Burden and standard of proof 31
Burden of proof 31
Standard of proof 32

CHAPTER 4 HISTORICAL APPROACHES TO SECURITY FOR COSTS IN ARBITRATION 35
Introduction 35
ICC tribunal decisions 36
Swiss tribunal decisions 38
UK court decisions 1934–1997 40
LCIA statistics 44
Annexure 4A: ICC and Swiss tribunals' security for costs decisions 50

CHAPTER 5 TOTAL CIRCUMSTANCES FACTORS 53
Introduction 53
Financial factors in favour of security for costs 54
Liability factors in favour of security for costs 59
Conduct factors in favour of security for costs 62
Fairness factors against security for costs 64

CHAPTER 6 THE MECHANICS 70
Applications 70
Establishing the financial and compliance condition 70
Estimating costs 70
Seeking security from the claimant 71
Claimant's response to request 71
Making the application 71
Responding to the application 71
Orders 72
Costs of applications 72
Cross-undertakings 73
Quantum 73
Form of security 75

CHAPTER 7 PARTY CONSENT AND SECURITY FOR COSTS 77
No further barriers to arbitration and fees exhaust the issue 78
Assumption of the risk 80
(1) Unsupported by the juridical basis 81
(2) Freedom of contract is no longer unconstrained 81
(3) Consent to the transaction vs risk to being sued 83
(4) It assumes knowledge unlikely to be held 83

(5) It involves a non sequitur in assuming the claimant will not pay 83
(6) It assumes third party funding is not available 84
(7) It is inconsistent with the assumption of good faith 85
(8) It assumes higher risks of international trade 85
(9) It assumes freedom of choice 86
(10) The risk is unidentified, unquantified, un-correlated 86
(11) It applies only one aspect of the legal relationship 88
(12) It undermines the purpose of security for costs 88
(13) It fails to take account of the subtleties of each situation 89
(14) It presents an unnecessarily binary choice 89

CHAPTER 8 PARTY AUTONOMY, PROCEDURAL FAIRNESS, AND THE NATURE OF ARBITRATION 91
Introduction 91
(1) Party autonomy 91
(1a) Choices have consequences 92
(1b) The law chooses when the parties do not 94
(1c) Right to agree, not to veto retrospectively 96
(1d) Party autonomy has limits 96
Summary of party autonomy 99
(2) Security for costs and procedural fairness 99
(2a) Equal treatment and proper opportunity 100
(2b) Prejudgment of the merits 101
The nature of the merits enquiry 101
The requirements of the Model Law 101
The authoritative sources 102
(3) Contrary to the international nature of international commercial arbitration 103
(3a) Inhibits international trade 103
(3b) Counter to the transnationalisation of international arbitration 104
(3c) A misplaced English idiosyncrasy 104
(3d) Security for costs is out of place in an ICC arbitration 105
Reasons for choosing institutions 105
Reasons for choosing seats 106
Conclusion – security for costs is not out of place in ICC arbitration 106
(4) Enforcement issues 107
(4a) Enforcement is adequate without security for costs 107
(i) The modern basis of security for costs is not enforceability 107
(ii) The law should not withhold an additional remedy 108
(iii) Enforceability is not guaranteed 108
(4b) Tribunal's power to stay arbitration 108
(5) Basis of security for costs 111
(5a) Unfair to creditors 111
(5b) Inappropriate where no costs shift 112

CHAPTER 9 UTILITY OF SECURITY FOR COSTS IN INTERNATIONAL COMMERCIAL ARBITRATION 113
Introduction 113
A. For the immediate benefit of the parties 113

(1) Enforcement of costs awards 113
(2) Control mechanism against unmeritorious claims, improper conduct, and excessive cost and delay 115
(2a) Unmeritorious claims 116
(2b) Improper conduct 117
(2c) Cost and delay 117
(3) Procedural fairness and access to justice 119
(3a) Equality of treatment 119
(3b) Opportunity to present case 121
(3c) Access to justice 122
(4) Enabling tribunals to correct injustices 122
(5) Counter-balancing the judicialisation of arbitration 122
(6) Facilitate settlement 123
B. For the institution of arbitration 124
(7) A rich source of jurisprudence and guidance 124
(8) Uniformity within international commercial arbitration 124
(9) Attraction and competitiveness of international commercial arbitration 124
(10) Harmonisation of arbitration and litigation 125

CHAPTER 10 SECURITY FOR COSTS IN INTERNATIONAL INVESTMENT ARBITRATION 126
Introduction 126
The need 126
Juridical basis 127
Power 127
(1) Treaties 127
(2) ICSID 127
(3) UNCITRAL 128
(4) Institutional rules 128
(5) Inherent powers 128
(6) Court rules 128
Burden and standard of proof 129
Standard 129
UNCITRAL 129
ICSID 131
Exceptional circumstances 132
Quantum, form, orders, and costs 134

Index 135

ACKNOWLEDGEMENTS

This work is an adaptation of a doctoral thesis that was prompted by having to rule on an application for security for costs in an international commercial arbitration. It was seen then how little guidance there was for practitioners and tribunals on the topic and the apparently different approaches taken. Research for the thesis began with no preconception of what was or should be the approach and with a conscious effort to overcome any inherent bias towards the common law version of the facility. A view formed during the process of writing that international commercial arbitration would not be disadvantaged by a multifactorial approach taking the total circumstances into account without predisposition for or against security and with fairness as the touchstone. That formula contains the controls necessary to ensure justice in each case.

Particular thanks go to my three supervisors for their valued discipline and direction – Professor Jeff Giddins and Dr Benjamin Hayward of Monash University, and Justice Clyde Croft AM of the Supreme Court of Victoria who has kindly agreed to write a foreword.

I am grateful, too, for the authors on whom I have relied for their experience, insight and research. It is unfair to single out any for special mention, but Samaa Haridi's perceptive analysis of ICC decisions was particularly timely and valuable, Christine Sim's comprehensive coverage of investor-state arbitration was insightful, and Alan Redfern and Sam O'Leary's article gave additional reasons and encouragement for the approach taken.

Thanks also go to Arijit Sanyal for his much appreciated editing, proofreading and suggestions. Any oversights remain mine.

This book is dedicated to my father, Gordon, and to my younger brother, Mitchell, who would have been proud if its publication, and to my mother, Tess, who is.

Cameron Ford
June, 2024

FOREWORD

An order for a security for costs is well accepted as part of the procedural armoury of the common law courts to protect parties, defendants and third parties from expending time and money in litigation brought by an unsuccessful plaintiff with no funds or resources. In more recent times the latter may include access to the support of a litigation funder. These courts have utilised the security for costs measure, it seems, since the late 18th century, apparently in response to Continental courts applying such measures to English plaintiffs.[1] Against this background it may seem incongruous that international commercial arbitration, generally thought to be procedurally innovative and forward looking, should have neglected adopting an interim measure by way of security for costs. It is to this apparent paradox and the controversies that arise in the context of international commercial arbitration that Dr Cameron Ford addresses in this extremely valuable work.

The nature and extent of these controversies are examined in general and in more particular terms in Dr Ford's work. First, it is observed that international commercial arbitration is by its international nature attended by controversies. Its very purpose involves participants, lawyers and parties in different states who may bring with them different cultural attitudes and legal traditions. As observed by Dr Ford these drivers have been exacerbated by the very significant growth in international arbitration since the 1970s and, in part, due to the lack of a supranational authority which could address, particularly, delays and costs issues.

More directly linked to controversy in relation to the utilisation of security for costs orders as interim measures is the more general controversy as to the scope and powers which international arbitral tribunals should have to grant interim measures more broadly. As Dr Ford observes, it was only in 2006 that the *UNCITRAL Model Law on International Commercial Arbitration* was amended to provide a detailed suite of provisions for interim measures; provisions which sought to address then prevailing uncertainty with respect to the power and scope of any power in international arbitral tribunals to order such measures.

As a result, orders for security for costs have only been permitted and utilised to a very limited extent in international commercial arbitration. Consequently, this international disputes regime generally lacks an effective means of discouraging proceedings by impecunious claimants, with consequent detriment to respondents and others involved.

1 See *Fitzgerald v Whitmore* [1786] 1 TR 352.

Having contextualised the paradox, Dr Ford turns to consider the overarching question, 'Is security for costs as practised in international commercial litigation appropriate for international commercial arbitration?' The author's broad answer to this question is that significant benefits would flow to international commercial arbitration were security for costs orders added to the interim measures available to international arbitral tribunals.

In considering this question, Dr Ford explores a series of subsidiary questions, the discussion of which makes this work particularly valuable and informative. These are:

- Does international commercial arbitration take a more restrictive approach to security for costs and common law litigation, and, if so, why is that appropriate?
- Does any feature of international commercial arbitration or security for costs make either incompatible with the other or require a more restrictive approach for security for costs in international commercial arbitration than in common law litigation?
- What should be the approach of international arbitral tribunals, and the test to be applied, in determining applications for security for costs?

As I have sought to emphasise, this work by Dr Ford is an extremely valuable contribution to the jurisprudence, law and practice of international commercial arbitration. As such it is an essential addition to the library of academics, researchers and practitioners involved in international commercial litigation or international commercial arbitration.

The Hon. Justice Clyde Croft AM
Supreme Court of Victoria
6 June 2024

TABLE OF CASES

A. S.p.A. (Italy) v B AG (Germany) (Decision, Geneva Chamber of Commerce and Industry, 25 September 1997) 1.1, 4.8, 4.18, 4.19, 4.20, 4.26
ABC AG v Mr X Procedural Order, 27 November 2002 reported in (2005) 3.13, 4.20
Abigroup Limited v Sandtara Pty Limited [2002] NSWCA 45 .... 5.26
Ackerman v Ackerman [2011] EWHC 2183 (Ch) 5.21
ACN 006 577 162 Pty Ltd v Beauville Pty Ltd [2014] VSC 298 .... 5.30, 5.53
Adarsh Pandit v Viking Engineering Sdn Bhd [1998] 2 AMR 1009 .... 5.5
Adelaide (SA Pools and Spa) Manufacturing and Installation Pty Limited v Westcourt General Insurance Brokers Pty Limited [2016] SASC 60 .... 5.58
ADS Advertising v Central West Business Park [2005] VSC 265 .... 5.17
Al Jaber v Al Ibrahim [2019] EWHC 1136 (Comm) 5.21
Al-Koronky v Time-Life Entertainment Group Ltd [2006] EWCA Civ 1123 .... 5.29, 5.57, 9.19, 9.22, 9.34
Al-Koronky v Time-Life Entertainment Group Ltd [2007] 1 Costs LR 57 .... 2.46, 8.8
ALS & Assocs v AGM Marine Constructors Inc 557 F Supp 2d 180 (D Mass 2008) 9.33
Andrews v Zuccubarr Pty Ltd [2020] VSC 675 .... 2.45, 5.56, 5.58
Anglo Petroleum Ltd v TFB Mortgages Ltd [2004] EWHC 1177 (Ch) 5.14
Ansa Enterprises Pty Ltd v Australian Finance Group Ltd [2001] WASC 233 .... 5.19
Ansford v Plymouth Finance Co Ltd [1933] NLR 209 .... 5.68
Aoun v Bahri [2002] EWHC 29 (Comm); [2002] CLC 776 .... 5.21
Arcambel v Wiseman (1796) 3 US 306 .... 2.3
The Argenpuma [1984] 2 Lloyd's Rep 563 (CA) 8.59
Ariss v Express Interiors Pty Limited (In Liq) [1996] 2 VR 507 .... 5.58
Armstrong Strategic Management and Marketing Pty Ltd v Expense Reduction Analysts Group Pty Ltd [2013] NSWSC 457 .... 3.2
Asian Shield Warehousing Sdn Bhd (dalam likuidasi) v Leopad Holdings Sdn Bhd [2019] 1 AMR 456 .... 5.42
ASM Shipping Ltd of India v TTMI Ltd of England [2005] EWHC 2238 (Comm) 9.33
Astley v Austrust Ltd (1999) 197 CLR 1 .... 7.40
Atlantic Triton Company Limited v People's Revolutionary Republic of Guinea (ICSID Case No ARB/84/1) unreported decision (1984) 10.15
Attorney-General (Botswana) v Aussie Diamond Products Pty Ltd [2009] WASC 299 .... 2.42
Augusta Ventures Limited v Mt Arthur Coal Pty Limited [2020] FCAFC 194 .... 2.46, 5.7
Australian Battery Distributors Pty Ltd v Robert Bosch (Australia) Pty Ltd [2015] FCA 1164 .... 5.30, 5.48, 5.50, 5.52, 5.53, 5.54, 5.57, 5.58, 5.61, 6.26, 6.29, 7.44, 7.45, 8.32, 8.73
Australian Equity Investors v Colliers International (NSW) Pty Limited [2012] FCAFC 57 .... 5.30, 8.32

AWB Limited v Cole (No 2) [2006] FCA 913 ... 5.68
Bailey v Glaxosmithkline UK Ltd [2017] EWHC 3195 (QB); [2018] 4 WLR 7 ... 5.23
Ballard v Brookfield Australia Investments Ltd [2012] NSWCA 434 ... 2.47, 5.59
Bank Mellat v Helliniki Techniki SA [1984] 1 QB 291 ... 2.10, 4.22, 4.24, 4.26, 4.36, 5.8, 10.15
Bank of China (Hong Kong) Ltd v Twin Profit Ltd [2011] 3 HKC 59 ... 5.26
Barrow v Bankside Agency Ltd [1996] 1 SLR 257 ... 2.13
Barton v Minister for Foreign Affairs (1984) 2 FCR 463 ... 5.5, 5.7
Battenberg v Phillips [2017] NSWSC 1813 ... 5.5
Baygol Pty Ltd v Huntsman Chemical Co Australia Pty Ltd [2004] FCA 1248 ... 5.23
Bell Wholesale P/L v Gates Export Corporation (No 2) (1984) 8 ACLR 588 ... 8.73
Berry v Innovia [2014] FCA 357 ... 6.34, 6.39
Bevwizz Group Pty Ltd v Transport Solutions Pty Ltd [2008] NSWSC 1399 ... 5.14
Bhagat v Murphy [2000] NSWSC 892 ... 2.13, 5.35, 5.40
Bhattacharya v Freedman [2001] NSWSC 498 ... 2.8, 5.20, 5.21
Bilcon Ltd v Fegmay Investments Ltd [1966] 2 QB 221 ... 4.36
Birbilis Bros Pty Ltd v Chubb Fire and Security Pty Ltd [2018] QSC 3 ... 5.23, 6.30
BJ Crabtree (Insulation) Ltd v GPT Communications Systems (1990) 59 BLR 43 (CA) ... 5.15
Blue Oil Energy Pty Limited v Tan [2014] NSWCA 81 ... 6.33, 6.35
BNA v BNB [2020] 1 Lloyd's Rep 55 ... 8.12
Borrelli v Chan 2017 ONSC 1815 ... 5.23, 6.30
Bowring & Company (Insurance) Ltd v Corsi Partners Ltd [1994] 2 Lloyd's Rep 567 ... 2.6
BP Refinery (Westernport) Pty Ltd v Hastings Shire (1977) 180 CLR 266 ... 8.66
British Movietone News Ltd v London & District Cinemas Ltd [1952] AC 166 ... 2.28
Bruce Pie & Sons Pty Ltd v R H Mainwaring, English & Peldan [1985] 1 Qd R 401 ... 6.24
Bruder Expedition Pty Ltd v Leigh [2020] QCA 67 ... 5.62
Bryan E Fencot & Associates Pty Ltd v Eretta Pty Ltd (1987) 16 FCR 497 ... 2.47, 5.6, 5.44
Buckley v Bennell Design and Constructions Pty Ltd (1974) 1 ACLR 301 ... 1.4, 5.9
Burrows v Houda (No. 2) [2021] NSWDC 127 ... 5.46
Byrnes v John Fairfax Publications Pty Limited [2006] NSWSC 251 ... 5.19
Calderbank v Calderbank [1975] 3 All ER 333 (CA) ... 7.39
Carter v Mehmet [2021] NSWCA 32 ... 9.2
CBS v CBP [2021] SGCA 4 ... 3.9, 9.19
Cervo v Kingsley's Pty Ltd [2018] ACTSC 179 ... 5.26
Chang v Comcare Australia [1999] FCA 1677 ... 5.7
Chapel Road Pty Ltd v Australian Securities & Investments Commission (No 2) [2012] NSWSC 511 ... 5.44
Chaplair Limited v Kumari [2015] EWCA Civ 798 ... 5.26
Chapman v Michaelson [1908] 2 Ch 612, affirmed [1909] 1 Ch 238 ... 5.68
Charles Construction v Deriderian, 412 Mass 14 (1992) 16 ... 8.7
Chavez v Moreton Bay Regional Council [2009] QCA 348 ... 3.2
Cheffick Ltd v JDM Associates (1989) 43 BLR 52 (CA) ... 5.21
Chen Siew Lee v Tan Bak Lee [2018] AMEJ 0540; [2018] 11 MLJ 34 ... 5.1
Chen v Kevin McNamara & Son Pty Ltd [2012] VSCA 229 ... 5.26
Cherry v Read (Full Court of the Federal Court of Australia, 21 November 1996) ... 5.7, 5.21
China Machine New Energy Corp v Jaguar Energy Guatemala LLC [2020] SGCA 12 ... 9.33
Choice Constructions Pty Ltd v Janceski [2011] WASCA 358 ... 5.26
Christou v Stanton Partners Australasia Pty Ltd [2011] WASCA 176 ... 1.4
Chuku v Chuku [2017] EWHC 541 (Ch) ... 5.11
Citizens for Foreign Aid Reform Inc v Canadian Jewish Congress (1999) 36 CPC (4th) 266 (BCSC) ... 2.9

City of Moscow Gas Co v International Financial Society (1872) 7 Ch App 225 .... 5.16
CJSC Golden East Co. and CJSC Vostokneftegaz Co. v Mongolia, Order on Interim Measures (UNCITRAL, 2 September 2008) 10.21
Claimants 1–2 v Respondents 1–16 (Order, ZCC, 19 December 2008) reported in (2010) 1.4, 3.13, 4.20
Classic Ceramic Importers Pty Ltd v Ceramic Antiga SA (1994) 13 ACSR 263 .... 5.47
Clubb v Edwards [2019] HCA 11 .... 2.39
CNLT (Far East) Berhad v JCT Limited [2018] 1 LNS 1127 .... 5.19
Co-operative Central Bank Ltd v YM Raja Tan Sri Aznam Raja Hj Ahmad [2004] 5 CLJ 375 .... 5.42
Coca-Cola Amatil Victoria Ltd v P A A Enterprises Pty Ltd [2003] VSCA 135 .... 2.38, 5.54, 7.19, 7.45
Codelfa Construction Pty Ltd v State Rail Authority of NSW (1982) 149 CLR 337 .... 2.28
Cody v Live Board Holdings Ltd [2015] NSWSC 1790 .... 5.30, 8.32
Cody v Live Board Holdings Ltd [2017] NSWSC 308 .... 5.30, 8.32
Colmax Glass Pty Ltd v Polytrade Pty Ltd [2013] VSC 311 .... 5.15
Concrete Constructions v Dalma Formwork [1999] NSWCA 16 .... 5.15
Concrete Mining Structures Pty Ltd v Cellcrete Australia Pty Ltd (No 2) [2018] SASC 27 .... 5.57
Coonwarra Pty Ltd v Cornonero Pty Ltd [2018] VSC 333 .... 2.38, 6.24
Copson v DCM Coffee & Donuts Pty Ltd (1996) ATPR 41–505 .... 5.14
Cowell v Taylor (1885) 31 ChD 34 .... 5.6
Craven v Globe Valley Pty Ltd [2018] QDC 155 .... 5.19, 5.38, 5.56, 5.68
Crocker v Toys 'R' Us (Australia) Pty Ltd (No 3) [2015] FCA 728 .... 5.38
Crozat v Brogden [1894] 2 QB 30 .... 2.6
The Cultural Intelligence Project Pty Ltd v The Entourage Education Group Pty Ltd (No 2) [2021] FCCA 1317 .... 2.38
Cunningham v Olliver (Federal Court of Australia, 21 November 1994) 5.7
D'Hormusgee & Co v Grey (1882) 10 QBD 13 .... 5.66
Daimler AG v Bauman 571 U S 117 (2014) 8.22
Dalian Huarui Heavy Industry International Company Ltd v Clyde & Co Australia [2020] WASC 132 .... 6.31
Dalma Formwork Pty Limited v Concrete Constructions Group Ltd [1998] NSWSC 472 .... 5.49
David Clarke Air Conditioning Pty Ltd v Quann [No 2] [2016] WASC 176 .... 5.25
David v Loblaw 2018 ONSC 6469 .... 5.23, 6.30
Davis Contractors Ltd v Fareham Urban District Council [1956] AC 696 .... 2.28, 2.29
Dee-Tech Pty Ltd v Neddam Holdings Pty Ltd [2009] NSWSC 1095 .... 5.47
Del Bosco v Outtrim [2008] NSWSC 105 .... 5.50
Dennis v Joukhador [2021] NSWSC 870 .... 5.58
Dense Medium Separation Powders Pty Ltd v Gondwana Chemicals Pty Ltd [2011] NSWCA 84 .... 6.39
Dermajaya Properties Sdn Bhd v Permium Properties Sdn Bhd and another [2002] SGHC 53 .... 6.23
DIF III Global Co-Investment Fund LP v BBLP LLC [2016] VSC 401 .... 2.44, 5.23, 6.30, 6.34, 6.37, 6.39
Donoghue v Stevenson [1932] AC 562 .... 7.16
Doree Industries (M) Sdn Bhd v Sri Ram & Co [2007] 1 MLJ 722 .... 5.6
DSQ Property Co Ltd v Lotus Cars Ltd [1987] 1 WLR 127 .... 2.6, 2.7, 2.8, 2.9, 2.10, 5.8, 8.54
Dumrul v Standard Chartered Bank [2010] EWHC 2625 .... 5.15
Dymocks Franchise Systems (NSW) Pty Ltd v Chapter Three Pty Ltd [2022] NSWSC 35 .... 5.26

Edenham Pty Ltd v Meares (No 2) [2016] WASC 302 .... 5.15, 5.16
Enagic Co Ltd v Horizons (Asia) Pty Ltd (No 2) [2020] FCA 1240 .... 5.25
Enka Insaat Ve Sanayi AS v OOO Insurance Company Chubb [2020] UKSC 38 .... 4.47, 7.6, 8.7, 8.12, 8.13, 8.15, 8.16
Equity Access Ltd v Westpac Banking Corporation [1989] ATPR 40–972 .... 5.61
Eugene Kazmin v Republic of Latvia, ICSID Case No. ARB/17/5, Procedural Order No. 6 .... 10.3, 10.16, 10.17, 10.27, 10.31, 10.32, 10.33, 10.40, 10.41, 10.42
The Eugenia [1964] 2 QB 226 .... 2.29
Everwarm Ltd v BN Rendering Ltd [2019] EWHC 1985 (TCC) 5.41
FA Tamplin Steamship Co Ltd v Anglo-Mexican Petroleum products Co Ltd [1916] 2 AC 397 .... 2.28
Façade Treatment Engineering Pty Ltd (in liq) v Brookfield Multiplex Constructions Pty Ltd [2015] VSCA 169 .... 5.62
Faridah Begum bte Abdullah v Dato' Michael Chong [1995] 2 AMR 1191 .... 5.1
Faridah Begum bte Abdullah v Dato' Michael Chong [1995] 2 MLJ 404 .... 5.1, 5.6
Fat Mel's Restaurant Ltd v Canadian Northern Shield Insurance Co (1993) 76 BCLR (2d) 231 (CA) 2.9
Fat-sel Pty Limited v Brambles Holdings Limited (1985) 3 ACLC 312 .... 5.52
Ferris v Plaister (1994) 34 NSWLR 474 .... 3.2, 7.5, 7.31, 7.32, 8.20, 8.39
Fiduciary Ltd v Morningstar Research Pty Ltd (2004) 208 ALR 564 .... 5.11, 5.50, 5.66
Fiduciary v Morningstar Research [2004] NSWSC 664 .... 2.6
Firehold Land Co v Spargo [1868] WN 94 .... 5.16
Firth v Halloran (1926) 38 CLR 261 .... 2.28
Fitzgerald v Whitmore (1786) 1 TR 362 .... 2.7, 2.8, 5.1, 8.38, 8.39, 8.43
Flender Werft AG v Aegean Maritime Ltd [1990] 2 Lloyd's Rep 27 .... 2.9, 2.44, 2.46, 4.36, 5.58, 7.22, 7.24, 7.26, 7.42, 7.44, 8.39, 8.59, 9.5
Flower & Hart v White Industries (Qld) Pty Limited (1999) 87 FCR 134 .... 5.36
Forest Pty Ltd v Keen Bay Pty Ltd (1991) 4 ACSR 107 .... 8.73
Frantonios Marine Services Pte Ltd v Kay Swee Tuan [2008] 4 SLR 224 .... 5.31
Frigger v Banning (No 11) [2020] FCA 1257 .... 5.46
G.M. Combined (U) Limited v A.K. Detergents (U) Limited [1996] SCC OnLine UGSC 14 .... 5.10
Gateway Kand Pte Ltd v Turner (East Asia) Pte Ltd [1988] 1 MLJ 416 UK 5.55
General Trade Industries Pty Ltd (in liquidation) v AGL Energy Limited (No 2) [2023] FCA 556 .... 5.35
George Mitchell (Chesterhall) Ltd v Finney Lock Seeds Ltd [1983] QB 284, affirmed on appeal in [1983] 2 AC 803 .... 7.14, 7.15
Gerald Metals SA v Timis [2016] EWHC 2327 (Ch) 8.23
Global Access Ltd v Educationdynamics LLC [2009] QSC 373 .... 5.31
Global Finance Group Pty Ltd (in liq) v Marsden Partners [2004] WASC 52 .... 5.23
Gobain RF Pty Ltd v Maax Spa Corporation Pty Ltd [2004] VSC 335 .... 5.13
Goldquest International Ltd v Teh Leong Kiat [2003] AMEJ 0021; [2003] 2 CLJ 402 .... 5.1
Goldtrail Travel Ltd v Aydin [2017] UKSC 57 .... 5.55, 5.58
Goldus Pty Ltd (Subject to a Deed of Company Arrangement) v Cummins [2020] FCA 959 .... 9.38
Goldus Pty Ltd v Cummins (No 2) [2020] FCA 971 .... 5.19
Gomba Holdings (UK) Ltd v Minories Finance Ltd (No 2) [1993] Ch 171 .... 5.26
Grace Christian Chapel v Canaan Holdings Pty Ltd (Security for Costs) [2019] VSC 5 .... 5.13, 5.16

Green (as liquidator of Arimco Mining Pty Ltd) v CGU Insurance Ltd [2008] NSWCA 148 ... 2.8
Green (as liquidator of Arimco Mining Pty Ltd) v CGU Insurance Ltd [2008] NSWSC 449 ... 2.8
Green v CGU Insurance Ltd [2008] NSWCA 148 ... 5.9, 5.10, 5.11, 5.21, 5.23, 5.34, 5.43, 5.58, 6.24, 7.3, 7.42, 8.73
Grey v Harrison [1997] 2 VR 359 ... 2.39
Grocon Group Holdings Pty Limited v Infrastructure NSW [2020] NSWSC 1194 ... 2.47, 3.10, 5.58, 6.24
Guaranteed Asphalt (London) Ltd (in Administrative Receivership) v Taylor Woodrow Construction Ltd [1998] EWHC Technology 317 ... 8.62
Haidakota (M) Sdn Bhd v Tan Tiam Chai [2009] 1 CLJ 699); [2008] MLJU 654 ... 5.55
Han v Cho 2008 BCSC 1229 ... 2.8, 2.37, 7.44, 8.38, 8.39, 8.43
Hapisun Pty Ltd v Rikys & Moylan Pty Ltd [2013] VSC 730 ... 5.27
Hardingham v RP Data Pty Limited [2020] FCA 1062 ... 5.58
Harlequin Property (SVG) ltd v Wilkins Kennedy [2015] EWCA 1122 (TCC) ... 6.40
Harris v Wallis [2006] EWHC 630 (Ch) ... 5.21
Healy Air-conditioning Pty Ltd v Oracle Corporation Pty Ltd (2003) 21 ACLC 866 ... 5.23
Heller Factors Pty Ltd v John Arnold's Surf Shop Pty Ltd (in Liq) (1979) 4 ACLR 492 ... 5.47
Hello Quo the Movie Ltd v Duroc Media [2014] EWHC (Ch) 4622 ... 5.66
Hercules Carparking Systems 2004 Pty Ltd v Gennie Holdings Pty Ltd [2021] NSWDC 50 ... 9.18
Hession v Century 21 South Pacific Limited (1992) 28 NSWLR 120 ... 5.10
Hitachi Shipbuilding & Engineering Co Ltd v Viafiel Compania Naviera SA [1981] 2 Lloyd's Rep 498 (CA) ... 4.36
Hogan v Hogan (No 2) [1924] 2 IR 14 ... 5.64
Hong Kong Company v Vendor Company (Award, SIAC, 21 October 2011) reported in [2012] 1 Singapore Arbitration Awards 127 ... 9.16, 9.18
Hudson Strumpffabrik GMBH v Bentley Engineering Co Ltd [1962] 2 QB 587 ... 2.44, 2.46, 4.26, 4.30, 4.36, 7.6, 8.59
Hutchison Telephone (UK) v Ultimate Response Ltd [1993] BCLC 308 ... 5.14, 5.18, 5.48
I J R Homes Pty Ltd v Toma (Building and Property) [2016] VCAT 1626 ... 5.21
ICC Case No 6632 of 1993 ... 4.48
ICC Case No 6697 (1990) Societe Casa v Societe Cambior 1992 Rev Arb 135 ... 1.9, 4.48
ICC Case No 7047 (1994), Final Award reported in ICC, Special Supplement 2014: Procedural Decisions in ICC Arbitration 70 (ICC, 2014) ... 4.12
ICC Case No 7489 (1994), Final Award, reported in (1999) 8(2) ICC International Court of Arbitration Bulletin 68 ... 4.12, 4.42, 7.29
ICC Case No 11399 (2001), Interim Award, reported in ICC, Special Supplement 2011: Interim, Conservatory and Emergency Measures in ICC Arbitration 36 ... 4.12, 4.13
ICC Case No 11405 (2002), Interim Award, reported in (2006) 17(2) ICC International Court of Arbitration Bulletin 96 ... 4.12
ICC Case No 300273– 2103, Procedural Order No 7, Swiss Chambers' Arbitration Institution, (4 September 2014) reported in (2018) ... 5.57
ICC Case No 14661, Procedural Order No. 1, December 2007, reported in ICC, Special Supplement 2014: Procedural Decisions in ICC Arbitration 74 (ICC, 2014) ... 4.12, 4.13
ICC Case No 14661, Procedural Order No. 1, December 2008, reported in ICC, Special Supplement 2014: Procedural Decisions in ICC Arbitration 76 (ICC, 2014) ... 4.12, 4.13
ICC Case No 12228, Procedural Order of 11 June 2003, reported in ICC, Special Supplement 2010: Decisions on ICC Arbitration Procedure: A Selection

of Procedural Orders Issue by Arbitral Tribunals Acting Under the ICC Rules of Arbitration (2003–2004) (ICC, 2010) 4.9, 4.12
ICC Case No 12393, Procedural Order of 30 July 2003, reported in ICC, Special Supplement 2010: Decisions on ICC Arbitration Procedure: A Selection of Procedural Orders Issue by Arbitral Tribunals Acting Under the ICC Rules of Arbitration (2003–2004) (ICC, 2010) 4.12
ICC Case No 12035, Procedural Order, 6 June 2003, reported in ICC, Special Supplement 2010: Decisions on ICC Arbitration Procedure: A Selection of Procedural Orders issue by Arbitral Tribunals acting under the ICC Rules of Arbitration (2003–2004) (ICC, 2010) 1.14, 4.9, 4.12, 4.13
ICC Case No 12732, Procedural Order, January 2006, ICC Special Supplement 2014: Procedural Decisions in ICC Arbitration 62 (ICC, 2014) 4.12
ICC Case No 12853, Procedural Order, December 2003, ICC Special Supplement 2010: Decisions on ICC Arbitration Procedure: A Selection of Procedural Orders Issue by Arbitral Tribunals Acting Under the ICC Rules of Arbitration (2003–2004) 4.12, 4.13
ICC Case No 13359, Procedural Order, February 2006, ICC Special Supplement 2014: Procedural Decisions in ICC Arbitration 63 (ICC, 2014) 4.9, 4.12, 4.13
ICC Case No 13620, Procedural Order, May 2006, reported in ICC, Special Supplement 2014: Procedural Decisions in ICC Arbitration 65 (ICC, 2014) 4.12
ICC Case No 14020, Procedural Order, November 2006, reported in ICC, Special Supplement 2014: Procedural Decisions in ICC Arbitration 67 (ICC, 2014) 4.12
ICC Case No 14355, Procedural Order, January 2007, reported in ICC, Special Supplement 2014: Procedural Decisions in ICC Arbitration 70 (ICC, 2014) 1.14, 4.9, 4.12, 4.13, 7.30
ICC Case No 14433, Procedural Order, October 2008, reported in ICC, Special Supplement 2014: Procedural Decisions in ICC Arbitration 73 (ICC, 2014) 1.9, 4.12, 4.13, 4.42
ICC Case No 14993, Procedural Order, reported in ICC, Special Supplement 2014: Procedural Decisions in ICC Arbitration 77 (ICC, 2014) 4.10, 4.12, 4.13, 7.9
ICC Case No 15218, Procedural Order, July 2008, reported in ICC, Special Supplement 2014: Procedural Decisions in ICC Arbitration 79 (ICC, 2014) 1.14, 4.12, 4.13
ICC Case No 23904, Procedural Order, 27 March 2020 .... 2.42
ICC Case No ICC 12542/EC, Procedural Order, 19 December 2003, reported in (2005) 3.10, 3.12, 3.13, 4.15, 4.19, 4.20
ICC 2020–227, Procedural Order, reported in (2020) 2 ICC Dispute Resolution Bulletin 77 .... 3.13
ICC-PO-2020–224, Procedural Order, Security for Costs and Claim Under the ICC Rules of Arbitration: Rare, But Possible' (2020) 2 ICC Dispute Resolution Bulletin 98 .... 4.12
ICC-PO2–2020–225Procedural Order, Security for Costs and Claim under the ICC Rules of Arbitration: Rare, But Possible (2020) 2 ICC Dispute Resolution Bulletin 100 .... 4.13
ICC-PO3–2020–227, Procedural Order, Security for Costs and Claims Under the ICC Rules of Arbitration: Rare But Possible (2020) 2 ICC Dispute Resolution Bulletin 106 .... 4.12
ICC-PO6–2020–226, Procedural Order, Security for Costs and Claims Under the ICC Rules of Arbitration: Rare But Possible' (2020) 2 ICC Dispute Resolution Bulletin 105 .... 4.12
ICC, PO3–2020–228, Procedural Order, Security for Costs and Claim under the ICC Rules of Arbitration: Rare, But Possible (2020) 2 ICC Dispute Resolution Bulletin 109 .... 7.30
Idoport Pty Limited & Anor v National Australia Bank Limited [2001] NSWSC 744 .... 1.4, 2.44,

2.47, 5.42, 5.58, 7.24, 7.26
Indigenous Business Australia v Kani (No 2) [2012] NTSC 37 ... 5.26
Infinity Distribution Ltd (in administration) v The Khan Partnership LLP [2021] EWCA Civ 565 ... 1.13, 2.9, 2.11
Inforica Inc v CGI Information Systems and Management Consultants Inc 2008 CanLII 60706 ... 7.7
Ingot Capital Investments Pty Ltd v Macquarie Equity Capital Markets Ltd [2002] NSWSC 609 ... 2.6
Insigma Technology Co Ltd v Alstom Technology Ltd [2009] 3 SLR 936 ... 8.17
Intertoll Ics Cecons. O & M Co. Pvt. Ltd. v National Highways Authority of India [2013] 135 DRJ 160 ... 5.9, 5.13, 5.23, 5.68
Interwest Ltd v Tricontinental Corporation Ltd (1991) 5 ACSR 621 ... 5.13, 5.14, 5.66
J & M O'Brien Enterprises Pty Ltd v Shell Company of Australia Ltd (1983) 70 FLR 261 ... 5.65
James v Australia and New Zealand Banking Group Ltd (1985) 9 FCR 422 ... 8.65
Jana Pty Ltd v Ezistripdemo Pty Ltd [2017] NSWSC 1286 ... 5.26
Jazabas Pty Ltd v Haddad [2007] NSWCA 291 ... 5.50, 8.32
Jebb v Superior Lawns Australia Pty Ltd [2019] WASCA 208 ... 5.19
Jenred Properties Ltd v Ente Nazionale Italiano per it Turismo (1985) Financial Times, October 29 (CA) ... 5.41
Jivraz v Hashwani [2010] EWCA Civ 712 ... 8.22
Jivraz v Hashwani [2011] UKSC 40 ... 8.22, 8.23
John Bishop (Caterers) Ltd v The National Union Bank Ltd [1973] 1 All ER 707 ... 5.66
Johnson v Gore Wood and Co [2002] 2 AC 1 ... 2.13
Jones v Gurney [1913] WN72 ... 5.11
JS Ocean Liner LLC, Bur Dubai (UAE) v m.v. Golden Progress [2007] 2 Bom CR 1 ... 5.38
K/S A/S Bani v Korea Shipbuilding and Engineering Corporation [1987] 2 Lloyd's Rep 445 ... 4.26, 4.32, 4.36, 9.39
Kabab-Ji SAL v Kout Food Group [2021] UKSC 48 ... 8.3, 8.12, 8.13
Kassiopi Maritime Co. Ltd. v MTAL Layyah [2014] 5 Bom CR 566 ... 5.1
Keary Developments Ltd v Tarmac Construction Ltd [1995] 3 All ER 534 (CA) ... 2.9, 2.47, 4.36, 5.29, 5.55, 5.58, 8.32
Keary Developments v Tarmac Construction Ltd (Court of Appeal, 13 April 1994) ... 7.26
Kejuruteraan Taipan (M) Sdn Bhd v Loh & Loh Construction Sdn Bhd [2006] AMEJ 0071; [2007] 1 MLJ 578 ... 5.42
Kelly, re Halifax Investment Services Pty Ltd (in liq) (No 10) [2020] FCA 1146 ... 5.46
Kiefel v Victoria [2014] FCA 604 ... 2.11, 5.21, 5.38
King v Burdett (1820) 4 B & Ald 140 ... 5.57
Knight v Beyond Properties Pty Ltd [2005] FCA 764 ... 5.6, 5.7
Kolyada v Yurov [2014] EWHC 2575 (Comm) ... 5.21
KP Cable Investments Pty Ltd v Meltglow Pty Ltd (1995) 56 FCR 189 ... 2.47
Kronemann v Papaioannou [2020] VSCA 275 ... 2.38
Kropp v Swaneset Bay Golf Course Ltd (1997) 29 BCLR (3d) 252 (CA) ... 2.9
Kupang Resources Ltd v Elias [2018] NSWSC 1553 ... 6.29
KVC Rice Intertrade Co Ltd v Asian Mineral Resources Pte Ltd [2017] SGHC 32 ... 8.12
Lall v 53–55 Hall Street Pty Ltd [1978] 1 NSWLR 310 ... 5.35, 5.38
Launer v Sommerfeld (1964) 45 DLR (2d) 293 ... 2.8
LCIA, Case No. 132551, Procedural Order No. 4, (2014) reported in (2018) ... 1.4, 2.44, 2.46, 4.15
Le Mesurier v Ferguson (1903) 20 TLR 32 ... 5.6

Lee v Australia and New Zealand Banking Group Ltd [2013] QCA 284 .... 5.26
Les & Zelda Investments Pty Ltd v Whitehaven Coal Ltd [2020] 1 NSWSC 1091 .... 1.4, 2.44, 5.43, 5.59, 6.21, 6.22, 6.25, 6.28, 6.29
Levi v Swaab [2020] NSWSC 1119 .... 5.46
Li v New South Wales [2013] NSWCA 165 .... 2.47
Liberty Grove (Concord) Pty Ltd v Mirvac Projects Pty Ltd [2008] NSWSC 48 .... 5.44
Lima Orthopaedics Australia Pty Ltd v Proactive Ortho Pty Ltd [2021] NSWSC 1014 .... 5.14, 6.26
Lina Soo (F) v Ngu Chu Chiong & Ngu Choo Chiong [1999] 1 LNS 76; [1999] MLJU 442 .... 5.1
Ling v Beyond Development Group Pty Ltd [2021] NSWSC 1251 .... 2.42
Liu v Resi Ventures Leakes Pty Ltd (No 2) [2019] VSC 638 .... 5.7
Live Board Holdings Ltd v Cody Live Pty Ltd [2017] NSWCA 302 .... 5.30
Lo Surdo v Public Trustee [2003] NSWSC 837 .... 5.5
Lobster Group Ltd v Heidelberg Graphic Equipment Ltd [2008] EWHC 413 (TCC) 6.27
Loque v Hansen Technologies Ltd [2003] FCA 81; (2003) 125 FCR 590 .... 5.5, 5.7, 5.21
LPH Developments Pty Ltd v Jamieson Moore Pty Ltd [2015] WASC 416 .... 5.15, 5.16
LRSM Enterprise Pty Ltd v Zurich Australian Insurance Limited [2014] NSWCA 88 .... 5.56, 5.58
Lucas v Yorke (1983) 58 ALJR 20 .... 2.49
Luminous Crossroads Sdn Bhd v Lim Kong Huat Construction [2001] 4 AMR 4861; [2002] 5 CLJ 100; [2001] MLJU 475 .... 5.1
Lynx Engineering Consultants Pty Ltd v The ANI Corporation Limited (No 3) [2010] FCA 32 .... 5.31
M A Productions Pty Ltd v Austarama Television Pty Ltd (1982) 7 ACLR 97 .... 5.50
Maatschappij voor Fondsenbezit v Shell Transport and Trading Co [1923] 2 KB 166 .... 5.48
Madgwick v Kelly [2013] FCAFC 61 .... 5.48
Maharashtra State Electricity Board v Datar Switchgear Ltd. [2003] 2 Bom CR 81 .... 5.20, 5.29
Manassen Holdings Pty Ltd v Commercial & General Corporation Pty Ltd (No 2) [2019] SASC 183 .... 5.26
Manuel García Armas et al. v Bolivarian Republic of Venezuela, PCA Case No. 2016–08, Procedural Order 9, Decision on Respondent's Request for Provisional Measures (20 June 2018) 10.3, 10.32, 10.33
Maples v Hughes [2002] NSWSC 617 .... 5.66
Marjorie Ilma Knox v John Vere Evelyn Deane [2011] CCJ Appeal No. 8 .... 5.6, 5.12
Maronis Holdings Ltd v Nippon Credit Australia Ltd [2000] NSWSC 994 .... 5.23
Martin v State of New South Wales [2011] NSWLEC 20 .... 5.68
Matthews v SPI Electricity Pty Ltd & Ors (No 9) [2013] VSC 671 .... 7.11, 7.42, 8.65
Mavani v Ralli Bros Ltd [1973] 1 WLR 468 .... 4.36
Maxim's Caterers Limited v Magnona Pty Ltd (No 1) [2010] FCA 450 .... 6.34, 6.37, 6.39
Mayfair Trading Co Pty Ltd v Dreyer (1958) 101 CLR 428 .... 5.68
Mbuzi v Hall [2010] QSC 359 .... 5.20, 5.38, 5.40, 5.56
McHenry v Lewis (1882) 22 Ch D 397 .... 5.34
Mechanalysis Sdn Bhd v Appraisal Property Management Sdn Bhd [2016] AMEJ 1263; [2016] 11 MLJ 566 .... 5.11
Mecrus Pty Ltd v Industrial Energy Pty Ltd (2015) 327 ALR 523 .... 7.45
Melioruchy v Melioruchy (1750) 2 Ves Sen 24 .... 2.6, 2.8
Melunu Pty Ltd v Claron Constructions Pty Ltd [2004] NSWSC 1064 .... 5.49

Melville v Craig Nowlan and Associates Pty Limited [2002] NSWCA 32; 54 NSWLR 82 ... 2.49, 5.7, 5.34, 5.62, 7.42
Merribee Pastoral Industries Pty Ltd v Australia and New Zealand Banking Group Ltd (1998) 193 CLR 502 ... 1.13, 2.11, 2.40, 5.4
Metal Storm Limited (in liquidation), Re [2018] NSWSC 900 ... 5.57
Metropolitan Bank Ltd v Pooley (1885) 10 App Cas 210 ... 2.2
Michael Wilson & Partners, Limited v Emmott [2020] NSWCA 139; [2020] NSWCA 245 ... 2.44, 5.46, 9.38
Milfoil Pty Ltd v CBA [2020] VSCA 223 ... 5.41, 6.24, 6.26
Minister for Immigration and Ethnic Affairs of the Commonwealth of Australia, Re; Ex parte Lai Qin (1997) 186 CLR 622 ... 9.6
Mio Art Pty Ltd v Mango Boulevard Pty Ltd [2018] QSC 31 ... 5.16
Mohareb v Fairfax Media Publications Pty Ltd [2019] NSWSC 1685 ... 2.49, 5.7, 5.21, 5.58
Mohareb v Harbour Radio Pty Ltd [2020] NSWCA 231 ... 2.49, 5.6, 5.7, 5.19, 5.21, 5.37, 5.42, 5.59, 6.26
Morris v Hanley [2000] NSWSC 957 ... 2.2, 2.8, 5.7, 5.34, 5.35, 5.42, 7.42
Morton v Palmer (1882) 9 QBD 89 ... 5.19
Motakov Ltd v Commercial Hardware Suppliers Pty Ltd (1952) 70 WN (NSW) 64 ... 5.14
Mr D v Ms P [2020] NSWCA 174 ... 5.6
Mr X v Mrs Y, Decision, 2003 reported in (2010) ... 4.20
Muga Developers Limited v Njehu Gatabaki [2017] SCC OnLine Ken 1164 ... 5.21
Nasser v United Bank of Kuwait [2002] 1 WLR 1868 ... 9.18, 9.30
National Bank of New Zealand Ltd v Donald Export Trading Ltd [1980] 1 NZLR 97 ... 6.24
National Carriers Ltd v Panalpina (Northern) Ltd [1981] AC 675 ... 2.28, 2.29
Neck v Taylor [1893] 1 QB 560 ... 5.14
Neo Modular Pty Ltd v Enderby Apartments Pty Ltd (No 2) [2020] WASC 375 ... 6.13
New Fenix Compagnie Anonyme D'Assurances de Madrid v General Accident, Fire, and Life Assurance Corp Ltd [1911] 2 KB 619 ... 5.14, 5.16
Ninan v Westpac Banking Corporation [2015] WASCA 94 ... 5.56
Northampton Coal, Iron, and Waggon Co v Midland Waggon Co (1878) 7 Ch D 500 ... 5.10
Notcutt v Universal Equipment Co (London) Ltd [1986] 1 WLR 641 ... 2.28
Nylex Corporation Pty Ltd v Basell Australia Pty Ltd [2009] VSC 97 ... 2.44, 5.23
Nyoni v Pharmacy Board of Australia [2018] FCA 1313 ... 5.19, 5.37, 5.38, 5.40, 5.56
NZX Limited v Ralex Commodities Pty Limited [2012] NZHC 1585 ... 5.16
Omar Ali bin Mohd v Syed Jafaralsadeg bin Abdulkadir Alhadad [1995] 3 SLR 388 ... 5.31
Omni Bridgeway (Fund 5) Cayman Invt. Ltd v Bugsby Property LLC [2023] EWHC 2755 (Comm) ... 6.30
Organizing Committee Commonwealth Games v Nussli (Switzerland) Ltd. [2014] SCC OnLine Del 883 ... 5.5
Orr v Lusute Pty Ltd (1987) 72 ALR 617 ... 2.8
Oswal, Re [2016] VSC 52 ... 5.41, 5.43, 5.44, 5.45, 6.24
Owens v Midway Amusements Pty Ltd [1986] ACTSC 64 ... 7.40
Owners Corporation PS623721 v Shangri-La Construction Pty Ltd (Building and Property) [2021] VCAT 581 ... 5.27
Owners of the Panamax Alexander v Registered Owners of the NYK Falcon [2022] EWHC 478 (Admlty) ... 5.41
Pacific Mirage Limited v Le Breton [2014] FCAFC 46 ... 5.26
Palermo Seafoods Pty Ltd v Lunapas [2014] NSWSC 792 ... 5.68
Pathway Investments Pty Ltd v National Australia Bank Limited [2012] VSC 97 ... 6.27

Payne v Australian Pacific Airports (Melbourne) Pty Ltd [2020] VCC 1458 .... 6.13
Pearson v Naydler [1977] 1 WLR 899 .... 1.4, 2.6, 2.9, 2.20, 2.44, 4.25, 4.36, 5.8, 5.9, 5.11, 5.66, 7.23, 7.42, 8.39, 9.5
Pelechowski v Registrar, Court of Appeal (1999) 198 CLR 435 .... 8.66
Petromin SA v Secnav Marine Ltd [1995] 1 Lloyd's Rep 603 .... 2.44, 2.46, 4.34, 5.58, 7.24, 7.25, 7.26, 8.32, 8.59, 8.60
Pfennig v R (1995) 182 CLR 461 .... 2.39
Pilkin v Sony Australia Limited [2018] FCA 1018 .... 2.38
Pioneer Park (in liq) v ANZ [2005] NSWSC 832 .... 5.50
Platinum United II Pty Ltd v Mortgage Management Ltd (in liq) [2011] QCA 229 .... 5.26
Porrier v Carter [1789] 1 H BL 106; 126 ER 64 .... 2.6, 2.8
Port of Melbourne Authority v Anshun Pty Ltd (1981) 197 CLR 589 .... 2.13
Porzelack KG v Porzelack (UK) Ltd [1987] 1 All ER 1074 .... 5.30, 8.32
Powell v Taylor (1885) 31 Ch D 34 .... 2.8
PPK Willoughby Pty Ltd v Baird [2019] NSWCA 48 .... 5.41
Pray v Edie (1786) 99 ER 1087 .... 2.6, 2.7, 2.8
Precise Training Pty Ltd v Chief Commissioner of State Revenue [2020] NSWSC 1202 .... 2.13, 5.43, 5.44, 6.6, 6.12, 6.13, 6.15, 6.16, 6.24, 6.26
Prima Paint Corp v Flood & Conklin Mfg Co 388 US 395 (1967) 3.2, 7.5, 8.20, 8.39
Printing and Numerical Registering Co v Sampson (1875) 19 Eq 462 .... 7.14
Printing Circles Inc v Compass Group Canada Ltd (2007) 88 OR (3d) 685 .... 5.23, 6.30
Procedural Order No 4, ICC, (April 2009) reported in (2010) 28(1) ASA Bulletin 59 .... 1.4, 2.33, 2.44, 2.46, 3.12, 4.16, 4.17, 4.20, 4.53, 6.15
Project 28 Pty Ltd v Barr [2005] NSWCA 240 .... 2.4, 2.5, 5.11
PS Chellaram (1991) 102 ALR 321 .... 6.34
Public Transport Ticketing Corporation v Integrated Transit Solutions Ltd [2009] NSWSC 54 .... 5.47, 5.48
Punters Show Pty Limited, In the Matter of [2017] NSWSC 605 .... 1.4
Pure Spirit Co v Fowler (1890) 25 QBD 235 .... 5.10, 5.16
Quality Tractors (M) Sdn Bhd v United Asian Bank Bhd [1980] 1 MLJ 95 .... 5.49
Queensland v JL Holdings Pty Ltd (1997) 189 CLR 146 .... 9.37
Rad Drill Services Pty Ltd v Warrego Energy EP469 Pty Ltd [2021] NSWSC 214 .... 5.14
Rafferty v Time 2000 West Pty Ltd (No 3) (2009) 257 ALR 503 .... 1.4
Rahman (Prince Abdul) v Abu-Taha (1980) 3 All ER 409 .... 7.43
Rajski v Computer Manufacturer & Design Pty Ltd [1982] 2 NSWLR 443; [1983] 2 NSWLR 122 .... 2.8, 5.7, 7.42
Ramsay International Ltd v Scientific Control Systems Iran Ltd [1980] WL 612943 3 (CA) 4.31, 4.36, 8.32
RBIL v Ryhurst [2011] EWHC 2209 (TCC); [2011] BLR 721 .... 5.41
RBS (Rights Issue Litigation), Re [2017] EWHC 1217 (Ch); [2017] 1 WLR 4635 .... 5.23
Regia Autonoma De Electricitate Renel v Gulf Petroleum International Ltd [1996] 1 Lloyd's Rep 67 .... 2.9, 4.35, 8.32
Resilium Pty Ltd v Nest Insurance Consult Pty Ltd [2021] NSWSC 974 .... 6.19, 6.20
Rickard Constructions v Rickard Hails Moretti [2005] NSWSC 481 .... 2.38
Rock JV Pty Ltd v Thiess Pty Ltd [2020] WASC 324 .... 6.19
Rodwin v Bahadur v CIMB Bank Berhad [2018] 6 AMR 803 .... 5.6
Rogers v Interpacific Resorts (Australia) Pty Ltd [2007] QSC 239 .... 7.40

Rogers v Rogers [2018] NSWSC 1982 ... 2.39
Rosengrens Limited v Safe Deposit Centres Limited [1984] 3 All ER 198 ... 6.33, 6.35
Rowe v Andrews [2021] TASSC 34 ... 2.49, 5.6
Rowe v Ingenious Media Holdings plc [2021] EWCA Civ 29 ... 2.44, 2.46, 4.33, 5.23, 5.25, 6.17, 6.30, 8.8, 9.22, 9.31, 9.34
RSM v St Lucia (ICSID ARB/12/10) ... 10.3, 10.10, 10.32
S A Coppée–Lavalin NV v Ken–Ren Chemicals and Fertilizers Ltd (in liquidation in Kenya) [1995] 1 AC 38 ... 1.7, 1.14, 2.2, 2.8, 2.30, 2.44, 2.46, 4.27, 4.29, 4.30, 4.32, 4.34, 4.35, 4.42, 4.48, 7.3, 7.31, 8.2, 8.6, 8.11, 8.28, 8.40, 8.44, 8.46, 8.49, 8.53, 8.54, 8.55, 8.59, 8.60, 8.63, 9.35, 9.39
Sabaza Pty Ltd v AMP Society (1981) 6 ACLR 194 ... 6.24
Salex NSW Pty Ltd v Congredior Pty Ltd [2021] NSWSC 732 ... 5.53, 5.57, 7.44, 7.45
Saloman v Saloman [1897] AC 22 ... 2.20
Sands v South Australia [2013] SASC 105 ... 5.38
Sarayiah v Williams [2019] EWCA Civ 1387 ... 5.56
Saric v Vukasovic [2019] VSCA 57 ... 2.38
Sax v Campbell [2020] NZHC 1297 ... 2.44, 5.56, 5.68
Security for Costs and Associated Costs Orders [2011] NSWLRCCP 13 ... 2.6
Shannon v ANZ Banking Group Ltd (No 2) [1994] 2 Qd R 563 ... 5.21
Shared Network Services Limited v Nextiraone UK Limited [2012] EWCA Civ 1171 ... 2.9
Sharjade v Darwinia Estate [2006] NSWSC 708 ... 5.50
Sheather v Staples Waste Removals Pty Limited [2012] FCA 998 ... 3.2
Shiell v Coach House Hotel Ltd (1982) 136 DLR (3d) 470 (CA) ... 2.8
Sinclair v British Telecommunications plc [2000] 2 All ER 461 ... 5.19, 5.58
Sir Lindsay Parkinson & Company Ltd v Triplan Ltd [1973] 1 QB 609 (CA) ... 2.9, 4.25, 4.36, 5.6, 5.49, 5.55, 5.64
SL Mining Limited v Republic of Sierra Leone, ICC Case No. 24708/TO ... 10.42
Slazengers Ltd v Seaspeed Ferries Ltd; The Seaspeed Dora [1998] 1 WLR 221; [1987] 3 All ER 967 (CA) ... 5.66
Smith Ltd v H International [1991] 2 Lloyd's Rep 127 ... 8.13
Société Pirelli & Cie Spa v Société Licensing Projects et autres, Supreme Court of Cassation of France, First Civil Law Chamber, Arrêt no. 392 FS-P+B+I, pourvoi no. N 11–27.770, 28 March 2013, Revue de l'Arbitrage 746 (No 3, 2013) ... 8.8
SolarBlue LLC v Aus 2013 ONSC 7638 ... 5.23, 6.30
South American Silver Ltd (Bermudas) v Bolivia (PCA Case no 2013–15), Procedural Order No 10 (11 January 2016) ... 10.23
Southbank Liquor Stores Vic Pty Ltd, Re [2021] VSC 404 ... 2.9, 7.45
Spy Academy Ltd v Sakar International Inc [2009] EWCA Civ 985 ... 5.49
Street v Luna Park Sydney Pty Ltd [2006] NSWSC 1317 ... 5.66
Strong v Carlyle Press (No 2) [1893] WN 51 ... 5.13
Strukturmas (Selangor) Sdn Bhd v Majlis Perbandaran Petaling Jaya [2001] AMEJ 0167; [2001] 3 MLJ 344 ... 5.41
Stuart v Mordialloc Sporting Club Inc [2020] VSC 658 ... 5.57
Stuart v Rabo-bank Australia Ltd (No 2) [2021] FCA 1626 ... 5.26
Stuart v Said [2021] VSCA 226 ... 2.13, 2.49
Sulamérica Cia Nacoinal de Seguros SA v Enesa Eugenharia SA [2012] EWCA Civ 638 ... 8.12

Sun Asia Group Pty Ltd ATF v Invigor Group Ltd [2021] NSWSC 1082 .... 5.47, 5.48, 5.66
Swiss entity v Dutch entity (Award, HKZ Case No 415, 20 November 2001) 1.14
Sydmar Pty Ltd v Statewise Developments Pty Ltd (1987) 73 ALR 289 .... 5.15, 5.16, 5.17
Sykes v Sacerdoti (1885) 15 QBD 42 .... 5.47
Sykes v Sykes (1869) LR 4 CP 645 .... 5.66
T Reasuransi Umum Indonesia v Evanston Ins Co, XIX YB Comm Arb 788 (US District Court, SDNY 1992) 9.33
T Sloyan & Sons (Builders) Ltd and another v Brothers of Christian Instruction [1974] 3 All ER 715 .... 5.16
Tasman Charters Inc (in liq) v Kamphuis [2006] NZHC 64 .... 2.38
Taurus Mining Finance Fund AIV LP v Sandfire Resources Ltd [2021] WASC 52 .... 2.45, 5.25
TC Developments (South East) Ltd v Investin Quay House Ltd [2019] EWHC 1432 (TCC) 5.16
Telesis Technologies Inc v Sure Controls Systems Inc 2010 ONSC 5288 .... 5.23, 6.30
Terna Bahrain Holding Co v Ali Marzook Ali Bin Kamil Al Shamsi [2012] EWHC 3283 (Comm) 9.33
Testel Australia Pty Ltd v KRG Electrics Pty Ltd [2013] SASC 91 .... 5.26
Thames Investment & Securities plc v Benjamin [1984] 1 WLR 1381 .... 5.19
Thistle Hotels Ltd v Gamma Four Ltd [2004] EWHC 322; [2004] BCLC 174 .... 5.16
Tim Barr Pty Ltd v Narui Gold Coast Pty Ltd [2009] NSWSC 563 .... 5.42, 5.43, 5.44
Tito v Waddell (No 2) [1977] Ch 106 .... 5.68
Togo Electricité v Togo (ICSID Case No. ARB/06/07) (ARB/06/07) 10.9
Tolstoy Miloslavsky v United Kingdom (1995) 20 EHRR 442 .... 2.46, 8.8
Tomanovich Holdings Limited v Gibbston Community Water Company (2014) Limited [2018] NZHC 990 .... 2.44
Tonstate Group Ltd, Re [2020] EWHC 328 (Ch) 5.21
Traderight Pty Ltd v Bank of Queensland Ltd [2010] NSWSC 1502 .... 5.23, 6.30
Trailer Trash Franchise Systems Pty Ltd v Fascia [2017] VSCA 293 .... 6.19
Travelodge Australia Ltd, Re (1978) 21 ACTR 17 .... 5.47
Travis Coal Restructuring Holdings LLC v Essar Global Fund Limited [2014] EWHC 2510 (Comm) 8.68, 9.10
Treloar Constructions Pty Limited v McMillan [2016] NSWCA 302 .... 5.58
Trident International v Manchester Ship Canal [1990] BCLC 263 .... 7.25
Trility Pty Ltd v Ancon Drilling Pty Ltd [2013] VSC 577 .... 5.1, 5.56, 5.58, 7.44
Trustees of Rotoaira Forest Trust v Attorney-General [1999] 2 NZLR 452 .... 9.33
Tsakiroglou & Co Ltd v Noblee Thorl GmbH [1962] AC 93 .... 2.29
Unionmatex Industrieanlagen GmbH v Turkmenistan (UCSID Case No. ARB/18/35 Decision on Security for Costs on) (27 January 2020) 10.3, 10.10, 10.26, 10.28, 10.30, 10.32
Union Stearinerie Lanza v Wiener [1917] 2 KB 558 .... 7.7
University of Canberra v Zierholz @ UC Pty Ltd [2020] ACTCA 45 .... 2.13, 2.47
Versloot Dredging BV v HDI Gerling Industrie Vesicherung AG [2013] EWHC 658 (Comm) 2.44, 5.23
Visco v Minter [1969] 2 All ER 714 .... 5.14, 5.16
Warren v Marsden [2014] EWHC 4410 (Comm) 5.44
Washoe Mining Co v Ferguson (1866) LR 2 Eq 371 .... 5.16
Watteen v Billam (1841) 3 DG & Sm 516 .... 5.47
Westonia Earthmoving Pty Ltd v Cliffs Asia Pacific Iron Ore Pty Ltd [2013] WASC 57 .... 5.1, 5.4, 5.49, 5.55, 5.56, 5.58, 5.64, 5.65
Westpac New Zealand Limited v Adams [2013] NZHC 3112 .... 2.44

Westralian Gold Mines Ltd v Westralian Mineral & Drilling Pty Ltd (In Liq) (1986) 4 ACLC 167 ....5.65
Whitelaw v Hookey [2020] QCA 145 ....5.30
Willey v Synan (1935) 54 CLR 175 .... 5.47, 5.48
Williams v Spautz (1992) 174 CLR 509 ....5.36
Winnote Pty Ltd (in liq) v Page (2005) 64 NSWLR 244 ....5.23
Winthorp v Royal Exchange Assurance Company (1755) Dick 282; 21 ER 277 ....2.6
Wizdoms Naik International Limited v DSV Gerimal [2020] SCC OnLine Bom 7646 ....5.68
Wollongong City Council v Legal Business Centre Pty Ltd [2012] NSWCA 245 ....5.52
WorkPac Pty Ltd v Rossato (2021) 95 ALJR 681 ....2.28
X Panama v Une personne physique domiciliée à Genève (Award, Zürich Chamber of Commerce, 1995), reported in (1995) 13(3) ASA Bulletin 529 .... 1.1, 4.8, 4.16, 4.18
X SA v A B and others, Commerce/Industry/and Chamber of Commerce of the Canton of Ticino, Ccia-Ti No 103/00, 25 July 2003 reported in (2010) 4.20
XXX Inc v YYY SA, Procedural Order No 2, 2009 in ICC Case 15951, reported in (2010) 2.23, 4.20
XY International v Company Z, Procedural Decision in ICC Arbitration No.....1995 reported in (1997) 15(2) ASA Bulletin 363 ....4.20
Yandil Holdings Pty Ltd v Insurance Co of North America (1985) 3 ACLC 542 ....2.47
Yara Australia Pty Ltd v Oswal (2013) 41 VR 245 .... 6.30, 6.35, 6.36, 6.38
Yee Hua Holdings Sdn Bhd v Chin Yew Nam [1999] 2 CLJ 63 ....5.42

TABLE OF LEGISLATION

Australia
ACICA (Australian Centre for International Commercial Arbitration) Arbitration Rules (2021)
r 37.2(e) 7.7
ACICA (Australian Centre for International Commercial Arbitration) Expedited Arbitration Rules (2021)
r 25.2(e) 7.7
Commercial Arbitration Acts of the Australian States and Territories
s 17 .... 3.7
Competition and Consumer Act 2010 7.16
Corporations Act 2001
s 1335(1) 2.9
s 588G 2.18
ss 588J–K 2.18
Foreign Proceedings (Excess of Jurisdiction) Act 1984
s 12 .... 5.5
International Arbitration Act 1974
s 18 .... 8.26, 8.61
s 23K 3.7, 7.6, 10.15
s 23K(2) 2.11, 8.54
Personal Property Securities Act 2009 .... 6.32
Trade Practices Act 1974 .... 7.16
Uniform Civil Procedure Rules 2005
r 51.50(1) 2.49
r 42.21(1)(a) 2.9
r 42.21(1)(d) 2.9

Belgium
CEPANI (Belgian Centre for Arbitration and Mediation) Arbitration Rules 2020
art 27(1) 7.7

Canada
Arbitration Act, SBC 2020, c 2
s 32(2)(b)(iii) 2.11
Business Corporations Act, SBC 2002, c 57
s 236 .... 2.9

China, People's Republic of
国际商事法庭 [Arbitration Law of the People's Republic of China] National People's Congress, Order No 31, 31 August 1994
art 5 .... 8.4
art 28 .... 7.7

Hong Kong
Arbitration Ordinance (Cap 609)
s 26(1) 8.24
s 40 .... 3.7
s 46(2) 8.24
s 46(3)(a) 8.24
s 46(3)(b) 8.24
s 46(3)(c) 8.24
s 56 .... 3.7, 8.49
s 56(1)(a) 4.46, 10.15
s 56(2) 2.11, 8.54
s 2GB 3.7
ss 56(1)(a) 10.15
Code of Civil Procedure 8.49
Companies Ordinance (Cap 622)
s 905(1) 2.9
HKIAC Administered Arbitration Rules 2018
art 23.1 .... 8.23
art 24 .... 4.46, 7.7
art 43 .... 9.13
Sch 4 .... 8.23

Indonesia
Law on Arbitration and Alternative Dispute Resolution (No 30 of 1999)
art 3 .... 8.4
art 4(1) 8.4
art 32(1) 7.7

Kazakhstan

Law of the Republic of Kazakhstan on International Commercial Arbitration (28 December 2004, No. 23-III ZRK)
art 25(1) 7.7

Malaysia

Arbitration Act 2005
s 11(1)(a) 7.6
s 19 ..... 3.7
s 19(10(a) 7.6

New Zealand

AMINZ Arbitration Rules 2017
art 66(1) 7.7
Arbitration Act 1996 (SR 1996/99) 4.37
s 17A 3.7
s 17B 7.7
Arbitration Amendment Act 2007 (SR 2007/94)
Sch 1 art 17 ..... 7.6
High Court Rules 2016
r 5.45(1)(a) 2.9
r 5.45(1)(b) 2.9

Singapore

Code of Civil Procedure 8.49
Companies Act (Cap 50) (rev. ed. 2006)
s 388(1) 2.9
Insolvency, Restructuring and Dissolution Act (No 40 of 2018)
s 239 ..... 2.18
s 241 ..... 2.18
International Arbitration Act (Cap 143A) (rev ed 2002)
s 12 ..... 8.49
s 12(1)(a) 4.46
s 12(4) 2.11, 8.54
s 24(b) 8.26
International Arbitration Act (Cap 143A) (rev ed 2007)
s 12 ..... 3.7
s 12(1) 10.15
s 12(1)(a) 7.6
s 12(1)(4) 7.6
Reciprocal Enforcement of Commonwealth Judgments Act (Cap 264) (rev ed 1985) 5.5
Reciprocal Enforcement of Foreign Judgments Act (Cap 265) (rev ed 2001) 5.5
SIAC Investment Rules 2017
r 27(1) 10.13
SIAC Rules 2016
r 5 ..... 7.4
r 27(j) 4.46, 7.7
r 28 ..... 7.4
r 29 ..... 9.13
r 30.2 ..... 8.23
r 41.2 ..... 9.3
Sch 1 ..... 7.4, 8.23

South Africa

International Arbitration Act 2017
Sch 1, art 17 ..... 3.7

Sweden

Stockholm Chamber of Commerce Arbitration Rules 2017
art 37(4) and app II 8.23
art 38 ..... 3.8, 7.7
art 39 ..... 9.13
Stockholm Chamber of Commerce Rules for Expedited Arbitrations 2017
art 39 ..... 7.7

Switzerland

Swiss Rules of International Arbitration
art 26(3) 3.6

Thailand

Thailand Arbitration Centre Rules on Arbitration Rules 2015
art 66(5) 7.7

United Arab Emirates

DIFC Arbitration Rules
art 25.2 ..... 7.7

United Kingdom

Arbitration Act 1950 ..... 4.35
Arbitration Act 1996 ..... 4.47, 8.34, 8.62
s 1(b) 8.4
s 33 ..... 8.23
s 33(1)(b) 8.24
s 34 ..... 8.23
s 38 ..... 3.7, 4.22, 8.49, 9.42, 10.15
s 40 ..... 8.23
s 41(6) 2.44, 2.46
s 59(1)(c) 5.28
s 69 ..... 2.16, 5.33
s 38(3) 7.6
s 38(3)(a) 2.11
s 38(3)(b) 2.11

s 39A 9.10
s 39(2)(b) 7.6
Arbitration Bill 2023
s 7 .... 9.10
Civil Procedure Rules 1998, SI 1998/3132
r 25.13(2)(a) 2.9
r 25.13(2)(a)(ii) 5.5
r 25.13(2)(c) 2.9
r 25.13(2)(c) 2.9
Code of Civil Procedure 8.49
Companies Act 1929 .... 4.24
s 275 .... 2.18
Companies Act 1985
s 726(1) 2.9
Insolvency Act 1986
s 123 .... 2.21
s 214 .... 2.18
s 218 .... 2.18
Judicature Act 1925
s 38 .... 5.68
Limited Liability Act 1855 .... 2.9
London Court of International Arbitration Rules 2020
art 22.1 .... 9.13
art 25.2 .... 7.7
art 28(3) 5.28
art 9B 8.23
r 14.7 .... 4.49
r 25.2 .... 4.48, 7.7
r 26.5 .... 4.49
London Court of International Arbitration Rules 2021
art 32(2) 9.3
Sale of Goods Act 1979 .... 7.16
Supply of Goods (Implied Terms) Act 1973 .... 7.16
Unfair Contract Terms Act 1977 .... 7.16

United States of America
Ted Stevens Olympic and Amateur Sports Act 7.8
36 U.S. Code §
s 220509 .... 7.8

Vietnam
Rules of Arbitration of the Vietnam International Arbitration Centre 2017
art 33(6) 7.7

International Agreements, Conventions, and Treaties
Convention on the Contract for the International Carriage of Goods by Road 1956
art 31(5) 2.1
Convention on the Settlement of Investment Disputes between States and Nationals of other States 1965
art 47 .... 10.7
Convention relative aux Transports Internationaux Ferroviaires (Obereinkommen über den internationalenEisenbahnverkehr) 1980
art 18(4) 2.1
Convention Réviseé pour la Navigation sur le Rhin (Revidierte Rheinschiffahrtsakte) 1868
art 36(1) 2.1
European Convention for the Protection of Human Rights and Fundamental Freedoms 1950
art 6(1) 8.8
European Convention on Establishment 1955
art 9(1) 2.1
European Convention on Human Rights
art 6 .... 9.22, 9.34
Hague Convention 1905 .... 4.18
Hague Convention 1954 .... 4.18
Hague Convention 2005 .... 5.5
Hague Convention on Civil Procedure 1954
art 17 .... 2.1
ICC Internal Rules of the Court of Arbitration
art 5(2) 8.68
International Arbitration Centre Arbitration and Mediation Rules 2018
art 23.1(10) 7.7
International Centre for the Settlement of Investment Disputes Arbitration Rules 2022
r 53 .... 10.7, 10.9, 10.30, 10.38
International Chamber of Commerce Arbitration Rules 2017
art 41 .... 9.3
International Chamber of Commerce Arbitration Rules 2021
App X, art 7(2) 8.61
art 4(4) 8.61
art 11(7) 7.4
art 12(9) 7.4
art 17(1) 7.4
art 17(2) 7.4

art 22 .... 7.4, 8.68, 9.13
art 22(1) 8.68, 8.69
art 26(1) 7.4
art 29 .... 8.23
art 37(1) 5.28
art 37(6) 8.61
JAMS Comprehensive Arbitration Rules & Procedures 2010
r 18 .... 9.13
Regulation (EC) No 593/2008 of the European Parliament of the Council of 17 June 2008 on the law applicable to contractual obligations 8.15
art 3(1) 8.15
art 4(1) 8.15
art 4(1)(a) 8.15
art 4(3) 8.15
art 4(4) 8.15
rec (6) 8.17
Treaty of Rome
art 6 .... 2.1
UNCITRAL Arbitration Rules 2010 .... 8.51
UNCITRAL Arbitration Rules 2021 .... 10.18
art 26(2)(c) 10.7, 10.12
art 42(1) 10.7, 10.12, 10.34
UNCITRAL Model Law on International Commercial Arbitration 1985 .... 1.2, 2.18, 2.19, 3.14, 8.26, 8.31, 8.51, 8.53, 8.71, 10.18
art 1(2) 8.6, 8.11, 8.13
art 2(e) 7.6, 8.6
art 7 .... 8.22
art 8(1) 8.4, 8.60
art 9 .... 10.15
art 11(2) 8.23
art 11(4) 8.23
art 11(5) 8.23
art 12 .... 8.24
art 12(1) 8.23
art 17 .... 1.2, 3.3, 3.4, 3.6
art 17(2)(a) 3.4
art 17(2)(b) 3.4
art 17(2)(c) 3.4, 3.5, 10.12
art 18 .... 8.23, 8.24, 8.26, 8.61, 9.10, 9.23, 9.32
art 18, 34(2)(a)(ii) 5.33
art 19(1) 8.4
art 19(2) 8.23
art 34(1) 8.4
art 34(2)(a)(ii) 8.26, 9.10
art 34(2)(b)(i) 8.21
art 35 .... 8.4
art 36(1)(a)(ii) 5.33, 8.26
art 36(1)(b)(i) 8.21
art 2A 3.15
art 17A 3.3, 3.4, 3.6
art 17A (1) 7.41
art 17A(1)(a) 3.5
art 17A(1)(b) 8.33
art 17A-J 3.3
art 17C(5) 8.23
art 17D 8.35
art 17E 6.17
art 17G 6.17, 9.31
art 17H 8.23, 8.70
United Nations Convention on Contracts for the International Sale of Goods
art 35(3) 7.40
United Nations Convention on the Recognition and Enforcement of Foreign Arbitral Awards 1958 (New York Convention) 4.19, 8.2, 8.52, 8.53, 8.56, 9.9, 9.23
art II(1) 8.3, 8.60
art II(2) 8.22
art II(3) 8.60
art II(I) 8.21
art III 8.3, 8.56
art V(1)(a) 8.6, 8.11
art V(1)(d) 8.6, 8.11, 8.29
art V(1)(e) 8.6, 8.11
art V(2)(a) 8.21
art V(b) 5.33, 8.26

CHAPTER 1

Introduction to the controversy

Introduction

1.1. Security for costs is an interim measure in international commercial arbitration by which a claimant is ordered to provide financial security for the respondent's costs of defending the proceedings. It is said to be at the 'forefront of the clash of cultures', a 'vexed and complicated' issue,[1] 'one of the most neglected and misunderstood forms of interim relief',[2] contentious and deserving of separate treatment[3] and 'an interim measure to which international commercial arbitration has been hostile'.[4]Interim measures are themselves contentious, and security for costs rides like a teacup in the interim measures squall on the unsettled waters of international commercial arbitration.

1.2. Certain of these issues apply to interim measures more generally, of which security for costs is one. Doubts have attended the existence and scope of power, and the propriety of tribunals granting interim measures in place of state courts. Questions remain as to whether the law governing a tribunal's jurisdiction to grant interim measures should also guide its exercise of it.[5] Despite desirability in the uniformity of application,[6] trans-national standards have only emerged recently for some interim measures. It was not until 2006 that the 1985 UNCITRAL *Model Law on International Commercial Arbitration*[7] was amended to contain detailed provisions on interim measures.[8]

1 Christopher Kee, 'International Arbitration and Security for Costs – A Brief Report on Two Developments' (2006) 17 *American Review of International Arbitration* 273, 280.

2 Noah Rubins, 'In God We Trust, All Others Pay Cash: Security for Costs in International Commercial Arbitration' (2000) 11 *American Review of International Arbitration* 307.

3 Jeffrey Waincymer, *Procedure and Evidence in International Arbitration* (Kluwer, 2012) 643 [8.3.1].

4 Samaa AF Haridi, 'Security for costs and Claim under the ICC Rules of Arbitration – Rare, But Possible' (2020) 2 *ICC Dispute Resolution Bulletin* 77; Alan Redfern and Sam O'Leary, 'Why It Is Time for International Arbitration to Embrace Security for Costs' (2016) 32 *Arbitration International* 397, 400; *X Panama v Une personne physique domiciliée à Genève* (Award, Zürich Chamber of Commerce, 1995) (1995) ASA Bulletin 529, 531, quoted in *A. S.p.A. (Italy) v B AG (Germany)* (Decision, Geneva Chamber of Commerce and Industry, 25 September 1997) (2001) 19(4) ASA Bulletin 745 [7].

5 Gary Born, *International Commercial Arbitration* (Kluwer, 3rd ed, 2021) [17.02] [F].

6 Ibid.

7 UNCITRAL, *Model Law on International Commercial Arbitration*, adopted 3–21 June 1985, 40 GAOR Supp No 53 A/40/53 (entered into force 11 December 1985, GA Res 40/72) ('*Model Law*').

8 *Model Law* art 17.

DOI: 10.4324/9781003479628-1

The significance of security for costs

1.3. Both an application and an order for security for costs impose pressures on a claimant, and the refusal of an order has consequences for the respondent. Time, distraction and cost pressures are applied to a claimant facing an application for security for costs.[9] Financial stresses are magnified if an order is made and the claimant must provide security or have its claim stayed, raising issues of access to justice. If an order is not made, the respondent may not recover its costs if it succeeds, raising issues of abuse of process in failing to preserve the costs jurisdiction.

1.4. Security for costs is a 'powerful',[10] 'highly effective weapon'[11] for respondents, an order resulting in 'certain immediate damage'[12] to the claimant, or a stay[13] and ultimate dismissal[14] of its claim without a determination on the merits. Reluctance to order security where it is warranted can become 'a weapon whereby the impecunious company can use its inability to pay costs as a means of putting unfair pressure on a more prosperous company'.[15] However, there are apprehensions that applications for security for costs may be deployed tactically as part of interlocutory 'warfare'[16] 'to exhaust the financial resources of' the claimant.[17]

1.5. On the other hand, the facility can be deployed as an aid in dealing with guerrilla tactics and as a more moderate means of controlling apparently unmeritorious claims than by summary judgment. Security could be ordered as a condition of a party taking a step that smacks of delay or obstruction, and it could be used where the claim appears weak but the high standard required to grant summary judgment is not met and the claimant appears unlikely to be able to pay an ultimate order for costs.

The controversy

1.6. Two principal questions underpin the controversy as to security for costs in international commercial arbitration. The first is whether it is suited to and should be

9 ICCA–Queen Mary Task Force, *Report on Third-Party Funding in International Arbitration* (Report, ICCA and QMUL, April 2018) 165 ('ICCA Report on Third-Party Funding').

10 *Buckley v Bennell* (1974) 1 ALCR 301, 309 (Moffitt P); *Christou v Stanton Partners Australasia Pty Ltd* [2011] WASCA 176.

11 Redfern and O'Leary (n 4) 397.

12 Waincymer (n 3) 644 [8.3.1]. Cf *Les & Zelda Investments Pty Ltd v Whitehaven Coal Ltd* [2020] NSWSC 1091 [49] where Parker J noted that the 'cost of financing an extra $100,000 or $200,000 in security would be a mere bagatelle in the scheme of this litigation'.

13 Colin YC Ong and Michael Patrick O'Reilly, *Costs in International Arbitration* (LexisNexis, 2013) 167 [9.7]; Procedural Order No 4, LCIA, Case No. 132551, 2014 reported in (2018) 36(3) ASA Bulletin 664 [25]; *Claimants 1–2 v Respondents 1–16* (Order, ZCC, 19 December 2008) reported in (2010) 28(1) *ASA Bulletin* 47, 58–9 [7.4.6]; Procedural Order No 4, ICC, April 2009 (2010) 28(1) *ASA Bulletin* 59 [159], stating that '[t]he normal sanction for an eventual failure to comply with an order for security for costs is a refusal to proceed with the case'.

14 Waincymer (n 3) 653 [8.3.10].

15 *Pearson v Naydler* [1977] 1 WLR 899, 906–7, quoted in *Idoport Pty Limited & Anor v National Australia Bank Limited* [2001] NSWSC 744 [59].

16 Hon Mr Justice BH McPherson CBE, 'Foreword' in Stephen Colbran (ed), *Security for Costs* (Longman, 1993); Klaus Sachs, 'Time and Money: Cost Control and Effective Case Management' in Loukas Mistelis and Julian DM Lew (eds), *Pervasive Problems in International Arbitration* (Kluwer, 2006) 113 [5.37]; Lucy Ferguson Reed, 'Sanctions Available for Arbitrators to Curtail Guerrilla Tactics' in Günther J Horvath and Stephan Wilske (eds), *Guerilla Tactics in International Arbitration* (Kluwer, 2015) 94, 95.

17 *Rafferty v Time 2000 West Pty Ltd (No 3)* (2009) 257 ALR 503 [20]; *In the Matter of Punters Show Pty Limited* [2017] NSWSC 605 [93].

applied in international commercial arbitration at all; the second is, if it is, what tests or standards are to be applied.

1.7. These issues have manifested themselves in different approaches being taken by tribunals, and a lack of clear guidance,[18] with relatively few resources available to guide counsel and tribunals[19] and a norm against making applications.[20] These compounding problems are perpetuating a vicious cycle leading to a continued dearth of guidance[21] and reinforcement of the norm.

1.8. Doubts as to the facility's suitability to international arbitration have resulted in a more restrictive approach being taken to applications in arbitrations administered by the International Chamber of Commerce Court of Arbitration (**ICC**) – whose attitude to the facility has been described as hostile[22] – than would be taken in common law litigation or, apparently, in arbitrations administered by the London Court of Arbitration (**LCIA**). An approach between that of arbitrations administered by the ICC and the LCIA can be observed in arbitrations seated in Switzerland or administered under Swiss arbitral rules (**Swiss arbitrations**) published by the Swiss Arbitration Association (**ASA**).

1.9. As an illustration of the contrasting approaches of ICC and LCIA arbitrations, in the century of the existence of the ICC from 1923 to 2023,[23] it has published 23 tribunal decisions on security for costs,[24] with two more yet to be published at the time of writing.[25] Five of those applications were successful,[26] yielding a success rate of 17%.[27] In the three years from 2019 to 2021, LCIA tribunals dealt with 96 applications for interim measures where applications for security for costs accounted for at least half.[28] The success rate of such applications to LCIA tribunals is at least double that of those in ICC tribunals.[29]

1.10. The source of the difference in the number of applications and their success appears to lie in the difference in the tests applied by tribunals. In the case of LCIA arbitrations, it is only possible to refer to the test *apparently* applied, gleaned from the number of applications and their outcome, due to the LCIA not publishing reasons for those decisions.

18 Gu Weixia, 'Security for Costs in International Commercial Arbitration' (2005) 22(3) *Journal of International Arbitration* 167.

19 Haridi (n 4) 78.

20 Redfern and O'Leary (n 4) 399, quoting Lord Mustill saying 'in the international arbitrating community, security for costs is very much a minority measure' in *Coppée–Lavalin v Ken–Ren* (n 5). 63G, and citing Alan Redfern and Martin Hunter, *Law and Practice of International Commercial Arbitration* (Sweet & Maxwell, 4th ed, 2004) 349 [7–40].

21 Haridi (n 4) 78.

22 Ibid.

23 'History' (Web Page, undated) <http://www.iccwbo.org/about-icc/history/>.

24 Haridi (n 4). It is evident from occasional references to apparently unpublished decisions that these are not the entirety of decisions of ICC tribunals regarding security for costs, for example, ICC Award No 4126 of 1984 and ICC Award No 6697 of 1990 *Societe Casa v Societe Cambior* 1992 Rev Arb 135 [9].

25 The writer was involved in both applications as counsel and has a copy of the decisions from which the ruling and reasons are extracted without identifying the parties. Security for costs was refused in the 24th and granted in the 25th, the first successful application in an ICC arbitration against a natural person claimant.

26 Including the yet-to-be-reported 25th application in 2021 in which the writer was involved.

27 This accords approximately with the estimate of a 20% success rate given in PO of October 2008 in ICC Case No 14433, ICC Special Supplement 2014 [45].

28 See the respective Casework Report.

29 Ibid.

1.11. Three broad tests can be discerned – the 'exceptional circumstances' test, the 'special circumstances' test, and the 'total circumstances' test. ICC tribunals tend to require exceptional circumstances before granting security, usually evidenced by a change of circumstances since the transaction was entered into. Swiss tribunals, generally but with some exceptions, take a slightly more relaxed approach which requires something less exceptional than ICC tribunals, referred to here as special circumstances. LCIA tribunals take an even more liberal approach *indicating* that LCIA tribunals take into account the total circumstances of the case in a multifactorial discretion without a predisposition for or against security.

1.12. This work proposes the 'total circumstances' multifactorial approach, without a predisposition for or against security, as a transnational standard for security for costs in international arbitration. That standard is appropriate for both commercial and investment arbitration as the fact that the arbitration is one or the other is one of the circumstances to be taken into account.

1.13. The result is a broad, multifactorial discretion to be exercised judicially, founded on the protection of the integrity of the arbitral process, with fairness, or justice, as the touchstone,[30] enlivened when it appears that there is an appreciable risk the respondent will not be able to recover a costs order against the claimant if successful.[31] The factors traditionally considered in the exercise of this discretion are summarised in Chapter 5.

The arguments

1.14. Some 14 arguments have been made, either against the reception of security for costs into international commercial arbitration, or supporting the narrower exceptional or special circumstances tests, and can be placed into five non-exclusive categories. They are that security for costs is contrary to:

(1) Party autonomy;
(2) Party consent;
(3) The summary nature of arbitration;
(4) International nature of arbitration;[32] and
(5) Procedural fairness[33] and access to justice.[34]

1.15. Those arguments and possible responses to them are given in Chapters 7 and 8 to assist practitioners and tribunals dealing with applications.

30 *Infinity Distribution Ltd (in administration) v The Khan Partnership LLP* [2021] EWCA Civ 565 [10] [34]; *Merribee Pastroral Industries Pty Ltd v Australia New Zealand Banking Group Ltd* (1998) 193 CLR 502 [26].

31 Redfern and O'Leary (n 4) 397, 410.

32 *Coppée–Lavalin v Ken–Ren* (n 5) 62C-D.

33 Waincymer (n 3) 643 [8.3.1]; *Coppée–Lavalin v Ken–Ren* (n 5).

34 Born (n 8) [17.02[G][4][e]]; Procedural Order, ICC, Case No 12035, 6 June 2003, reported in ICC, *Special Supplement 2010: Decisions on ICC Arbitration Procedure: A Selection of Procedural Orders issue by Arbitral Tribunals acting under the ICC Rules of Arbitration (2003–2004)* (ICC, 2010) ('PO 12035'); Procedural Order, ICC, Case No 14355, January 2007, reported in ICC, *Special Supplement 2014: Procedural Decisions in ICC Arbitration* 70 (ICC, 2014) ('PO 14355'); Procedural Order, ICC, Case No 15218, July 2008, reported in ICC, *Special Supplement 2014: Procedural Decisions in ICC Arbitration* 79 (ICC, 2014) ('PO 15218'); *Swiss entity v Dutch entity* (Award, HKZ Case No 415, 20 November 2001) reported in (2002) 20(3) *ASA Bulletin* 467 ('HKZ 415').

1.16. As ICC and Swiss decisions on security for costs are the only ones routinely published, they have become the jurisprudence on the topic (particularly the ICC cases), with their approach reflected in the literature[35] and professional association guidelines.[36] The approach of ICC tribunals is thereby reinforced in future ICC arbitrations, and may be transmitted to *ad hoc* arbitrations or to those administered by other institutions and under other rules which may draw influence from already available publications on such issues.

1.17. This work conducts a comprehensive review and analysis of literature and court and tribunal decisions on security for costs in international arbitration. It includes a systematic review of the reasons given by tribunals, courts, and commentators for restricting the facility of security for costs in international commercial arbitration in Chapter 4 and gives possible responses in Chapters 7 and 8. In Chapter 9, potential benefits of the multifactorial, total circumstances approach to security for costs for parties in arbitration and the institution of arbitration are raised for consideration.

35 See [4.7].

36 *Chartered Institute of Arbitrators, Applications for Security for Costs* (Chartered Institute of Arbitrators, undated) 2 [2], 7–8 (b)–(d) ('CIArb SFC Guidelines').

ANNEXURE 1A

Arbitral legislation provisions relating to security for costs or interim measures

Australia

Commercial Arbitration Act 2017 (ACT) s 17(3)(a)
Commercial Arbitration Act 2010 (NSW) s 17(3)(a)
Commercial Arbitration Act 2013 (Qld) s 17(3)(a)
Commercial Arbitration Act 2011 (SA) s 17(3)(a)
Commercial Arbitration Act 2011 (Tas) s 17(3)(a)
Commercial Arbitration Act 2011 (Vic) s 17(3)(a)
Commercial Arbitration Act 2012 (WA) s 17(3)(a)
Commercial Arbitration (National Uniform Legislation) Act 2011 (NT) s 17(3)(a)

Austria

Austrian Code of Civil Procedure ss 585, 593

Brazil

Brazilian Arbitration Law 1996 art 22A

Egypt

Egyptian Arbitration Law, Law 27 of 1994 art 24

France

French New Code of Civil Procedure 1981, Title V (International Arbitration) art 1468

Germany

*Code of Civil Procedure (*Zivilprozessordnung (ZPO)) ss 1033, 104(1)

India

Arbitration and Conciliation Act 1996 s 17

Indonesia

Law No. 30 of 1999 on Arbitration and Alternative Dispute Resolution art 32

Japan

Arbitration Act (No 138 of 2003) art 24.1

Kazakhstan

Law on Arbitration (Law No. 488-V) dated 8 April 2016. Article 20 is said to confer inherent jurisdiction to order provisional measures.[37]

Malaysia

Arbitration Act 2005 (as amended 2018) s 19(2)(e)

New Zealand

Arbitration Act 1966 (NZ) sch 2 art 3(d)

People's Republic of China – Mainland

Arbitration Law of the People's Republic of China

People's Republic of China – Hong Kong SAR

Arbitration Ordinance (Hong Kong) cap 609 s 56(1)(a)

Russia

Russian Law on International Commercial Arbitration dated 7 July 1993 art 9

Singapore

International Arbitration Act (Singapore, cap 143A, 2002 rev ed) s 12(1)(a)

South Africa

International Arbitration Act sch 1 art 17

South Korea

Korean Arbitration Act 1966 art 18

Sweden

Swedish Arbitration Act 1999 s 25

Switzerland

Swiss Private International Law Act 1987 arts 182, 183

37 'International Arbitration in Kazakhstan', *Aceris Law* (Web Page, 13 November 2021) <https://www.acerislaw.com/international-arbitration-in-kazakhstan/>.

United Arab Emirates

Federal Law No. 6 of 2018 on Arbitration

United Kingdom

Arbitration Act 1966 (UK) s 38(3)

United States of America

Federal Arbitration Act, 9 USC (1925)

ANNEXURE 1B

Arbitral rules relating to security for costs or interim measures

Rules Providing Expressly for Security for Costs	*Institution Acronym*
2018 HKIAC Administered Arbitration Rules, effective 1 November 2018 art 24	HKIAC
ACICA Arbitration Rules incorporating Emergency Arbitration Provisions, adopted 1 April 2021 r 25.2(e)	ACICA
ACICA Expedited Arbitration Rules, adopted 1 April 2021 r 25.2(e)	ACICA
AIFC International Arbitration Centre Arbitration and Mediation Rules 2018 art 23.1(10)	IAC
AMINZ Arbitration Rules, adopted 22 May 2017 art 66(1)	AMINZ
Arbitration Rules of CEPANI, the Belgian Centre for Arbitration and Mediation, effective 1 January 2020 art 28(1)	CEPANI
Arbitration Rules of the Arbitration Institute of the Stockholm Chamber of Commerce, adopted 1 January 2017 art 38	SCC
Arbitration Rules of the London Court of International Arbitration, effective 1 October 2020 art 25.2	LCIA
Arbitration Rules of the Singapore International Arbitration Centre (6th Edition), effective 1 August 2016 r 27j	SIAC
DIAC Arbitration Rules 2022, effective 21 March 2022 Appendix II art 1.2(e)	DIAC
DIFC-LCIA Arbitration Rules, effective 1 January 2021 r 25.2	DIFC-LCIA
Rules for Expedited Arbitrations of the Stockholm Chamber of Commerce, adopted 1 January 2017 art 39	SCC
Thailand Arbitration Centre Rules on Arbitration Rules BE 2558, effective 1 July 2015 art 66(5)	THAC
The LMAA Terms, effective 1 May 2021 Second Schedule para 7	LMAA
VIAC Rules of Arbitration 2021, effective 1 July 2021 art 33(6)	VIAC
RULES ADOPTING MODEL LAW PROVISION FOR INTERIM MEASURES	
Arbitration Rules of the Cairo Regional Centre for International Commercial Arbitration, effective March 2011 art 26	CRCICA
UNCITRAL Arbitration Rules, effective 15 August 2010 art 26	UNCITRAL
RULES ADOPTING OTHER PROVISION FOR INTERIM MEASURES	
2018 DIS Arbitration Rules, effective 1 March 2018 art 25	DIS

American Arbitration Association Commercial Arbitration Rules, effective 1 October 2013 r 37	AAA
Arbitration Rules and Procedures of the Badan Arbitrase Nasional Indonesia, effective 1 January 2018 art 20(5)	BANI
Arbitration Rules of the Center for Arbitration and Mediation of the Chamber of Commerce Brazil-Canada, effective 28 April 2016 art 8	CAM-CCBC
Arbitration Rules of the Milan Chamber of Arbitration, effective 1 July 2020 art 26	CAM
Arbitration Rules of the Mumbai Centre for International Arbitration, 2nd edition effective 15 January 2017 r 15	MCIA
Arbitration Rules of the Netherlands Arbitration Institute, effective 1 January 2015 art 9.1	NAI
Beijing Arbitration Commission Arbitration Rules, effective 1 April 2015 art 62	BAC
China International Economic and Trade Arbitration Commission Arbitration Rules, effective 1 January 2015 art 23	CIETAC
Commercial Arbitration Rules of the Japan Commercial Arbitration Association, effective 1 July 2021 art 71	JCAA
ICC Rules of Arbitration, effective 1 January 2021 art 28	ICC
International Arbitration Rules of the Korean Commercial Arbitration Board, effective 1 June 2016 art 32	KCAB
JAMS Comprehensive Arbitration Rules and Procedures, effective 1 June 2021 r 24(2)	JAMS
Procedural Regulations of Arbitration of the Ab Dhabi Commercial Conciliation & Arbitration Center, effective 20 October 2013 art 25	ADCCAC
Rules of Arbitration of the Vietnam International Arbitration Centre, effective 1 March 2017 art 21(1)	VIAC
Swiss Rules of International Arbitration, effective June 2021 art 29	SAC
The Rules of Arbitration of International Commercial Disputes of the International Commercial Arbitration Court at the Chamber of Commerce and Industry of the Russian Federation, effective 11 January 2017 § 34	ICAC
RULES WITH NO EXPRESS PROVISION FOR INTERIM MEASURES	
Shanghai International Economic and Trade Arbitration Commission (Shanghai International Arbitration Centre) Arbitration Rules, effective 1 January 2015	SHIAC

CHAPTER 2

The evolution and nature of security for costs

The historical background and evolution of security for costs

2.1. A version of security for costs – the *legis actio sacramentum* – existed in Roman law from before 450 BC in the form of a deposit paid by both parties, with the victor's being returned and the vanquished's forfeited to the temple.[1] In Europe, security for costs – or *cautio judicatum solvi* – existed by statute in many states.[2] This practice became forbidden by a series of treaties and court decisions where the sole basis of the *cautio* was the residence of a plaintiff in another contracting state.[3] Article 6 of the Treaty of Rome prohibits any discrimination on the grounds of nationality.[4] The substantive contract law of countries such as Switzerland and Germany forbade *cautio* being awarded either absolutely, or unless there was a change in circumstances from the time of contracting.[5] The facility disappeared wholly from French procedural law by two statutes, one in 1972 and another in 1975.[6]

2.2. Security for costs emerged in England after the unification of the courts[7] under the Crown, the emergence of a paid legal profession in the beginning of the 13th century[8]

1 Werner Pfennigstorf, 'The European Experience with Attorney Fee Shifting' (1984) 47 *Law and Contemporary Problems* 37, 41; Bernhard Berger, 'Security for Costs: Trends and Developments in Swiss Arbitral Case Law' (2010) 28 *ASA Bulletin* 7, noting that the Roman original required the respondent rather than the claimant to provide security because the respondent's representative – the *cognitor* or *procurator* – was considered to defend in his own name. The text of G. Inst 4 101 read: 'However, the party against whom an action is brought must always give security if another person is acting on his behalf, for no one is considered to be a sufficient defendant of another person's case without security'.

2 Claude Reymond, 'Security for Costs in International Arbitration' (1994) 10 *Law Quarterly Review* 503.

3 Otto Sandrock, 'The Cautio Judicatum Solvi in Arbitration Proceedings or the Duty of an Alien Claimant to Provide Security for the Costs of the Defendant' (1997) 14 *Journal of International Arbitration* 17, 20, referring to art 17 of the *Hague Convention on Civil Procedure* of 1 March 1954, art 9(1) of the *European Convention on Establishment* of 13 December 1955, art 31(5) of the *Convention on the Contract for the International Carriage of Goods by Road* (CMR) of 19 May 1956, art 18(4) of the *Convention relative aux Transports Internationaux Ferroviaires (COTIF) (Obereinkommen über den internationalenEisenbahnverkehr)* of 5 May 1980, art 36(1) of the *Convention Réviseé pour la Navigation sur le Rhin (Revidierte Rheinschiffahrtsakte)* of 17 October 1868, and in a number of international bilateral conventions.

4 David Altaras, 'Security for Costs' (2003) 69(2) *Arbitration: The International Journal of Arbitration, Mediation and Dispute Management* 81.

5 Sandrock (n 3) 24–7.

6 Ibid 19; Thomas Webster and Michael Bühler, *Handbook of ICC Arbitration* (Thomson Reuters, 4th ed, 2018) 455 [28.33].

7 The Court of Common Pleas, the Court of Kings Bench and the Court of Chancery in the 11th and 12th centuries: See Theodore FT Plucknett, *A Concise History of the Common Law* (Lawbook Exchange, 5th ed, 2001) 83–157.

8 Paul Brand, *The Origins of the English Legal Profession* (Blackwell, 1992) 51–69; James A Brundage, *The Medieval Origins of the Legal Profession* (University of Chicago Press, 2008) 1, 283, 328.

DOI: 10.4324/9781003479628-2

that 'was only just sufficiently aware of the existence of other systems to glory in its isolation',[9] and the ability of the courts to award costs.[10] Failure to pay costs was regarded as a new species of abuse of process that the common law courts[11] countered by creating the facility of security for costs by drawing on their inherent jurisdiction to prevent abuse.[12]

2.3. The USA took a different position on costs, with the Supreme Court in 1796 confirming that each party was to bear its own costs in US litigation,[13] reflecting a policy of prioritising access to justice, manifested also in limits on lawyers' fees for litigation.[14] The English policy was also different from that adopted in France where the courts had power to award costs to the victor but did so only in about half the cases, reflecting a social value choice of access over costs.[15]

2.4. The English approach to costs is known as 'costs-shifting', 'costs following the event', or the 'English rule',[16] while the America approach is known as 'no costs-shifting', 'each party bearing its own costs', or the 'American rule'.[17] These approaches are the subject of this work as they are the predominant approaches to costs in international commercial arbitration.

2.5. Justification for the English, costs-shifting rule has been in the incremental wholistic development of the English legal system and the discouragement from taking points that are barely or not arguable, against other possible excesses in the conduct of litigation and unscrupulous attempts to manipulate the system.[18]

2.6. The earliest reported English decision on security for costs appears to be in 1750,[19] with another reference in 1755 to a developing rule,[20] but the facility was not

---

9 Plucknett (n 7) 83–105.

10 Created for the common law courts by the *Statute of Marlborough* in 1267 and the *Statute of Gloucester* in 1278, and for the courts of equity by *17 Rich 2 c 6* in 1393.

11 Parliament granted the courts of equity the power to require security for costs in 1436 in *15 Hen 6 c 4,* as a condition of commencing chancery proceedings to discourage claims for which there was a remedy at common law: Stephen E Colbran, *Security for Costs* (Longman, 1993) 4, 5–7 [2.2], [2.9]–[2.18].

12 Ibid 4 [2.4]. See also *Morris v Hanley* [2000] NSWSC 957 [11]–[13] ('*Morris v Hanley*') where it was said that the inherent power to order security for costs had its origins in the court's power to see that its process was not abused by proceedings without reasonable grounds so as to be vexatious and harassing, quoting Lord Blackburn in *Metropolitan Bank Ltd v Pooley* (1885) 10 App Cas 210, 220–1. The House of Lords gave the same purpose as the basis of security for costs in international commercial arbitration: *S A Coppée–Lavalin NV v Ken–Ren Chemicals and Fertilizers Ltd (In liquidation in Kenya)* [1995] 1 AC 38, 71F ('*Coppée–Lavalin v Ken–Ren*').

13 *Arcambel v Wiseman* (1796) 3 US 306; see John Yukio Gotanda, 'Awarding Costs and Attorneys' Fees in International Commercial Arbitrations' (1999) 21(1) *Michigan Journal of International Law* 1, 10–11; Werner Pfennigstorf, 'The European Experience with Attorney Fee Shifting' (1984) 47 *Law and Contemporary Problems* 37, 40–1. *Cf* Christopher Koch, 'Is There a Default Principle of Cost Allocation in International Arbitration: The Importance of the Applicable Provisions and Legal Traditions' (2014) 31(4) *Journal of International Arbitration* 485, 490 that the true purpose of the American rule is 'as an insurance policy to ensure the financial risk that the claimant's attorney assumes [in acting on a contingency basis] remains calculable and limited'.

14 Koch (n 13), 490–1.

15 Ibid 489.

16 *Project 28 Pty Ltd v Barr* [2005] NSWCA 240 [112] ('*Project 28*').

17 Colin YC Ong and Michel Patrick O'Reilly, *Costs in International Arbitration* (LexisNexis, 2013) 13–14 [1.6].

18 *Project 28* (n 16) [112].

19 Lawrence Collins, *Dicey and Morris on the Conflict of Laws* (Sweet & Maxwell, 13th ed, 1999) 213 [8–080], referring to *Meliorucchy v Meliorucchy* (1750) 2 Ves Sen 24.

20 Security for costs would not be ordered where one of a number of claimants resides in the jurisdiction: *Winthorp v Royal Exchange Assurance Company* (1755) Dick 282; 21 ER 277. See *Pearson v Naydler* [1977] 1 WLR 899, 902 ('*Pearson v Naydler*'); *Ingot Capital Investments Pty Ltd v Macquarie Equity Capital Markets Ltd* [2002] NSWSC 609 [61]; *Fiduciary v Morningstar Research* [2004] NSWSC 664 [54].

fully received into the common law courts until 1786.[21] Before that time '[t]he policy was one of free access to our courts for all, rich and poor, English and foreign', the courts seldom exercising the security for costs jurisdiction and then only in special circumstances such as the claimant being nominal.[22] By degrees it was extended to claimants who were misdescribed, whose address was misstated, or who were abroad.[23] Security for costs was not available against respondents who should be allowed to defend the allegations against them.[24] By 1894[25] it had become 'the inflexible rule of the court' to require security for costs from any claimant resident outside the jurisdiction with insufficient means within it; no enquiry was permitted into the merits of the case.[26]

2.7. It is not apparent what caused the change in English policy from one of free access to protecting citizens from claims by residents abroad. *Pray v Edie*[27] gave the difficulty of enforcement of a costs order as the sole reason, but this difficulty was not new.[28] Tidd said in 1793 that security for costs was not formerly granted because of the fear that it might affect trade and clog the course of justice.[29] Counsel in *Fitzgerald v Whitmore*[30] suggested that the recent deployment of the facility in England was in response to English claimants in Continental proceedings being required to provide security for costs due to their residence abroad. Berger records that, from 1761, the Canton of Bern required security for costs from those who were insolvent or were domiciled or habitually resident outside the canton, lending some support to counsel's suggestion.

2.8. In summary, the modern form of security for costs in England began in the mid-18th century,[31] grounded in the inherent power of the court[32] to protect its processes from abuse by ensuring orders for costs against claimants would be satisfied.[33] Emanating from the court's inherent power, it is a discretionary interlocutory remedy.[34] Initially based on the nominal nature

---

21 *Pray v Edie* (1786) 99 ER 1087 ('*Pray v Edie*') accepted that the power to order security for costs was part of superior courts' inherent jurisdiction: New South Wales Law Reform Commission, *Security for Costs and Associated Costs Orders* [2011] NSWLRCCP 13, 22 [2.11]. It also marked a dramatic change in practice, rapidly established, to order security for costs against claimants solely because they were resident outside the jurisdiction: *DSQ Property Co Ltd v Lotus Cars Ltd* [1987] 1 WLR 127, 129 ('*DSQ Property*').

22 *DSQ Property* (n 21) 129; Colbran (n 11) 7 [2.22].

23 Colbran (n 11) 8 [2.23]. For example, in 1789 the court held that a resident of England would not be required to give security if he was a foreigner or insolvent: *Porrier v Carter* [1789] 1 H BL 106; 126 ER 64.

24 *Bowring & Company (Insurance) Ltd v Corsi Partners Ltd* [1994] 2 Lloyd's Rep 567.

25 *Crozat v Brogden* [1894] 2 QB 30.

26 *DSQ Property* (n 21) 129. Incidentally, this describes the traditional operation of *cautio judicatum solvi* in civil law jurisdictions where the facility is applied almost automatically based solely on the claimant's foreign residence: Sandrock (n 3) 17, 18.

27 *DSQ Property* (n 21).

28 Ibid 129.

29 Willam Tidd, *The Law of Costs in Civil Actions* (Wheeldon and Butterworths, 1793) 61, repeated verbatim in Willam Tidd, *The Practice of the Courts of King's Bench and Common Pleas in Personal Actions and Ejectment* (Butterworth, Butterworth and Cooke, 8th ed, 1824) 579.

30 *Fitzgerald v Whitmore* [1786] 1 TR 352 ('*Fitzgerald v Whitmore*').

31 Collins (n 19) 213 [8–080], referring to *Meliorucchy v Meliorucchy* (1750) 2 Ves Sen 24.

32 Keith Mason, 'The Inherent Jurisdiction of the Court' (1983) 57 *Australian Law Journal* 449, 455. Similarly in Canada: see *Han v Cho* 2008 BCSC 1229 [12] ('*Han v Cho*'), citing *Launer v Sommerfeld* (1964) 45 DLR (2d) 293; *Shiell v Coach House Hotel Ltd* (1982) 136 DLR (3d) 470 (CA).

33 *Morris v Hanley* (n 12) [11]–[13]; *Bhattcharya v Freedman* [2001] NSWSC 498 [27]; *Rajski v Computer Manufacturer and Design Pty Ltd* [1982] 2 NSWLR, 447–8; [1983] 2 NSWLR 122, 128; *Green as Liquidator of Arimco Mining Pty Ltd (in Liq) v CGU Insurance Limited* [2008] NSWSC 449 ('*Green*')]; *Coppée–Lavalin v Ken–Ren* (n 12) 71F.

34 *Pray v Edie* (n 21); *DSQ Property* (n 21) 129.

of the claimant, it grew to respond to the foreign residence of the claimant and the resultant difficulty of enforcing costs orders and recovering costs.[35] Over time, as cases threw up different circumstances, other factors began to gain relevance.[36] Poverty of natural claimants, alone, was not a sufficient reason to order security for costs,[37] and is still not sufficient of itself.[38]

2.9. When the limited liability corporation was created in England in the mid-19th century, the Legislature expressly made the remedy available against corporate claimants where there was reason to believe, by credible evidence, the company would likely be unable to pay an adverse costs order.[39] This was to protect respondents from the limited liability of corporations enabling natural persons to shelter behind empty shells and corporations to 'privatize their gains while externalizing or "socializing" their losses' and to 'impose taxes or costs on other people without their direct consent'.[40] That reason to believe did not *require* the court to grant security for costs but enlivened the court's power to grant the discretionary remedy after considering all relevant factors.[41] Similar legislation or rules of court have been enacted in common-law costs-shifting jurisdictions[42] with the effect that the apparent impecuniosity of a corporate claimant is a primary factor in the exercise of the discretion.[43]

2.10. Where the corporate claimant is not incorporated in the jurisdiction, the statutory factor is relied on by analogy 'as a makeweight to the exercise of the court's discretionary power'.[44] To put it another way, a corporate claimant's impecuniosity is a statutorily recognised factor factually relevant to the question of the likelihood of the respondent recovering costs.[45]

---

35 *Fitzgerald v Whitmore* (n 30).

36 Colbran (n 11), 8 [2.23]. For example, in 1789 the court held that a resident of England would not be required to give security if he was a foreigner or insolvent: *Porrier v Carter* [1789] 1 H BL 106; 126 ER 64.

37 *Powell v Taylor* (1885) 31 Ch D 34, 38; *Orr v Lusute Pty Ltd* (1987) 72 ALR 617.

38 *Green (as liquidator of Arimco Mining Pty Ltd) v CGU Insurance Ltd [2008] NSWCA 148 [6]) ('Green appeal').*

39 *Limited Liability Act 1855* (UK). See *Pearson v Naydler* (n 20) 904–5, 906G; *Flender Werft AG v Aegean Maritime Ltd* [1990] 2 Lloyd's Rep 27, 30 ('*Flender Werft*'); *DSQ Property* (n 21) 129. The most recent such provision in the *Companies Act 1985* (UK) s 726(1) was repealed on 1 October 2009, leaving respondents with the equivalent power in *Civil Procedure Rules 1998* (UK) 25.13(2)(c) (commonly referred to as 'Gateway C'): *Infinity Distribution Ltd (in administration) v The Khan Partnership LLP* [2021] EWCA Civ 565 [10] (*'Infinity Distribution'*). See Jane Ching, 'The Statutory Ground to Award Security for Costs Against an Impecunious Company: Should We Mourn Its Passing?' (2009) 28 *Civil Justice Quarterly* 470.

40 Ignacio Ferror, W Michael Hoffman and Robert E McNulty, 'Must Milton Friedman Embrace Stakeholder Theory?' (2014) 119(1) *Business and Society Review* 37, 38.

41 *Sir Lindsay Parkinson & Co Ltd v Triplan* Ltd [1973] QB 609, 626A-D, 627D-F, and 628H–629A ('*Lindsay Parkinson*').

42 For example, *Corporations Act 2001* (Cth) s 1335(1); *Companies Act* (Singapore, cap 50, 2006 rev ed) s 388(1); *Companies Ordinance* (Hong Kong) cap 622, 905(1); *Business Corporations Act*, SBC 2002, c 57, s 236; *Uniform Civil Procedure Rules 2005* (NSW) r 42.21(1)(a) and (d), the *Civil Procedure Rule 1998* (UK) 25.13(2) (a) and (c), and the *High Court Rules 2016* (NZ) r 5.45(1)(a) and (b).

43 *Pearson v Naydler* (n 20); *Lindsay Parkinson* (n 41); *Keary Developments Ltd v Tarmac Construction Ltd* [1995] 3 AER 534, 539h ('*Keary*'); *Regia Autonoma De Electricitate Renel v Gulf Petroleum International Ltd* [1996] 1 Lloyds Rep 67, 71; *Shared Network Services Limited v Nextiraone UK Limited* [2012] EWCA Civ 1171 [3], [29]; *Re Southbank Liquor Stores Vic Pty Ltd* [2021] VSC 404 [28], [77(a)] and the cases there cited. In British Columbia, the Court of Appeal has held that once the application for security has shown that the claimant will not be able to pay costs should the claim fail, security is generally ordered unless the court is satisfied that there is no arguable defence: *Fat Mel's Restaurant Ltd v Canadian Northern Shield Insurance Co* (1993) 76 BCLR (2d) 231 (CA) [16]; *Kropp v Swaneset Bay Golf Course Ltd* (1997) 29 BCLR (3d) 252 (CA). See also *Citizens for Foreign Aid Reform Inc v Canadian Jewish Congress* (1999) 36 CPC (4th) 266 (BCSC) 14].

44 *Bank Mellat v Helliniki Techniki SA* [1984] 1 QB 291, 300G ('*Bank Mellat*').

45 *DSQ Property* (n 21) 130.

2.11. To render the facility suitable to international commercial arbitration, the foreign residence of a corporate claimant has been statutorily removed in a number of common law jurisdictions as the sole determinant of the availability of the facility.[46] Security for costs is now a broad, multifactorial, judicial discretion founded on the protection of the integrity of the judicial process, with fairness, or justice, as the touchstone,[47] enlivened when it appears that there is an appreciable risk the respondent will not be able to recover a costs order against the claimant if successful.[48]

The juridical bases of the facility

2.12. The juridical basis of the security for costs facility in the common law is given as the prevention of abuse of process.[49] An additional socio-economic basis is proposed in this work of the protection of creditors. In international commercial arbitration it has been suggested that the legal basis of the facility lies in the *clausula rebus sic stantibus* ('things thus standing') rule, applicable where there has been a fundamental change in circumstances.[50] These three bases are considered next.

Prevention of abuse of process

2.13. Security for costs is said to prevent abuse of process and to preserve the integrity of proceedings by 'the protection of the efficacy of the exercise of the jurisdiction to award costs'.[51] It may be used 'to prevent abuse of the court's processes by putting a brake on proceedings which would otherwise operate oppressively and vexatiously against a defendant'.[52] That rationale grounds the facility in public policy, similar to the public interest in finality of litigation, also founded on the prevention of abuse of process in England.[53] This has relevance to arguments that security for costs denies claimants access to justice.

2.14. There are instructive parallels between the public interest in the finality of litigation and in the prevention of abuse of process in relation to the public interest in access to justice. There is a similar tension between finality and access to justice as there is between security for costs and access to justice. That tension is resolved by granting

46 For example, *Arbitration Act 1996* (UK) s 38(3)(a) and (b); *International Arbitration Act 1974* (Cth) s 23K(2); *International Arbitration Act* (Singapore, cap 143A, 2002 rev ed) s 12(4); *Arbitration Ordinance* (Hong Kong) cap 609, s 56(2); *cf Arbitration Act*, SBC 2020, c 2, s 32(2)(b)(iii).

47 *Infinity Distribution* (n 39) [34]; *Merribee Pastroral Industries Pty Ltd v Australia New Zealand Banking Group Ltd* (1998) 193 CLR 502 [26] ('*Merribee*'); *Kiefel v Victoria* [2014] FCA 604 [43], [88] (Mortimer J).

48 Alan Redfern and Sam O'Leary, 'Why It Is Time for International Arbitration to Embrace Security for Costs' (2016) 32 *Arbitration International* 397, 410.

49 See (n 12).

50 Marc D Veit, 'Note: Procedural Order No. 14 of 27 November 2002: Security for Costs in International Arbitration: Some Comments to Procedural Order No. 14 of 27 November 2002' (2005) 23(1) *ASA Bulletin* 116.

51 *Stuart v Said* [2021] VSCA 226 [26] ('*Stuart Appeal*'); *Precise Training Pty Ltd v Chief Commissioner of State Revenue* [2020] NSWSC 1202 [54].

52 *Bhagat v Murphy* [2000] NSWSC 892 [5]–[6]; *University of Canberra v Zierholz @ UC Pty Ltd* [2020] ACTCA 45 [16] ('*University of Canberra*').

53 *Johnson v Gore Wood and Co* [2002] 2 AC 1, 31; *Barrow v Bankside Agency Ltd* [1996] 1 SLR 257, 260. Cf in Australia where it is based on the legal principle of estoppel: *Port of Melbourne Authority v Anshun Pty Ltd* (1981) 197 CLR 589. Yet underpinning that application of the principle may be the broader public interest in finality and prevention of abuse of process: Murray Gleeson, 'Finality' (2013) *Bar News* 33, 34–5.

claimants finite access to justice, limited by economic and practical realities and by striking a balance of fairness between the parties.

2.15. The need for eventual finality of litigation results in 'a conscious rationing of judicial resources' by dictating the nature and number of appeals, reflecting 'a compromise between the desirability of correcting error or other injustice and the need for finality'.[54]

2.16. The international commercial arbitration community makes an even sterner compromise in favour of finality, one of its vaunted and perceived advantages,[55] by 'overwhelmingly' proscribing appeals and merits reviews in all but a small minority of jurisdictions.[56] The balance is weighed so heavily in favour of finality that, in the words of Chief Justice Sundaresh Menon of Singapore, in arbitration there is no right to a right answer,[57] paraphrasing Sir Michael Kerr's comment that 'when parties agree arbitration they buy the right to get the wrong answer'.[58] Sir Bernard Eder has said that, even where a right of appeal exists, the mere fact that an award is wrong does not justify judicial intervention.[59]

2.17. In other words, at a very early stage in the arbitral process, finality is viewed as being of greater importance than both justice and access to justice. Finality is seen as one element of the idea of justice,[60] creating an abiding tension between the parties' desire for right answers and the law's drive for finality.[61] In a similar way, prevention of abuse of process – and in particular, protection of the jurisdiction to award costs – places a limit on access to justice by the requirement to provide security for costs. Prevention of abuse could also properly be said to be one element of the idea of justice, perhaps even more fundamental than finality. Abuse of the process by which justice is secured tends to pervert the course of justice and subvert the system of ensuring justice.

Creditor protection

2.18. An additional contemporary juridical or policy basis for security for costs suggested here is in the socio-economic policy of preventing the incurrence of unpayable debts. Governments and international organisations are concerned for reasons of public and socio-economic policy to discourage companies from incurring debts that are unlikely

54 Gleeson (n 53) 35.

55 In *QMUL, 2018 International Arbitration Survey: The Evolution of International Arbitration ('QMUL 2018')*, 16% of respondents gave finality as one of the three most valuable characteristics of international arbitration: 7, Chart 3.

56 Nigel Blackaby and Constantine Partasides, with Alan Redfern and Martin Hunter, *Redfern and Hunter on International Arbitration* (Oxford University Press, 6th ed, 2015) 592 [10.67]. The UK is one of the few jurisdictions to permit an appeal, limited to a question of English law: *Arbitration Act 1996* (UK) s 69.

57 Sundaresh Menon, 'Arbitration's Blade: International Arbitration and the Rule of Law' (2021) 38 *Journal of International Arbitration* 1, 6, 15–17.

58 Bernard Eder, *Does Arbitration Stifle Development of the Law? Should s 69 Be Revitalised?* (Speech, CIArb AGM Keynote Address, 28 April 2016) [14].

59 Ibid.

60 Gleeson (n 55) 36.

61 Menon (n 59) 16.

to be paid.[62] 'Legislation has been enacted to that end,[63] the details of which are not relevant for present purposes, but include imposing personal liability on directors for debts incurred[64] or payments made[65] when the company is insolvent, or for losses caused by insolvent trading.[66] Criminal or civil penalties may be imposed in certain jurisdictions in addition to personal liability for the debt or damages.[67] UNCITRAL[68] and the World Bank[69] recommend discouraging companies that are approaching insolvency from incurring debts that are unlikely to be paid. The latter advocates implementing reliable procedures that enable credit providers and investors to more effectively assess, manage, and resolve default risks and to promptly respond to a state of financial distress of an enterprise borrower.[70] Security for costs could be seen as one such procedure.

2.19. Policies against the avoidable incurrence of unrecoverable debts serve economic efficiency, said to remain the dominant theoretical paradigm in contemporary corporate and commercial scholarship.[71] UNCITRAL recognises that effective insolvency regimes are important to prevent or limit financial crises, to reallocate resources from unviable to more efficient businesses, to preserve employment, reduce the costs of business, and

62 Andrew Keay and Michael Murray, 'Making Company Directors Liable: A Comparative Analysis of Wrongful Trading in the United Kingdom and Insolvent Trading in Australia' (2005) 14 *International Insolvency Review* 27; Paul Omar, 'The European Initiative on Wrongful Trading' (2003) 6 *Insolvency Lawyer* 239, noting legislation on the topic in UK, France, Belgium, Germany, Spain and The Netherlands. Cf Hong Kong where there is no similar provision: Howard Lam, Flora Innes and Jeffrey Wong, 'Restructuring and Insolvency in Hong Kong' in *ALB Asia Insolvency and Restructuring Handbook 2020* (ALB, 2020) 29, 32. UNCITRAL noted in 2020 that little has been done internationally to harmonise the various approaches of national law: UNCITRAL, 'Directors' Obligations in the Period Approaching Insolvency' in *Legislative Guide on Insolvency Law* (UNCITRAL, 2nd ed, 2020) 6 [3] ('UNCITRAL *Legislative Guide*').

63 One of the earliest being the prohibition against fraudulent trading in the *Companies Act 1929* (UK) s 275 following the report of the Company Law Amendment Committee, Parliament of the United Kingdom (Report, 6 January 1925) 28 (I Fraudulent Trading).

64 For example, *Insolvency Act 1986* (UK) s 214; *Corporations Act 2001* (Cth) s 588G; *Insolvency, Restructuring and Dissolution Act* (Singapore, No 40 of 2018) s 239.

65 For example, German law requires directors to file an application for insolvency proceedings within three weeks after the insolvency occurs and renders them liable for payments made if they do not: Christoph Schotte and Björn Grotebrune, 'Insolvency and Directors' Duties in Germany: Overview' in *Corporate Insolvency Proceedings* (Thomson Reuters, 2018) [22].

66 Markus Wolf, 'Dead Man Walking: Insolvent Trading Under Swiss Law' (2019) *Butterworths Journal of International Banking and Financial Law* 142; UNCITRAL *Legislative Guide* (n 62) 11–12 [3], 14 [7], 24–5 [30]–[33].

67 For example, *Insolvency Act 1986* (UK) s 218; *Corporations Act 2001* (Cth) ss 588J–K; *Insolvency, Restructuring and Dissolution Act* (Singapore, No 40 of 2018) s 241.

68 The UNCITRAL, *Legislative Guide* (n 62) suggests national legislation consider that, when a company is approaching insolvency, the directors act to minimise losses to creditors, avoid aggravating the situation, and take appropriate action to avoid the company sliding into insolvency such as reducing expenditure and focussing on the interests of creditors, employees, suppliers, customers, governments, shareholders, and even environmental concerns.

69 The World Bank *Principles for Effective Insolvency and Creditor Rights Systems* recommends that 'laws governing director and officer liability for decisions detrimental to creditors made when an enterprise is in financial distress or insolvent should promote responsible corporate behaviour while fostering reasonable risk taking': World Bank, *Principles for Effective Insolvency and Creditor Rights Systems* (World Bank, April 2001) 10 (Principle 7).

70 World Bank, *Principles for Effective Insolvency and Creditor/Debtor Regimes* (World Bank, 2016) 14 (Part A. Creditor/Debtor Rights, A1 Key Elements).

71 David Morrison, 'The Economic Necessity for the Australian Insolvent Trading Prohibition' (2003) 12 *International Insolvency Review* 171, 172.

increase the availability of credit.[72] Employment and taxation are stated to be public policy concerns.[73]

2.20. These policies have not previously been expressly identified as a basis of security for costs, yet the facility can be seen ultimately to serve economic efficiency and to evidence parallels with insolvent trading provisions. Both the facility and the provisions are necessitated by the twin concepts of corporate limited liability and separate legal identity.[74] It is not suggested that the insolvent trading criteria should be met for security for costs to be granted but that the policies underlying the insolvent trading provisions are served by an order for security.

2.21. Such an order is predicated on a reason to believe the corporate claimant will be unable to pay the successful respondent's costs. Companies are considered insolvent if they are unable to pay their debts when they fall due.[75] The signal differences between the test for security for costs and that for insolvency is that the former looks to the future and is contingent on the claimant's failure in the proceeding, while the latter may be determined as at the present. Those differences do not render the policies underlying the insolvent trading principles inapplicable to security for costs as the prediction of future inability to pay is largely dependent on present ability.[76]

2.22. Security for costs performs a more moderate function in relation to financially distressed companies than do the insolvent trading provisions, and on satisfaction of a lower standard. Its function is more moderate in that it merely requires provision of security or a stay of proceedings in the absence of security, rather than attributing personal liability; its standard of satisfaction is lower in that it requires only a reason to believe a future inability to discharge a contingent debt. In appropriate cases, it prevents the claimant from forcing the respondent to incur significant expenses the claimant will not be able to pay. It may also prevent the claimant from itself incurring debts it is unable to pay such as lawyers', experts', tribunal, and institutional fees. This socio-economic function of security for costs is performed regardless of legal tradition or dispute resolution system.

Clausula rebus sic stantibus

2.23. It has been suggested that the legal basis for granting security for costs is in many cases an application of the well-established *clausula rebus sic stantibus* rule because it is perceived to be grounded on and requiring a fundamental change in circumstances.[77]

---

72 UNCITRAL, 'UNCITRAL Legislative Guide on Insolvency Law' *United Nations Commission on International Trade Law* (Web Page, undated) (Relevance to international trade).

73 Ibid (Purpose).

74 Established by *Saloman v Saloman* [1897] AC 22. As to insolvent trading, see Morrison (n 71) 171. As to security for costs, see *Pearson v Naydler* (n 20).

75 For example, *Insolvency Act 1986* (UK) s 123. Statutory formulations may differ, but the concept is the same.

76 See [5.15].

77 Marc D Veit, 'Note: Procedural Order No. 14 of 27 November 2002: Security for Costs in International Arbitration: Some Comments to Procedural Order No. 14 of 27 November 2002' (2005) 23(1) *ASA Bulletin* 116. It is not clear if the requirement of a fundamental change is given as being indicative, or a result, of the foundation of the facility.

That suggestion was made following an observation that a fundamental change appears to be the common denominator of grounds in arbitral decisions on security for costs.[78]

2.24. *Clausula rebus sic stantibus* ('things thus standing' or 'under the circumstances') is a rationale underlying certain provisions of substantive contract law, mainly in civil law jurisdictions.[79] It as an exception to the universally accepted principle of *pacta sunt servanda* ('agreements must be kept').[80] Application of the *clausula* rationale depends upon its statutory expression but may be generalised as excusing a party from its obligations under a contract when there has been an unanticipated fundamental change of circumstances since the contract was formed.[81] The doctrine dates from Roman law and is said to have its roots in the philosophy of Cicero and Seneca in adapting agreements and promises to an unforeseeable and extraordinary change.[82] It relies on the principle in the substantive contract law of some civil law jurisdictions[83] that the parties assume certain risks of dealing with each other and that, accordingly, a change from the assumed risks is required to ground liability.[84] This, in turn, is based on fault-based contract law as opposed to the strict liability of common law contract law.[85] The perception that security for costs is grounded in the *clausula* rationale has arisen due to security for costs having been limited in many ICC arbitrations to situations where the financial condition of the claimant has deteriorated after the transaction was formed, principally on the basis that the respondent assumed the risk of dealing with the claimant.[86]

2.25. Nine problems attend ascribing the foundation of security for costs to the *clausula* doctrine. First, it is contrary to the historical development of the facility in both the civil and common law traditions. Second, it contains a logical fallacy that the observable

78 Webster and Bühler (n 6) 459 [28.49]; *XXX Inc v YYY SA*, Procedural Order No 2, 2009 in ICC Case 15951, reported in (2010) 28(1) *ASA Bulletin* 71) 75 [2.3].

79 Caslav Pejovic, 'Civil Law and Common Law: Two Different Paths Leading to the Same Goal' (2001) 32 *Victoria University of Wellington Law Review* 817, 824; Ingeborg Schwenzer, 'Force Majeure and Hardship in International Sales Contracts' (2008) 39 *Victoria University of Wellington Law Review* 709, 711, noting that the doctrine has found voice in theories of hardship in Germany, The Netherlands, Italy, Greece, Portugal, Austria, the Scandinavian countries, and USA insofar as it is accommodated within the doctrine of impracticability. For a more detailed history of the episodic development of the rule, see Konrad Zweigert and Hein Kötz, *Comparative Law* (Clarendon Press, 4th ed, 2011) 518–24.

80 Dionysios P Flambouras, 'The Doctrines of Impossibility of Performance and *Clausula Rebus Sic Stantibus* in the Convention on Contracts for the International Sale of Goods and the Principles of European Contract Law: A Comparative Analysis' (2001) 13 *Pace International Law Review* 261.

81 Ibid 277; Pejovic (n 79) 824; Valentin Jentsch, *The Law of Contracts in the Age of the Coronavirus Pandemic: Is the Statutory Risk Allocation Pursuant to the Swiss Code of Obligations Still Adequate?* (European University Institute, 2020) 12, noting that the concept exists in most civil law systems. It is said that the Swiss Federal Supreme Court usually uses the wording: 'The judge must amend or rescind a contract if, as a result of subsequent, unforeseeable circumstances, such as a manifest disproportion between performance and consideration has arisen that a party's insistence on its claim appears to be abusive' and that it follows that the concept of *clausula rebus sic stantibus* is applied only with reluctance and only in case an adjustment is justified from a good faith point of view: Peter Haas and Martin Rauber, 'Switzerland: Legal Considerations Relating to the COVID-19 Outbreak' (Web Page, *Eversheds Sutherland*, undated) [7] <https://ezine.eversheds-sutherland.com/force-majeure-global-guide/choose-a-location/overlay/switzerland/>.

82 Schwenzer (n 79) 710.

83 Noting that there is 'a great diversity' in the substantive laws among civil law jurisdictions, as there is among common law jurisdictions: John Henry Merryman and Rogelio Pérez-Perdomo, *The Civil Law Tradition* (Stanford University Press, 3rd ed, 2007) 1.

84 Melvin Aron Eisenberg, 'The Role of Fault in Contract Law: Unconscionability, Unexpected Circumstances, Interpretation, Mistake, and Non-performance' (2009) 107(8) *Michigan Law Review* 1413, 1418.

85 Ibid 1419.

86 See [4.10].

situations in which it has been granted reveals the juridical basis. Third, it is a civil law basis for a common law remedy, when that basis has been severely limited in its operation in the common law (and, in fact, is not acknowledged). Fourth, as such, it would replace a universal basis with a limited basis from a different system. Fifth, it operates on substantive contractual obligations rather than matters of procedure. Sixth, it would render a procedural remedy determinable by substantive law contrary to arbitral theory.[87] Seventh, it marginalises to the point of irrelevance many of the factors traditionally considered in exercising the discretion. Eighth, it dramatically and unnecessarily reduces the operation of the facility so as to undermine its purpose. Ninth, it excludes other deserving situations. These issues are explained next.

Contrary to the historical basis

2.26. Security for costs in the civil[88] and common law[89] traditions was originally grounded in the foreign residence of the claimant and the resultant difficulty in enforcing an order for costs against the claimant. This leads to its being founded in the prevention of abuse of process.[90]

Logical fallacy

2.27. It is a logical fallacy to infer that the juridical basis of the facility lies in the *clausula* rule from the observation that all or most orders for security in one type of arbitration have been made where there has been a change of circumstances. Apart from the limited and unrepresentative dataset, the juridical basis – the *explanandum* – cannot logically be deduced from that one isolated feature – the *explanans*.[91]

Civil law basis for common law remedy, and replacing a universal basis with a limited basis

2.28. These two problems may be dealt with together. While the *clausula* theory may inform analogous principles in various legal systems, in the common law system it is not a free-standing doctrine enabling contracts to be rewritten or judicial remedies to be devised on the basis of a change in circumstances. *Clausula* may be the unarticulated basis in the common law of the doctrine of frustration although it is not expressly acknowledged as such.[92] After years of debate,[93] the doctrinal basis of frustration has been accepted in the

87 Berger (n 1).

88 Sandrock (n 5) 18–21.

89 See [2.8].

90 See [2.2].

91 W Bradley Wendel, 'Explanation in Legal Scholarship: The Inferential Structure of Doctrinal Legal Analysis' (2011) 96(4) *Cornell Law Review* 1035, 1047.

92 *Davis Contractors Ltd v Fareham Urban District Council* [1956] AC 696, 719–21, 727–9 ('*Davis Contractors*'); *Codelfa Construction Pty Ltd v State Rail Authority of NSW* (1982) 149 CLR 337, 376.

93 See Tham Chee Ho, 'Frustration' in Andrew Phang Boon Leong (eds), *The Law of Contract in Singapore* (Academy Publishing, 2012) 1337, 1342–50 [19.010]–[19.025]; JD Heydon, *Heydon on Contract* (Thomson Reuters, 2019) 880–4 [23.200]–[23.280].

UK and Singapore as being one of contractual construction,[94] but not in Australia.[95] The suggestion that the courts have jurisdiction to make a curial determination as to what is just and reasonable when circumstances have changed has been emphatically rejected as an absolving power available to courts,[96] as contrary to authority,[97] as generating excessive uncertainty,[98] and as resting on no theoretical basis.[99] Common law courts regard it as no part of the judicial function to remake bargains for contracting parties when circumstances change or when terms are perceived to be or become unfair.[100]

2.29. Relief from contractual performance under the doctrine of frustration is extreme and is available only in limited circumstances. It is extreme in that it operates to discharge the contract and relieves the parties of any future obligations of performance or payment of damages.[101] It does not permit the terms of the contract to be amended to take account of the changed conditions.[102] It is limited in that it applies only where there has been such a fundamental change in circumstances to render performance impossible or so different as to be beyond the contemplation of the parties.[103] Absent statutory intervention, changes in economic conditions are expressly excluded from attracting its protection.[104]

2.30. It is evident that the doctrine of frustration – the only common law principle with any similarity to the *clausula* rule – would not produce a facility such as security for costs, and has not been identified as its juridical basis. To assign a theoretical basis to security for costs that does not exist in the common law world, from whence this version of security for costs has evolved, is to ascribe to it qualities, functions, and a *raison d'etre* it does not possess in that world. The effect would be to exclude from the discussion of its suitability considerations arising from the common law, and to appropriate the facility to the civil law system. It would subsume the facility – criticised as a common law idiosyncrasy[105] – to an equally idiosyncratic concept in civil law systems.[106]

Substantive law basis for procedural remedy

2.31. The *clausula* rule is expressed in civil law jurisdictions in substantive contract law.[107] It operates to vary the substantive obligations under a contract, for example, to

---

94 Tham (n 95) 1346–50 [19.017]–[19.025].

95 Heydon (n 95) 884 [23.280].

96 *FA Tamplin Steamship Co Ltd v Anglo-Mexican Petroleum products Co Ltd* [1916] 2 AC 397, 404.

97 *British Movietone News Ltd v London & District Cinemas Ltd* [1952] AC 166, 185; *Notcutt v Universal Equipment Co (London) Ltd* [1986] 1 WLR 641, 647.

98 *Firth v Halloran* (1926) 38 CLR 261, 270.

99 *National Carriers Ltd v Panalpina (Northern) Ltd* [1981] AC 675, 687 ('*Panalpina*').

100 In *WorkPac Pty Ltd v Rossato* (2021) 95 ALJR 681 [62]–[64], Kiefel CJ, Keane, Gordon, Edelman, Steward and Gleeson JJ stated emphatically that 'it is no part of the judicial function to reshape or recast a contractual relationship in order to reflect a quasi-legislative judgment as to the just settlement of an industrial dispute'.

101 *Panalpina* (n 101) 700; Anthony Groom, 'Force Majeure Clauses' (2004) *AMPLA Yearbook* 286, 290; Melvin Aron Eisenberg, 'The Role of Fault in Contract Law: Unconscionability, Unexpected Circumstances, Interpretation, Mistake, and Non-performance' (2009) 197(80) *Michigan Law Review* 1413, 1419.

102 Groom (n 103).

103 Ibid 286, 288–9.

104 *Davis Contractors* (n 92); *Tsakiroglou & Co Ltd v Noblee Thorl GmbH* [1962] AC 93; *The Eugenia* [1964] 2 QB 226.

105 *Coppée–Lavalin v Ken–Ren* (n 12) 62C-D.

106 Valentin Jentsch, 'The Law of Contracts in the Age of the Coronavirus Pandemic' *EU Working Papers* (European University Institute, 2020) 12.

107 Pejovic (n 81) 824; Schwenzer (n 81) 711.

relieve a party from performance, or to vary the price, in situations of economic hardship caused by changed circumstances.[108] To state the principle is to highlight its application: 'contracts *are binding* only so long as and to the extent that matters remain the same as they were at the time of the contract coming into force'.[109] The principle operates on the binding nature of the contract, not on procedural matters relating to its enforcement.

Arbitral procedure governed by lex arbitri

2.32. Matters of procedure in arbitration are governed by the *lex arbitri*, not the *lex contractus*, and it is improper to appropriate the latter to procedural issues.[110] To apply the *clausula* rule from substantive *lex contractus* would be contrary to arbitral legal theory.

Marginalises traditional discretionary considerations

2.33. Grounding security for costs in the *clausula* rule would render a fundamental change in circumstances of the claimant as the principal factor, which it is not in the modern version of the facility.[111] It would anchor the discretion in that factor and colour the relevance of all other factors with that necessity – again an approach which has not occurred in its modern application. As the tribunal in an ICC arbitration said in another context,[112] 'the answer to the classification controversy . . . will nonetheless determine the relevant process by which the Arbitral Tribunal should seek to identify relevant legal conditions for the request'.[113] A fundamental change in the plaintiff's circumstances is not a consideration under the civil law litigation version of the facility, being based solely on the foreign residence of the claimant.[114]

Undermines utility of the facility

2.34. As is evident from the comparison in Chapter 4 of the number of applications and orders for security for costs in ICC, Swiss, and LCIA arbitrations, restricting the facility to a change of circumstances severely limits its utility in preventing the incurrence of costs that are unlikely to be paid. That comparison revealed that applications for security occur 40 times more often in LCIA arbitrations than in ICC arbitrations, and orders are made two-to-three times more often, resulting in a ratio of orders for security in LCIA to ICC arbitrations of approximately 88 to 1.[115] Five recorded orders for security for costs

108 Ingeborg Schwenzer and Edgardo Muñoz, 'Duty to Re-negotiate and Contract Adaptation in Case of Hardship' (2019) 24(1) *Uniform Law Review* 1093, 1094 n 7.

109 Egidijus Baranauskas and Paulius Zapolskis, 'The Effect of Change in Circumstances on the Performance of Contract' (2009) 118(4) *Jurisprudencija: Mokslo darbu žurnalas* 197, 198.

110 Blackaby and Partasides (n 57) 167 [3.42]; Gary B Born, *International Commercial Arbitration* (Kluwer, 2021) 2462 [17.02][G][2].

111 See the discretionary factors catalogued in Chapter 5.

112 The question of whether security for costs is an 'interim measure or protection' under Swiss law or is a 'procedural institution': Procedural Order No 4, 2009 reported in (2010) 28(1) *ASA Bulletin* 59 [160].

113 Ibid [156].

114 Sandrock (n 3).

115 Orders for security are made in 30%–50% of LCIA applications but only in 17% of ICC applications. That yields 12–20 LCIA orders to 0.17 ICC orders. If 15 is taken as a representative number of LCIA orders for demonstration purposes, the ration becomes 15:0.17. Those numbers are multiplied by 5.89 to bring 0.17 to 1.

have been made in the 100 year history of the ICC compared to 46 in the LCIA in the four years 2017 to 2020 inclusive.[116] Had a change in circumstances not been required, approximately half of the applications rejected in ICC arbitrations would likely have resulted in an order for security.[117]

Excludes other deserving situations

2.35. Basing the facility in the *clausula* rule suggests security for costs is only available where there is a change in circumstances, rather than merely making it one of the situations in which the facility is available. There is no doubt that altered circumstances can justify an order for security, but other situations may also justify an order, such as proceedings that are an abuse of process,[118] proceedings with very low prospects of success,[119] the claimant's persistent non-payment of legal obligations,[120] the claimant's being a nominal party,[121] any of which may be combined or not with long-term financial difficulty.[122]

2.36. In summary, the juridical basis of security for costs in international commercial arbitration is not found in the *clausula* principle but in the concern to prevent abuse of process. As a consequence, the juridical basis of the facility does not limit considerations in the exercise of the discretion to identifying exceptional or changed circumstances.

The nature of the discretion

2.37. Security for costs is discretionary. A remedy is discretionary where its availability depends on the application of a very general standard – for example, what is 'just and equitable' in a given circumstance – and 'balancing of injustice is always a factor in the exercise of judicial discretion'.[123]

2.38. The security for costs discretion involves engaging in an instinctive synthesis of the various relevant criteria[124] and giving them due weight.[125] That weight depends upon the intrinsic persuasiveness of each factor and its impact on all the other circumstances which have to be weighed.[126] The factors are 'never more than pointers one way or another. Focussing too much on one factor can distort the overall assessment'.[127]

---

116 See [4.39] et seq.

117 See [4.8] et seq.

118 See [5.34].

119 See [5.29].

120 See [5.19].

121 See [5.11].

122 See [5.6]–[5.8].

123 *Han v Cho* (n 32) [26]. See also Lord Justice Bingham, 'The Discretion of the Judge' (1990) 5 *Denning Law Journal* 27, 28. According to his definition, 'an issue falls within a judge's discretion if, being governed by no rule of law, its resolution depends on the individual judge's assessment (within such boundaries as have been laid down) of what it is fair and just to do in a particular case. He has no discretion in making his findings of fact. He has no discretion in his rulings on the law'.

124 *Kronemann v Papaioannou* [2020] VSCA 275 [19], *Pilkin v Sony Australia Limited* [2018] FCA 1018 [34]; *The Cultural Intelligence Project Pty Ltd v The Entourage Education Group Pty Ltd (No 2)* [2021] FCCA 1317 [28]; *Coonwarra Pty Ltd v Cornonero Pty Ltd* [2018] VSC 333 [79], [81] (as to calculation of quantum); *Rickard Constructions v Rickard Hails Moretti* [2005] NSWSC 481 [39].

125 *Saric v Vukasovic* [2019] VSCA 57 [10]–[11].

126 *Coca-Cola Amatil Victoria Ltd v P A A Enterprises Pty Ltd* [2003] VSCA 135 [9].

127 *Tasman Charters Inc (in liq) v Kamphuis* [2006] NZHC 64 [63].

2.39. An instinctive synthesis involves 'an evaluative determination of a discretionary nature, not susceptible of complete exposition' and one which is 'inexact, non-scientific, not narrow or purely mathematical, and fact and circumstance specific'.[128] It considers all the relevant criteria together and makes a global judgment in a single step, rather than the contrasting structured, sequential process of adding and subtracting the effect of the applicable criteria one by one.[129] On occasion this may require the weighing of incommensurables but this is neither uncommon in the law nor inutile.[130] It is a value judgment, not a mathematical calculation.[131]

2.40. A discretion exercised within broad guidelines is preserved because it is neither possible nor desirable to attempt to devise a rule that would do justice in every situation.[132] Two cases are rarely identical and special aspects will strike different minds in different ways,[133] and flexibility to achieve fairness is preserved by having regard to the rules and principles applied by the courts carefully worked out over many years in a large amount of case law.[134]

The consequences of an order for security for costs

2.41. The consequences of an order for security for costs have relevance to the abuse sought to be prevented. This section outlines those consequences by considering the consequences of an application, the usual outcomes of an application and the consequences of an order.

Consequences of an application

2.42. A request for security for costs,[135] followed by an application, distracts the claimant[136] from preparing their case,[137] and forces expenditure on work that does not advance determination of the merits.

128 *Rogers v Rogers* [2018] NSWSC 1982 [162].

129 *Grey v Harrison* [1997] 2 VR 359, 367.

130 *Clubb v Edwards* [2019] HCA 11 [271].

131 *Pfennig v R* (1995) 182 CLR 461, 529.

132 *Merribee* (n 48) [26(1)].

133 Ibid.

134 Departmental Advisory Committee, Parliament of the United Kingdom, *Report on the Arbitration Bill* (Final Report, February 1996) [365] ('*DAC Report*').

135 See [6.6].

136 Incidentally or intentionally. The application might be brought tactically when the claimant is preoccupied with preparing substantive submissions, with the purpose or effect of distracting the claimant's attention and resources. An interruption by the potential intrusion of a stay during the pre-trial preparation for a hearing of the case: *Attorney-General (Botswana) v Aussie Diamond Products Pty Ltd* [2009] WASC 299 [15]–[16]; *Ling v Beyond Development Group Pty Ltd* [2021] NSWSC 1251 [44]. In Procedural Order, ICC, Case No 23904, 27 March 2020 ('PO 23904') the respondent brought the application after the claimant had requested an extension of time to make its submissions in reply and in defence of the counterclaim, some 12 months after the proceeding began.

137 The application process for security for costs can be slow and costly, particularly in international commercial arbitration where it is less common than in litigation: Alastair Henderson, 'Security for Costs in Arbitration in Singapore' (2011) 7 *Asian International Arbitration Journal* 54–5; ICCA–Queen Mary Task Force, *Report on Third-Party Funding in International Arbitration* (Report, ICCA and Queen Mary University of London, April 2018) 18, 26–7 ('ICCA Report on Third-Party Funding') 163, citing Born 2494; Samaa AF Haridi, 'Security for Costs and Claim Under the ICC Rules of Arbitration – Rare, But Possible' (2020) 2 *ICC Dispute Resolution Bulletin* 77, 78.

Usual outcomes of an application

2.43. There are three usual alternative outcomes of an application for security for costs:

(1) An order is made and the security is paid. This result may be termed 'paid';
(2) An order is made, the security is not paid and the proceeding is stayed. This result may be termed 'stayed';
(3) An order is not made and the proceeding continues in the usual way. This result may be termed 'not made'.

Consequences of an order

2.44. The consequences for the claimant ('C') of an order for security, using the preceding terminology, are:

C1. Paid – the claimant has fewer funds to finance the arbitration or must incur the cost of financing the security,[138] usually either by cash,[139] a loan, or bank guarantee,[140] a charge over assets,[141] by third party funding,[142] or by insurance.[143] Compounding these effects is that the claimant is being ordered to do something that it will likely find difficult to do,[144] which increases their difficulties.

C2. Stayed – the claimant's claim is not determined on the merits and may eventually be dismissed without prejudice to the claimant's rights.[145] The claimant may feel dissatisfied with the process in not having had the merits of its claim ventilated and the outcome may not be 'accepted with serenity'.[146]

---

138 Jeffrey Waincymer, *Procedure and Evidence in International Arbitration* (Kluwer, 2012) 644 [8.3.1].

139 Depositing cash until the conclusion of the proceeding deprives the claimant of use of those funds in its prosecution of the claim or otherwise.

140 Taking a loan or providing a bank guarantee requires payment of interest and reduces the ability of the company to raise finance for business purposes.

141 Granting a charge over assets limits the ability to utilise those assets for other fund-raising purposes and to dispose of the assets: *Rowe v Ingenious Media Holdings plcs* [2021] EWCA Civ 29 [47] ('*Rowe v Ingenious*').

142 Third party funders usually take a portion of the proceeds recovered under a judgment, typically around 30%–40%, diminishing the value of the proceeding to the claimant: *ICCA Report on Third-Party Funding* (n 137)18, 26–7. Security for costs is seen as a cost of the funder's business rather than the imposition of an additional burden on an impecunious claimant, and the funder's interests are not considered on an application for security: *Les & Zelda Investments Pty Ltd v Whitehaven Coal Ltd* [2020] 1 NSWSC 1091 [48] ('*Les & Zelda*'). Some funders enjoy a size or reputation enabling them to meet an order for security by simply giving an undertaking to the court to pay an adverse costs order: see [7.27].

143 *Nylex Corporation Pty Ltd v Basell Australia Pty Ltd* [2009] VSC 97 [58]–[62]; *Versloot Dredging BV v HDI Gerling Industrie Vesicherung AG* [2013] EWHC 658 (Comm); *DIF III Global Co-Investment Fund LP v BBLP LLC* [2016] VSC 401 [49].

144 *Pearson v Naydler* (n 20); *Idoport Pty Limited & Anor v National Australia Bank Limited* [2001] NSWSC 744 [59] ('*Idoport*').

145 *Coppée–Lavalin v Ken–Ren* (n 12) 48C; *Flender Werft* (n 39) 32; *Petromin SA v Secnav Marine Ltd* [1995] 1 Lloyd's Rep 603, 609–11 ('*Petromin*'); *Hudson Strumpffabrik GMBH v Bentley Engineering Co Ltd* [1962] 2 QB 587, 593 ('*Hudson*'); *Michael Wilson & Partners, Limited v Emmott* [2020] NSWCA 245 [5]; *Sax v Campbell* [2020] NZHC 1297 [32]; *Tomanovich Holdings Limited v Gibbston Community Water Company (2014) Limited* [2018] NZHC 990 at [68]–[85]; *Westpac New Zealand Limited v Adams* [2013] NZHC 3112 [92(c)]. For arbitration, see Procedural Order No 4, LCIA, Case No 132551 (2014) reported in (2018) 36(3) *ASA Bulletin* 664 [25]; Procedural Order No 4, ICC (April 2009) reported in (2010) 28(1) *ASA Bulletin* 59 [159]; Redfern and O'Leary (n 49); *DAC Report* (n 134) [198]; *Arbitration Act 1996* (UK) s 41(6).

146 Jan Paulsson, *The Idea of Arbitration* (Oxford University Press, 2013) 1 [1.1].

C3. Not made – the claimant is not at risk on costs, subject to the likelihood of successful enforcement of a costs award.

2.45. For the respondent ('R'), the immediate consequences of an order are:

R1. Paid – the respondent's costs are protected to the extent of the security[147] and the respondent may feel able to incur costs it might not otherwise have done, secure in the knowledge that if it succeeds on the merits, the security will cover those costs.
R2. Stayed – the respondent has effectively won the entire proceeding without having to fight a long and costly battle on the merits.[148]
R3. Not made – the respondent has no protection for its costs and may feel constrained to limit its expenditure if there is no realistic possibility of enforcement of a costs award.

Maintaining access to justice

2.46. The usual order accompanying an order for security for costs is that the claim be stayed until security is provided.[149] After a time of non-payment, the stay may be made permanent[150] or, in some jurisdictions, the proceeding dismissed.[151] This denial of access to justice is justified on three grounds. First, it is permissible to subject access to justice to limitations that are reasonable and proportionate, bearing in mind finite state resources.[152] Second, access to justice is bilateral and must be viewed from the respondent's point of view as well as from the claimant's.[153]

2.47. Third, appropriate access to justice is maintained by the stifling principle which holds that security for costs will not be ordered if it is established on the balance of probabilities that the claimant would be unable to raise the security, resulting in the claim being stayed.[154] This is a 'powerful factor' in the exercise of the discretion[155] founded on the fundamental notion of access to justice.[156]

2.48. Where the *European Convention on Human Rights* applies, it has been held that ordering security for costs does not infringe the guarantee of access to justice as that

---

147 *Taurus Mining Finance Fund AIV LP v Sandfire Resources Ltd* [2021] WASC 52 [18].

148 *Andrews v Zuccubarr Pty Ltd* [2020] VSC 675 [93].

149 *Coppée–Lavalin v Ken–Ren* (n 12) 48C; *Flender Werft* (n 39) 32; *Petromin* (n 145) 609–11; *Hudson* (n 145) 593. For arbitration, see Procedural Order No 4, LCIA, Case No 132551 (2014) reported in (2018) 36(3) *ASA Bulletin* 664 [25]; Procedural Order No 4, ICC (April 2009) reported in (2010) 28(1) *ASA Bulletin* 59 [159]; Redfern and O'Leary (n 48).

150 *Petromin* (n 145) 611.

151 *Augusta Ventures Limited v Mt Arthur Coal Pty Limited* [2020] FCAFC 194 [15]; *DAC Report* (n 134) [198]; *Arbitration Act 1996* (UK) s 41(6).

152 *Rowe v Ingenious* (n 141) [57]; *Tolstoy Miloslavsky v United Kingdom* (1995) 20 EHRR 442 [59], as explained in *Al-Koronky v Time-Life Entertainment Group Ltd* [2007] 1 Costs LR 57 [30].

153 See [8.6] and [8.8].

154 (n 152); *Keary* (n 43) 539–40; *Grocon Group Holdings Pty Limited v Infrastructure NSW* [2020] NSWSC 1194 [111]; *Li v New South Wales* [2013] NSWCA 165 [45].

155 *Ballard v Brookfield Australia Investments Ltd* [2012] NSWCA 434 [37]; *Idoport* (n 144); *Yandil Holdings Pty Ltd v Insurance Co of North America* (1985) 3 ACLC 542, 545; *Bryan E Fencot & Associates Pty Ltd v Eretta Pty Ltd* (1987) 16 FCR 497, 509; *KP Cable Investments Pty Ltd v Meltglow Pty Ltd* (1995) 56 FCR 189.

156 *University of Canberra* (n 52) [3].

guarantee applies as equally to respondents as it does to claimants and that it is subject to reasonable limitations.[157]

2.49. Exceptional circumstances are usually only required under the multifactorial approach in applications for security against natural persons,[158] and in appeals where required by statute or rules of court.[159] Requiring exceptional circumstances for security against natural persons was a result of the ancient and well-established rule that they should have unfettered access to justice and that should not be barred by their impecuniosity.[160] Something exceptional has been required to overcome that principle, although in recent years courts have moved more towards the total circumstances test in relation to natural persons.[161] What was once considered a rule, that poverty is no bar to a litigant, has come to be regarded as no more than a relevant consideration.[162]

2.50. Factors that have been held to be sufficiently exceptional to justify an order for security for costs against a natural person who is impecunious are:

(1) Low prospects of success of a claim;
(2) Any form of abuse of process;
(3) A claim not being stifled by an order for security; and
(4) Low prospects of success in combination with other factors, even if an order might stifle the claim.

157 See (n 152).

158 *Rowe v Andrews* [2021] TASSC 34 [7].

159 For example, *Uniform Civil Procedure Rules 2005* (NSW) r 51.50(1).

160 *Melville v Craig Nowlan & Associates Pty Ltd* (2002) 54 NSWLR 82 [21], [80], [84], [85].

161 *Stuart appeal* (n 51) [35(c)-(e)].

162 *Lucas v Yorke* (1983) 58 ALJR 20, 21; *Mohareb v Fairfax Media Publications Pty Ltd* [2019] NSWSC 1685 [54], affirmed in *Mohareb v Harbour Radio Pty Ltd* [2020] NSWCA 231 [15].

CHAPTER 3

Power and proof

Power

3.1. Tribunals' power to order security for costs derives from any of the following available sources:

(1) Agreement of the parties;
(2) *Lex arbitri*;
(3) Institutional rules;
(4) General, or 'inherent', case management powers.

(1) Agreement of the parties

3.2. In exercise of their autonomy, the parties may agree in their arbitration agreement or after the arbitration commences that security for costs will be available.[1] Parties do not usually condescend to such minute details[2] in their agreement,[3] nor is a claimant likely to agree when an arbitration arises, unless the case for security is strong.[4] For parties to include security for costs in their agreement, they would need to be aware of the facility, sufficiently concerned about its implications, and be able to predict which of them was likely to be the claimant and respondent. It has been suggested that scant regard is often had to arbitration clauses,[5] that security for costs is ignored in dispute resolution clauses

1 Neil Kaplan, 'Winter of Discontent' (2017) 34 *Arbitration International* 373, 385; Alan Redfern and Sam O'Leary, 'Why It Is Time for International Arbitration to Embrace Security for Costs' (2016) 32 *Arbitration International* 397, 401.

2 Gu Weixia, 'Security For Costs in International Commercial Arbitration' (2005) 22(3) *Journal of International Arbitration* 167, 170; Ali Yeşilirmak, *Provisions Measures in International Commercial Arbitration* (Kluwer, 2005) [3–8], citing Julian Lew, 'Commentary on Interim and Conservatory Measures in ICC Arbitration' (2000) 11(1) *ICC International Court of Arbitration Bulletin* 15 ('Lew *Commentary*') and Christopher R Drohazal, 'Party Autonomy and Interim Measure in International Commercial Arbitration' in Albert van den Berg (ed), *International Commercial Arbitration: Important Contemporary Questions* (ICCA, 2003) 179, 182.

3 David D Caron in Barry E Carter et al. (eds), 'Comparative Analysis of International Dispute Resolution Institutions' (1991) 85 *American Society of International Law* 64, 66.

4 For example, as in *Armstrong Strategic Management and Marketing Pty Ltd v Expense Reduction Analysts Group Pty Ltd* [2013] NSWSC 457 [83]; *Sheather v Staples Waste Removals Pty Limited* [2012] FCA 998 [56]; *Chavez v Moreton Bay Regional Council* [2009] QCA 348 [2]. A claimant may agree to provide security where the case for security is strong to avoid the costs of the interlocutory application or to minimise the risk of the forced imposition of a high quantum of security. The claimant may be able to negotiate a lower amount in exchange for its concession to give security.

5 *Ferris v Plaister* (1994) 34 NSWLR 474, 491G (Kirby P), agreeing with Black J in *Prima Paint Corp v Flood & Conklin Mfg Co* 388 US 395 (1967).

 DOI: 10.4324/9781003479628-3

probably because of the protracted and potentially costly negotiations involved in dealing with a minor procedural detail,[6] and that, at the negotiation stage, 'parties are generally not sufficiently focused on the procedural intricacies of future disputes to make provision for specialized issues, such as provisional relief'.[7]

(2) Lex arbitri

3.3. The *Model Law* is the paradigm *lex arbitri*, enacted by many states with or without modification.[8] Security for costs is an interim measure within art 17 of the *Model Law* which, when first adopted in 1985, was sparsely worded.[9] In 2006, the interim measures power was expanded into 11 articles,[10] including a test for their granting.[11] States have differed in their enactment of the *Model Law*, some following the bare 1985 provision, others applying the 2006 amendments, and others still taking their own path on security for costs.[12]

3.4. Neither the 1985 nor 2006 version of art 17 includes reference to security for costs. It was excluded from the 2006 amendments, despite being suggested by the USA delegation, for fear of its being interpreted as empowering an order against defendants.[13] Article 17 now reads:

> *Article 17. Power of arbitral tribunal to order interim measures*
> (1) Unless otherwise agreed by the parties, the arbitral tribunal may, at the request of a party, grant interim measures.
> (2) An interim measure is any temporary measure, whether in the form of an award or in another form, by which, at any time prior to the issuance of the award by which the dispute is finally decided, the arbitral tribunal orders a party to:
> (a) Maintain or restore the status quo pending determination of the dispute;
> (b) Take action that would prevent, or refrain from taking action that is likely to cause, current or imminent harm or prejudice to the arbitral process itself; or

6 Jeffrey Waincymer, *Procedure and Evidence in International Arbitration* (Kluwer, 2012) 645 [8.3.2].

7 Gary B Born, *International Commercial Arbitration* (Kluwer, 3rd ed, 2021) 2632 [17.02][A][6].

8 UNCITRAL, *Status: UNCITRAL Model Law on International Commercial Arbitration (1985), with Amendments as Adopted in 2006* (Web Page) <https://uncitral.un.org/en/texts/arbitration/modellaw/commercial_arbitration/status> (*Model Law Status*); Clyde Croft, 'The Arbitration Division of the Commercial Court' [2010] *Victorian Judicial Scholarship* 54, 6, referring to the *Model Law* as 'the arbitration law against which all other arbitration laws are judged'.

9 'Unless otherwise agreed by the parties, the arbitral tribunal may, at the request of a party, order any party to take such interim measure of protection as the arbitral tribunal may consider necessary in respect of the subject-matter of the dispute. The arbitral tribunal may require any party to provide appropriate security in connection with such measure'.

10 Articles 17 and 17A-J.

11 Articles 17 and 17A.

12 Peter Binder, *International Commercial Arbitration and Mediation in UNCITRAL Model Law Jurisdictions* (Kluwer, 4th ed, 2019) 803–10 Part C, Article 17; Klaus Peter Berger, 'Common Law v Civil Law in International Arbitration: The Beginning or the End?' (2019) 36(3) *Journal of International Arbitration* 295, 300 noting that as of January 2019, 11 jurisdictions in 80 states have adopted the Model Law and other jurisdictions such as England, France, Sweden, and Switzerland have sought inspiration and guidance from its text and systematic structure.

13 *Report of the Working Group on Arbitration on the Work of Its 37th Session*, UN Doc A/CN.9/523 (11 November 2002).

(c) Provide a means of preserving assets out of which a subsequent award may be satisfied; and

(d) Preserve evidence that may be relevant and material to the resolution of the dispute.

Article 17A. Conditions for granting interim measures

(1) The party requesting an interim measure under article 17(2)(a), (b) and (c) shall satisfy the arbitral tribunal that:

(a) Harm not adequately reparable by an award of damages is likely to result if the measure is not ordered, and such harm substantially outweighs the harm that is likely to result to the party against whom the measure is directed if the measure is granted; and

(b) There is a reasonable possibility that the requesting party will succeed on the merits of the claim. The determination on this possibility shall not affect the discretion of the arbitral tribunal in making any subsequent determination.

3.5. The leading authors agree that an order for security for costs does not fit neatly into the conditions for interim measures.[14] Nevertheless it is accepted that an order for security for costs falls within art 17(2)(c) as preserving assets out of which a subsequent award may be satisfied[15] and that the harm to satisfy art 17A(1)(a) is the inability of the respondent to recover its costs, which, although it may occur in the future, requires provision to be made now.[16] There need only be a 'reasonable possibility' of the respondent's success on the merits.

3.6. Nothing in the original or amended version of art 17 requires exceptional circumstances or a change in circumstances before an interim measure generally is granted, nor has any suggestion been found that it does or should.[17] By notable contrast, and throwing the absence of the requirement in art 17 into relief, some institutional rules permit *ex parte* applications for interim relief in exceptional circumstances.[18] In other words, such circumstances are not required for *inter partes* applications. The express requirement for exceptional circumstances only for *ex parte* applications – where one party is temporarily denied the right to be heard – strongly suggests, on normal principles of construction, that such circumstances are not required for *inter parties* applications, where both parties have the right to be heard and for which art 17A states the criteria.

14 Blackaby and Partasides say that '[s]ecurity for costs is a special form of interim relief to which the criteria outlined so far do not apply': Blackaby and Partasides with Redfern and Hunter, *Redfern and Hunter on International Arbitration* (Oxford University Press, 6th ed, 2015) 316 [5.35]). Born says that 'applications for security for legal costs typically do not require showings of an urgent risk of irreparable harm': Born (n 3) 2656 [17.02][G][3][b][i]. Waincymer says that 'the standard criteria for considering interim measure applications do not normally apply to security for costs' to which 'urgency and injunction relief is not relevant' and that '[t]he irreparable harm is simply the allegation that a losing claimant will not be able to pay a costs award': Waincymer (n 6) 647 [8.3.5].

15 Born (n 7) 2680 [17.02][G][4][e]; Howard M Holtzmann et al., *A Guide to the 2006 Amendments to the UNCITRAL Model Law on International Commercial Arbitration* (Kluwer, 2015) 168.

16 Waincymer (n 6) 647 [8.3.5].

17 For example, in Holtzmann et al. (n 15) 166–72; Waincymer (n 6) 625–8 [8.2.5]; Yeşilirmak (n 2); Lew, *Commentary* (n 2); Drohazal (n 2) 182; Joseph F Sanchez, 'Applying the *Model Law*'s Standard for Interim Measures in International Arbitration' (2020) 37(1) *Journal of International Arbitration* 49, 86.

18 Blackaby and Partasides (n 14) 316 [5.33] citing the Swiss Rules art 26(3).

3.7. Neither does any of the arbitral legislation specifically addressing security for costs addressed in this work require exceptional circumstances, nor a change in circumstances or similar.[19]

(3) Institutional rules

3.8. In their approach to security for costs, the rules of arbitral institutions fall into three categories – those that expressly provide for security for costs,[20] those that rely on a general interim measures provision,[21] and those that mention neither.[22] Unique among those in requiring exceptional circumstances is art 38 of the SCC Rules 2017. It has been suggested that the rules reflect current best practice in arbitration that security for costs should only be granted in the rarest of cases, referring to the ICC practice critiqued in this dissertation and the risks of prejudging the merits and stifling claims.[23] It has also been suggested that there may not be a need for material deterioration in the claimant's financial position to warrant an order for security, which has been one of the principal means of establishing exceptional circumstances in ICC arbitrations.[24]

(4) Case management powers

3.9. Tribunals have broad, general case management power to ensure the just, expeditious, economical, and final determination of the dispute, subject to the fundamental rules of natural justice,[25] which would encompass making orders for security for costs.[26]

Burden and standard of proof

Burden of proof

3.10. International commercial arbitration places the burden of proof in security for costs applications on the respondent.[27] Unlike common law litigation, international commercial arbitration does not expressly cast an evidential burden on the claimant once

---

19 Redfern and O'Leary (n 1) 401; *International Arbitration Act 1974* (Cth) s 23K and the uniform *Commercial Arbitration Acts* of the Australian States and Territories s 17; *Arbitration Act 1996* (UK) s 38; *Arbitration Act 1996* (New Zealand, SR 1996/99) s 17A; *International Arbitration Act* (Singapore, cap 143A, rev ed 2007) s 12; *Arbitration Ordinance* (Hong Kong) cap 609 ss 2GB, 40, 56; *International Arbitration Act 2017* (South Africa) sch 1, art 17; *Arbitration Act 2005* (Malaysia) s 19.

20 ACICA 2021, AMINZ 2017, DAIC 2022, HKIAC 2018, LCIA 2020, LMAA 2021, SIAC 2016, CEPANI 2020, DIAC–LCIA 2021, SCC 2017, IAC 2018, THAC 2015 and VIAC–2018. It is now reasonably clear that an arbitral tribunal appointed under any of these rules has the power to order security for costs: Redfern and O'Leary (n 1) 401.

21 AAA 2013, BANI 2018, CAM–CBC 2016, JAMS 2021, MCIA 2016, ADCCAC 2013, DIS 2018, ICC 2021, JCAA 2019, KCAB 2016, CAM 2019, NAI 2015, SAC 2021, V^{n}IAC 2017, ICAC 2017, BAC 2015, CIETAC 2015.

22 SHIAC-2015.

23 Carl Persson and Bruno Gustafsson, 'A Practitioner's Guide to Security for Costs at the SCC' (Global Arbitration Review, 13 November 2019) <https://www.josemigueljudice-arbitration.com/xms/files/02_TEXTOS_ARBITRAGEM/19_Financiamento_Arbitragem/A_practitioner_guide_for_security_for_costs_-SCC-_-GSR_nov_19-.pdf>.

24 Ibid; Samaa A F Haridi in Security for costs and Claim under the ICC Rules of Arbitration – Rare, but Possible (2020) 2 *ICC Dispute Resolution Bulletin* 77, 95.

25 *CBS v CBP* [2021] SGCA 4 [61]–[62] (Singapore Court of Appeal).

26 Sundaresh Menon (ed), *Arbitration in Singapore: A Practical Guide* (Thomson Reuters, 2014) 296 [11.082].

27 Procedural Order, ICC Case No ICC 12542/EC, 19 December 2003, reported in (2005) 23(4) ASA Bulletin 685 ('ICC 12542') [49].

the respondent establishes matters to a *prima facie* level. In litigation, while the burden rests on the applicant from first to last, the plaintiff should establish matters within its knowledge,[28] such as:

(a) Whether its financial situation is better than it appears on the applicant's evidence;
(b) Whether an order for security would stultify its capacity to conduct the litigation;
(c) Whether the plaintiff's impecuniosity was caused by the defendant, and
(d) Any other matters it relies on to avoid paying security.

3.11. This analysis of the tribunal decisions in Chapter 4 reveals that some eight of the applications refused by tribunals may have succeeded if an evidential burden had been cast on the claimant to show it would be able to pay costs once that had been *prima facie* established by the respondent.

Standard of proof

3.12. The standard of proof in applications for security for costs is the standard on applications for interim measures, as security for costs is generally considered to be a form of interim measure.[29] There is no clear expression of the standard of proof to be applied in applications for interim measures in international commercial arbitration.[30] Tribunals may refer to the *lex arbitri*,[31] to arbitral decisions, and to scholarly opinions[32] for assistance in determining the standard. Chan, Tan, and Poon rebut the adoption of a transnational standard[33] and suggest that it is important for tribunals to be consistent with the approach of courts at the seat.[34] Sim, on the other hand, argues that there is a strong case for a transnational approach, at least to applications for emergency measures[35] (of which security for costs is not one). It has been suggested that *prima facie* evidence is sufficient and that an interim measure may be granted where there is a mere probability of the existence of the asserted facts and rights,[36] in the sense of a substantial risk rather than a 50% or greater likelihood.[37]

---

28 For example, *Grocon Group Holdings Pty Limited v Infrastructure NSW* [2020] NSWSC 1194 [59].

29 *Cf* Procedural Order No 4, 2009 reported in (2010) 28(1) ASA Bulletin 59 [160] holding that security for costs is a procedural institution under Swiss law rather than an interim measure. See also, ICC 12542 (n 27) [51] doubting, but not deciding, whether security for costs is an interim measure under Swiss law.

30 Born (n 7) 2650 [17.01(b)]; Blackaby and Partasides (n 14) 315 [5.31]; Alastair Henderson and Vikas Mahendra, 'Interlocutory Applications' in Menon (ed) (n 26) 302 [11.100]; Darius Chan, Paul Tan and Nicholas Poon, *The Law and Theory of International Commercial Arbitration in Singapore* (Academy Publishing, 2022) [6.16]; Waincymer (n 6) 630 [8.2.7] noting that there is 'so much discretion as to timing, access to evidence, standard of proof and the relevance of inferences both positive and negative'.

31 Yeşilirmak (n 2) 172 [5.21]. Born notes that virtually no national arbitration legislation addresses the standards applicable for a grant of interim measures: Born (n 7) 2650 [17.01].

32 Yeşilirmak (n 2) 173 [5.22].

33 Advocated by Born (n 7) [17.02][G][2].

34 Chan, Tan and Poon (n 30) [6.26]–[6.31].

35 Cameron Sim, *Emergency Arbitration* (Oxford University Press, 2021) 224 [7.07].

36 Ibid 173 [5.23], citing Markus Wirth, 'Interim or Preventive Measures in Support of International Arbitration in Switzerland' (2000) 18 *ASA Bulletin* 31, 38. Born notes that some tribunals order interim measures based simply on a probability: Born (n 7) 2651 [17.01(b)].

37 Born (n 7) 2651 [17.01(b)].

3.13. Tribunals use varying verbal formulae to describe the standard of proof such as 'somewhat lower (no matter where exactly the threshold lies) than the standard applicable [to the] substance of the dispute',[38] whether there was a '*reasonable probability* [of] an impending injury',[39] and whether there was 'some likelihood' that the respondent's claims for costs were *not* at risk.[40] Another noted, without deciding, that the standard might be either 'the usual standard of the balance of probabilities' or 'the lower standard of plausibility according to a prima facie examination'.[41]

3.14. Guidance should be obtainable from the conditions for granting interim measures established by the *Model Law* as evidencing a level of international consensus,[42] yet few tribunals refer to those conditions. They are that the respondent:

> shall satisfy the arbitral tribunal that:
>
> (a) Harm not adequately reparable by an award of damages is likely to result if the measure is not ordered, and such harm substantially outweighs the harm that is likely to result to the party against whom the measure is directed if the measure is granted; and
>
> (b) There is a reasonable possibility that the requesting party will succeed on the merits of the claim. The determination on this possibility shall not affect the discretion of the arbitral tribunal in making any subsequent determination.

3.15. Three elements of those conditions are suggestive of a lower standard of proof than the balance of probabilities (that is, 50% or greater). First, the respondent is to 'satisfy' the tribunal. Second, harm 'is likely' to result. Third, there must be 'a reasonable possibility' of success on the merits. As this is an interpretative exercise, regard must be had to the standards in art 2A of the *Model Law*, namely its international origin, the promotion of uniformity, and observance of good faith. Reading 'satisfy' with 'is likely' and 'a reasonable possibility' suggests, on the face of the words, a less demanding standard than proof on the balance of probabilities. 'Satisfy' imports a level of subjectivity into the determination, although, in the context of the exercise of a judicial discretion, the outer limits of acceptability would be what would satisfy a reasonable tribunal.[43] That word was chosen by the drafters of the 2006 amendments as a 'neutral formulation' of the standard of proof.[44]

3.16. To establish that the prescribed degree of harm is 'likely' to result, it is usually sufficient to show that there is a 'material'[45] or 'sufficient'[46] risk of that harm.[47]

---

38 Procedural Order ICC 2020–227, reported in (2020) 2 ICC Dispute Resolution Bulletin 77.

39 *Claimants 1–2 v Respondents 1–16* (Order, ZCC, 19 December 2008) reported in (2010) 28(1) ASA Bulletin 47 [6.2.4] [emphasis added] ('*Claimants 1–2 v Respondents 1–16*').

40 *ABC AG v Mr X* Procedural Order, 27 November 2002 reported in (2005) 23(1) ASA Bulletin [4.9] ('*ABC AG v Mr X*').

41 ICC 12542 (n 27) [18].

42 At the same time, noting that some jurisdictions, such as Singapore, deliberately chose not to adopt the 2006 amendments to the Model Law, making those amendments formally irrelevant in Singapore although they were subject to due deliberation and extensive consultation with governments: Henderson and Mahendra (n 30) 302 [11.101].

43 See [2.37].

44 Holtzmann (n 15) 169.

45 Born (n 7) 2653 [17.01(b)(i)].

46 Ibid 2655 [17.01(b)(i)].

47 Sim (n 31) 246 [7.88], noting that it would usually be impossible for claimants to prove, literally, irreparable harm.

The formula of a 'reasonable possibility' of success on the merits began in the drafting of the 2006 amendments with a 'likelihood', then moved to a 'substantial possibility' before settling on 'reasonable possibility'. This equates to the applicant establishing a *prima facie* case or reasonable prospects of success,[48] said to be a low threshold.[49] It is to be remembered that success on the merits, like the projected inability to pay costs, is a prediction as to a future matter which is logically not susceptible of determination on the balance of probabilities.[50]

3.17. Faced with ambiguous and sometimes conflicting statements of uncertain content, it may be more useful to follow the advice of Sir Anthony Mason and look to what tribunals do, rather than to what they say they do.[51] Born takes this approach and observes that tribunals do not mechanically apply a particular level of probability but adopt a pragmatic enquiry balancing all aspects of the case – the fairness of who should bear the risks of granting and not granting the measure; the likelihood, degree, and character of that harm; and the prospects of success.[52] A reasonable chance of very serious harm may justify an interim measure where the prospects of success are lower than would be required to prevent less serious harm.[53]

3.18. This is substantially the same as the multifactorial, total circumstances approach, other than the apparent absence of an evidential burden passing to the claimant,[54] and no overt consideration of a different approach to determination of the probability of future events occurring (as opposed to past events having occurred), such as the asserted harm to the respondent of the claimant's posited inability to pay an adverse costs order.[55]

48 Born (n 7) 2660–3 [17.01(b)(iv)]; Yeşilirmak (n 2) 177 [5.28]; Holtzmann et al (n 15) 171; Sim (n 31) 250 [7.102] in relation to emergency arbitrations.

49 Chan, Tan and Poon (n 30) [6.21], citing Jose F Sanchez, 'Applying the Model Law's Standard for Interim Measures in International Arbitration' (2020) 37(1) *Journal of International Arbitration* 49, 52; Sim (n 35) 251–2 [7.108].

50 See [5.15].

51 Sir Anthony Mason, 'Declarations, Injunctions and Constructive Trusts; Divergent Developments in England and Australia' (1980) 11(2) *University of Queensland Law Journal* 121, 128.

52 Born (n 7) 2653, 2654, 2655 [17.01(b)(i)].

53 Ibid 2654 [17.01(b)(i)].

54 See [4.12].

55 See [3.16].

CHAPTER 4

Historical approaches to security for costs in arbitration

Introduction

4.1. Two principal approaches to security for costs are evident in arbitration, referred to here as the ICC approach and the LCIA approach. A third, intermediate approach is the Swiss approach.

4.2. ICC tribunals generally take a restrictive approach to security for costs in requiring applicants to demonstrate exceptional circumstances.[1] Typically, a fundamental change in circumstances from the time the transaction was entered into is required, relevant to the claimant's ability to pay the respondent's costs.[2]

4.3. An effect of the LCIA not publishing awards is that ICC decisions on security for costs have become the jurisprudence and create the impression of a uniform approach to the facility in arbitration.

4.4. The LCIA approach can only be gleaned through its statistics which show it typically deals with more applications each year than ICC has published in its 100-year history, and the success rate of applications in LCIA arbitrations is about twice that of those in ICC arbitrations.

4.5. From these figures it is possible to deduce that LCIA tribunals take a more liberal approach to security for costs than ICC tribunals in not requiring exceptional circumstances. It is reasonable to assume that the approach in LCIA arbitrations reflects the approach of courts in the United Kingdom, both to security for costs in arbitration when they had the power from 1934 to 1997, and in litigation generally.

4.6. Tribunals in Swiss arbitrations[3] tend to take a moderated ICC approach, requiring more than LCIA tribunals' statistics suggest they require, but less than ICC tribunals.

4.7. Scholarship on the topic may be divided into three categories – those neutrally recording that the test for security for costs in international commercial arbitration may be more stringent than in litigation, without mentioning a requirement of exceptional circumstances;[4]

1 Samaa AF Haridi, 'Security for Costs and Claims Under the ICC Rules of Arbitration: Rare But Possible' (2020) 2 *ICC Dispute Resolution Bulletin* 77, 78; Joseph and Foxton (n 5) 213 [6.2]; Alastair Henderson, 'Security for Costs in Arbitration in Singapore' (2011) 7 *Asian International Arbitration Journal* 54.

2 Haridi (n 1).

3 Referred to here as arbitrations seated in Switzerland regardless of the institution.

4 Jeffrey Waincymer, *Procedure and Evidence in International Arbitration* (Kluwer, 2012) 643–4 [8.3.1], 647–51 [8.3.5]; Gary B Born, *International Commercial Arbitration* (Kluwer, 3rd ed, 2021) 2679–80; Nigel Blackaby and Constantine Partasides, *Redfern and Hunter on International Arbitration* (Oxford University Press, 6th ed, 2015) 316–18 [5.35]–[5.39] ('Blackaby and Partasides'); Ali Yeşilirmak, *Provisional Measures in International*

DOI: 10.4324/9781003479628-4

those noting an historical need for exceptional circumstances in ICC arbitrations[5] or a substantial deterioration in the claimant's financial condition;[6] and one straddling the categories by suggesting that the approach should depend on the terms of the power – if the power expressly authorises security for costs, there should be no reluctance to make an order, but if the power is non-specific, a higher standard should be applied.[7] Redfern and O'Leary advocate for security for costs to be welcomed into international commercial arbitration.[8]

ICC tribunal decisions

4.8. ICC's traditional 'hostility'[9] to security for costs is said to have stemmed from different factors, in particular, the consensual nature of arbitration and the fear that meritorious claims would be impeded and security orders would prejudge the merits of a case. It may also have been informed by the arguments discussed in Chapters 7 and 8, and the traditional nature of arbitration as a simple process with few rules, guidelines, interlocutory processes, or interim measures, often no costs orders, and in an environment of the emerging European community.[10] Even in 2014, it was found that around half of tribunals ordered each party to bear its own costs,[11] thus eliminating any practical basis for security for costs.

4.9. By far the single most common reason given by ICC tribunals for refusing security was that exceptional circumstances are required, reflecting, or constituting, the test applied. The next four most common reasons given can be seen as either species of the genus 'exceptional circumstances', or matters said to justify requiring exceptional circumstances. They are that:

- The applicant assumed the risk of dealing with that claimant;
- The applicant assumed the risks of entering into the transaction;
- Mere financial weakness or insolvency is insufficient;[12] and
- There must be a fundamental change in the claimant's condition.

4.10. The need for a fundamental change in the claimant's condition has been identified as the common denominator of the majority of decisions rejecting applications for

Commercial Arbitration (Kluwer, 2005) 217–18 [5.85]; Julian Lew, Loukas Mistelis and Stefan Kröll, *Comparative International Commercial Arbitration* (Kluwer, 2003) 601–2 [23.54].

5 David Joseph and David Foxton, *Singapore International Arbitration* (LexisNexis, 2014) 213 [6.2]; Alastair Henderson and Vikas Mahendra, 'Interlocutory Applications', in Sundaresh Menon (ed) *Arbitration in Singapore* (Thomson Reuters, 2014) 298–9 [11.088].

6 Eric Schwartz and Yves Derains, *Guide to the ICC Rules of Arbitration* (Kluwer, 2nd ed, 2005) (374 n 22 in relation to ICC arbitrations); Thomas Webster and Michael Bühler, *Handbook of ICC Arbitration* (Thomson Reuters, 4th ed, 2018) 459 [28.49]. Or a deliberate organisation of corporate affairs to frustrate enforcement: Emmanuel Gaillard and John Savage (eds), *Fouchard, Gaillard, Goldman on International Commercial Arbitration*, (Kluwer, 1999) 686–8 [1256], cited by Colin YC Ong and Patrick O'Reilly, *Costs in International Arbitration* (LexisNexis, 2013) 164 [9.5].

7 Ong and O'Reilly (n 6) 159–66 [9.4]–[9.5].

8 Alan Redfern and Sam O'Leary, 'Why It Is Time for International Arbitration to Embrace Security for Costs' (2016) 32 *Arbitration International* 397.

9 Ibid 400; Haridi (n 1) 77; *X Panama v Une personne physique domiciliée à Genève* (Award, Zürich Chamber of Commerce, 1995) (1995) ASA Bulletin 529, 531, quoted in *A. S.p.A. (Italy) v B AG (Germany)* (Decision, Geneva Chamber of Commerce and Industry, 25 September 1997) (2001) 19(4) ASA Bulletin 745 [7].

10 See [2.1].

11 Christopher Koch, 'Is There a Default Principle of Cost Allocation in International Arbitration: The Importance of the Applicable Provisions and Legal Traditions' (2014) 31(4) *Journal of International Arbitration* 485, 496–7.

12 PO 12035 (n 166); PO 12228 (n 167); PO 13359 (n 171); PO 14355 (n 174). (All cross-references to tribunal decisions are to the decisions listed in Tables 4A1 and 4A2 for ease of reference).

security.[13] It can be seen to arise from the philosophy that the parties assume the risk of dealing with each other on the facts known at the time of the transaction.

4.11. This factor assumes less significance under the assumed LCIA multifactorial approach without predisposition for or against security for costs. It becomes a another factor to be weighed in the balance, rather than requiring a fundamental change.[14]

4.12. The nature and frequency of reasons given in ICC arbitrations for security for costs are set out in Table 4.1.

Table 4.1 Frequency of ICC reasons for refusing security

No.	*Reason*	*Number*
1.	Respondent assumed the risk	18[15]
2.	Exceptional circumstances required	14[16]
3.	Nature of security for costs	9[17]
4.	Party conduct	7[18]
5.	Power and proof	6[19]
6.	Nature of the claim	2[20]

13 PO 14993 (n 175), citing Derains and Schwartz (n 6) 297, in turn quoting Markus Veit, 'Security for Costs in International Arbitration – Some Comments to procedural Order No 14 of 27 November 2002' (2005) *ASA Bulletin* 116.

14 See [5.53].

15 Assumed the risk of dealing with that claimant (4): FA 7047 (n 163); IA 11399 (n 164); PO 12228 (n 167); PO 14020 (n 173) (security limited to future costs because of respondent's knowledge and acceptance of relevant issues). Assumed the risk of transacting generally (4): PO 12228 (n 167); PO 13359 (n 171); PO 14355 (n 174); PO 228 (n 184). Fundamental change of circumstances is required because respondent assumed the risk (4): PO 12228 (n 167); PO 14993 (n 174); PO 15218 (n 178); PO 14433 (n 179). Assumed the risk of claimant's financial weakness (3): PO 12228 (n 167); PO 12853 (n 170); PO 13359 (n 171). Assumed the risk of claimant's insolvency (2): PO 12035 (n 166); PO 15218 (n 178). Accept the risk of unenforceability (1): IA 11399 (n 164).

16 General statement (11): IA 11399 (n 164); PO 12035 (n 166); PO 12228 (n 167); PO 12732 (n 171); PO 12853 (n 170); PO 13620 (n 172); PO 14020 (n 173); PO 14993 (n 174); PO1 14661 (n 175); PO 14433 (n 179); PO 228 (n 184). Urgency and immediate danger of irreparable harm is required (2): PO 14433 (n 179); PO 228 (n 184). Claimant has third party funding (1): PO 225 (n 181).

17 Balance access to justice against risk of non-payment (3): PO 12035 (n 166); PO 14355 (n 174); PO 15218 (n 178). Security not granted for claimant's costs of claim (2): IA 11405 (n 165); PO 14020 (n 173). Security for costs leads to inequality (1): IA 11399 (n 164). Security is not granted for past costs (1): PO2 14661 (n 176). Security is not required for purely defensive counterclaims (1): PO 224 (n 180). Not needed because submission to arbitration is undertaking to carry out award (1): FA 7489 (n 162). A converse argument to the latter is that a claimant's commencing arbitration knowing or suspecting that it will be unable to pay a costs award violates the good faith agreement inherent in submission to arbitration to accept and honour awards: Waincymer (n 4), 644 [8.3.1].

18 Non-payment of respondent's share of the advances on costs may disqualify it from obtaining security (3): PO 13620 (n 172); FA 7047 (n 163); PO 227 (n 183); PO 227 (n 183). Respondent's causation of claimant's condition is relevant (2): PO 14355 (n 174); PO 225 (n 181). Previous arbitration on same claim unpaid and discontinued (1): PO 225 (n 181). Application too late: PO 12732 (n 171) – application made shortly before the final hearing on the merits.

19 ICC Rules do not provide for security of costs (1): FA 7047 (n 163). Express mention of security for costs in contract required (1): IA 11399 (n 164). Insufficient evidence of claimant's inability to pay costs (3): FA 7489 (n 162); PO 12393 (n 168); PO 226 (n 182). Respondent must show convincingly that claimant will almost certainly be unable to pay costs (1): PO 13359 (n 171), citing Alan Redfern and Martin Hunter, *Redfern and Hunter on International Arbitration* (Oxford University Press, 3rd ed, 2000) [7.32].

20 Inappropriate to consider merits (1): PO 227 (n 183). Claim not abusive or extravagant (1): PO 12035 (n 166).

4.13. In summary, circumstances that have been held to be sufficiently exceptional to justify ordering security have been:

- Something more than financial weakness or even bankruptcy, such as deliberately ordering affairs to defeat a costs award;[21]
- A fundamental deterioration in the financial standing of the claimant since the relationship began;[22]
- Manifest insolvency at the time the arbitration begins, amounting to a fundamental change in circumstances;[23]
- A claim that is fraudulent, abusive, or extravagant;[24]
- Including provisions for security for costs in the arbitration agreement;[25]
- Third party funding (perhaps in combination with another factor);[26] and
- Non-payment of the costs of a previous discontinued arbitration.[27]

4.14. ICC tribunals do not expressly cast an evidential burden on the claimant to rebut the respondent's evidence when that evidence establishes a *prima facie* case for security, as is done in the multifactorial, total circumstances approach.[28]

Swiss tribunal decisions

4.15. Decisions considered here are those published by the ASA which primarily reports decisions of tribunals seated in Switzerland or acting under the authority of procedural rules of Swiss origin. Occasionally it reports decisions made in arbitrations administered under ICC and LCIA rules which may affect the approach taken by the tribunal.[29]

4.16. A 2004 Swiss decision[30] traced the origins of the requirement for exceptional circumstances and appeared to doubt its necessity in Swiss arbitrations. It noted that the requirement appeared to have its origins in ZCC 1995[31] where Professor P.-A. Recordon, as sole arbitrator, drew for guidance on the then–recently adopted WIPO Rules which

21 Procedural Order, ICC Case No 12853, December 2003, ICC Special Supplement 2010: Decisions of ICC Arbitration Procedure – A Selection of Procedural Orders issued by Arbitral Tribunals acting under the ICC Rules of Arbitration (2003–2004); Procedural Order ICC Case No 13359, February 2006, ICC Special Supplement 2014; Procedural Order, ICC Case No14355, ICC Special Supplement 2014.

22 Procedural Order, ICC Case No 14993, ICC, Special Supplement 2014; Procedural Order, ICC Case No 15218 ICC Special Supplement 2014 ('PO 15218'); Procedural Order ICC Case No 14433 ICC Special Supplement 2014.

23 Procedural Order No. 1, ICC Case No 14661 ICC Special Supplement 2014; PO 15218 (n 23).

24 Procedural Order ICC Case No 12035, ICC Special Supplement 2010.

25 Interim Award in Case No 11399 (2001) reported in ICC, Special Supplement 2011.

26 Procedural Order ICC-PO2–2020–225 as noted in Haridi (n 1).

27 Ibid.

28 See [5.57].

29 For example, ICC 12542 (n 194); LCIA 132551 (n 199).

30 Procedural Order No 4, 2009, reported in (2010) 28(1) *ASA Bulletin* 59 ('PO 4').

31 (n 186).

authorised a tribunal to order security for costs 'if it considers it to be required by exceptional circumstances'.[32] His decision appears to have been influential, being referred to by a commentator in 2000[33] and two tribunals, one in Lausanne in 1996–7 and another in Zurich in 2001.[34]

4.17. After recounting the emergence of that requirement, the tribunal in PO 4 said that it 'is quite different in nature than the conditions that are commonly considered to be applicable to requests for interim measures (e.g. "risk of irreparable harm", "chance of success", "urgency", etc.)' and that it would render security for costs an exception to a general rule against the facility.[35] They refused security on the basis that insolvency alone is insufficient to justify an order, following previous decisions, and not on the basis of a lack of exceptional circumstances.[36] They expressly stated that there was no 'prevailing reason' to order security, instead of saying there was no 'exceptional reason', as they could have if that were the basis.

4.18. The tribunal in *A SpA v B AG* in 1997 noted the practical disappearance of security for costs in state courts of continental Europe due to the widespread acceptance of the Hague Conventions of 1905 and 1954, and expressed the view that this partly explained the reluctance of Swiss legal writers towards its use in arbitration.[37] That tribunal also referred to and appeared to disagree with Professor Recordon in ZCC 1995[38] who, they said, formed the view that '*d'une façon générale, doctrine et jurisprudence sont hostiles à la cautio judicatum solvi en matière d'arbitrage*'.[39]

4.19. Professor Recordon held that parties should not be required to provide security for costs unless it was included in the arbitration agreement, and that the ability to enforce an award under the New York Convention is an additional reason to refuse security. The tribunal in *A SpA v B AG* noted that 'international arbitration is not restricted to the shores of the Swiss lakes' and that 'in England, one of the major centres of international, mainly professional, arbitration, security for costs is in daily use'.[40]

4.20. The frequency of the reasons given by Swiss tribunals for refusing applications for security for costs are set out in Table 4.2.

32 PO 4 (n 197) [146].

33 Markus Wirth, 'Interim or Preventive Measures in Support of International Arbitration in Switzerland' (2000) 18 *ASA Bulletin* 31, 36.

34 PO 4 (n 34) [144]–[146].

35 Ibid [148].

36 Ibid [152]–[153], [172].

37 *A SpA v B AG* (n 188) [7]. See also Webster and Bühler (n 6) 454 [28.34]; Otto Sandrock, 'The Cautio Judicatum Solvi in Arbitration Proceedings or the Duty of an Alien Claimant to Provide Security for the Costs of the Defendant' (1997) 14 *Journal of International Arbitration* 17, 19–27.

38 (n 186).

39 '[I]n general, doctrine and jurisprudence are hostile to the *cautio judicatum solvi* in matters of arbitration'.

40 *A SpA v B AG* (n 188) [8], noted in ICC 12542 (n 194) [46].

Table 4.2 Swiss reasons for refusing security

No.	*Reason*	*Number*
1.	Respondent assumed risk	15[41]
2.	Exceptional circumstances are required	8+[42]
3.	Nature of security for costs	2[43]
4.	Party conduct	1[44]
5.	Nature of the claim	1[45]

UK court decisions 1934–1997

4.21. Decisions of the UK courts in security for costs in arbitration in this period are considered because it is a reasonable assumption that they have influenced the approach of LCIA tribunal and perhaps other tribunals seated in the UK and common law, costs-shifting jurisdictions. They are the only insight into the reasons of LCIA tribunals other than can be gleaned from the statistics.

4.22. The UK High Court's power to order security for costs was extended from litigation to UK-seated arbitrations in 1934,[46] and in 1997 was transferred from courts to tribunals by s 38 of the *Arbitration Act 1996* (UK). Decisions of UK courts between those years reveal an approach to the facility in international commercial arbitration different from that of ICC and Swiss tribunals.

4.23. The theory behind the conferral of exclusive power on the courts in 1934 was that it is the duty of an arbitral tribunal to decide the substantive merits of the dispute referred to it and that it would not be performing this duty if it stayed or struck out the proceedings pending the provision of security. The Departmental Advisory Committee under the chair of Saville LJ considering what became the 1996 Act disagreed with this theory, believing instead that an agreement to arbitrate does not necessitate an adjudication on the substantive merits, but an adjudication by the arbitral process.[47]

4.24. From 1934 to 1997, the High Court had, in relation to arbitration, 'the same power for making orders in respect – (a) security for costs . . . as it has for the purpose of and

41 Insolvency is not enough; it must be manifest, deceitful etc. (6): *XY International v Company Z* (n 187); *A SpA v B AG* (n 188); *Mr X v Mrs Y* (n 191); *X SA v A B* (n 197); *Claimants 1–2 v Respondents 1–16* (n 195); PO 4 (n 197). Applicant assumed the risk of transacting (6): *A SpA v B AG* (n 188); *Award 1998* (n 189); *Mr X v Mrs Y* (n 191); *X SA v A B* (n 197); ICC 12542 (n 194); *XXX Inc v YYY SA* (n 196). Fundamental change required (3): ICC 12542 (n 194); *Claimants 1–2 v Respondents 1–16* (n 195).

42 ZCC 1995 (n 186); *XY International v Company Z* (n 187); HKZ 415 (n 190); *ABC AG v Mr X* (n 191); *Mr X v Mrs Y* (n 191); *X SA v A B* (n 197); *Claimants 1–2 v Respondents 1–16* (n 195); *XXX Inc v YYY SA* (n 196). The discussion in PO 4 (n 197) suggests that a number of unpublished decisions may have taken that approach: see [144], [15].

43 Balance access to justice against risk of non-payment (1): HKZ 415 (n 190). Security is not granted for past costs (1): *ABC AG v Mr X* (n 191).

44 Applicants should come with clean hands (1): *ABC AG v Mr X* (n 191).

45 Merits must not be prejudged (1): *Claimants 1–2 v Respondents 1–16* (n 195).

46 *Bank Mellat v Helliniki Techniki SA* [1984] 1 QB 291, 300G ('*Bank Mellat*').

47 Departmental Advisory Committee, Parliament of the United Kingdom, Report on the Arbitration Bill (Final Report, February 1996) [191]–[192] ('*DAC Report*').

in relation to an action or matter in the High Court'.[48] That power was derived from the rules of court conferring the discretion and from a provision in various iterations of the *Companies Act* empowering the court to order security from English companies.[49] Where the claimant was a foreign corporation, the statutory power was relied on by analogy 'as a makeweight to the exercise of the court's discretionary power'.[50]

4.25. Flavouring the exercise of the discretion against foreign corporations were the terms of the statutory provision, empowering the court to order security where it appeared by credible testimony that there is reason to believe the corporation will be unable to pay the costs of the defendant if successful.[51] The Court of Appeal confirmed in 1973 that the provision conferred a discretion, enabling, but not requiring, the court to make an order if the condition were met.[52] Although not directly applicable to foreign corporate claimants in arbitration,[53] it was a common factor relied on by respondents and courts in combination with others. Megarry V-C said in 1977 that it 'is a matter which not only opens the jurisdiction but also provides a substantial factor in the decision whether to exercise it'.[54]

4.26. Commentators suggest UK courts approached security for costs in international commercial arbitration in the same manner as they approached the facility in litigation, without requiring exceptional circumstances and security being the norm where both parties or the claimant were resident outside England, unless the claimant was not impecunious or resided in a state protected from security for costs by a treaty.[55] In *A SpA v B AG* in 1997, the tribunal observed that security for costs was in daily use in England, with no comment that a different approach was taken to arbitration than to litigation.[56]

4.27. A signal decision is the controversial one of the House of Lords in May 1994 in *Coppée–Lavalin v Ken–Ren* where it was held that only in exceptional circumstances could security for costs be ordered by a UK court in an ICC arbitration seated in England, where neither party nor the arbitration had any other connection to the UK[57] (what might be called 'unconnected ICC arbitrations'). The decision related more to the degree of curial intervention in particular types of arbitrations than to security for costs simpliciter.[58]

48 *Bank Mellat* (n 50) 302A.

49 See (n 31).

50 *Bank Mellat* (n 50) 300G.

51 (n 53).

52 *Sir Lindsay Parkinson & Co Ltd v Triplan Ltd* [1973] 1 QB 609 (CA) 626A, 627E, 628H–629A ('*Lindsay Parkinson*'). Cairns LJ added that the discretion was to be exercised in special circumstances, a position with which the other members disagreed.

53 Redfern and O'Leary (n 8).

54 *Pearson v Naydler* (n 31) 906G.

55 NH Andrews, 'Arbitration Under ICC Rules and Security for Costs' (1994) 53(3) *Cambridge Law Journal* 470, 471–2, citing *K/S A/S Bani v Korea Shipbuilding and Engineering Corporation* [1987] 2 Lloyd's Rep 4 ('*Bani v Korea Shipbuilding*') and *Hudson Strumpffabrik GmbH v Bentley Engineering Co Ltd* [1962] 2 QB 587 ('*Hudson v Bentley*'). See also *Bank Mellat* (n 50) 309D.

56 (n 42).

57 *Coppée–Lavalin. NV v Ken–Ren Chemicals and Fertilizers Ltd (in Liquidation in Kenya)* [1995] 1 AC 38 69D–E (Lord Mustill) ('*Coppée–Lavalin v Ken–Ren*'). 45C–D; 45F; 63D–E; 66F–G. On a close reading of his speech, Lord Slynn did not require exceptional circumstances even in such an arbitration, saying only that there was no 'clear-cut distinction between the present type of arbitration and commercial arbitrations held in London where frequently orders for security for costs are made', and pointing to the claimant's impecuniosity and its being funded by a third party as sufficient grounds to make an order: 66B–C.

58 John Beechey, 'International Arbitration and the Award of Security for Costs in England' (1994) 12 *ASA Bulletin* 189; Brian Davenport, 'The Ken–Ren Case: Much Ado About Nothing Very Much' (1994) *Arbitration*

It was said at the time to have received universal condemnation for suggesting that the court should involve itself in such matters.[59]

4.28. Criticism of the decision was directed at its perceived unnecessary intervention in arbitration, rather than at the ordering of security *per se*. Counsel for Coppée–Lavalin in the arbitration complained of the Law Lords' useless interference with the work of international arbitrators and their assumed right, 'like over-grown boy scouts brimming with eagerness, to frog-march perfectly ambulatory arbitrators across the street'.[60] He said the decision 'lurches backwards towards pre-1979 interventionism'[61] and that the House of Lords should instead have ruled that arbitrators have the power to order security for costs.[62]

4.29. The factors the majority in *Coppée–Lavalin v Ken–Ren* considered to be sufficiently exceptional to warrant the court's intervention were not so exceptional, namely the claimant's being funded by a third party, the Government of Kenya.[63] This is the case with almost every impecunious claimant, with counsels' and other fees being paid by third parties such as shareholders or assignees.[64]

4.30. No mention was made in argument or in the speeches in *Coppée–Lavalin v Ken–Ren* of the courts taking a more restrictive approach to security for costs in international commercial arbitration generally than in litigation. To the contrary, Lord Woolf quoted Mocatta J in *Hudson v Bentley*[65] saying he could 'find no distinction between the circumstances of an action and those of an arbitration sufficient to warrant any departure in dealing with applications for security for costs in arbitrations from the rule of practice'.[66] Lord Mustill acknowledged there was no difference in approach from arbitration to litigation, saying that 'there are many international arbitrations in which it is, and may properly continue to be, the practice to make such orders'.[67] Lord Slynn, likewise, said he did 'not find it acceptable to draw an absolute or even a clear-cut distinction between the present type of arbitration and commercial arbitrations held in London where frequently orders for security for costs are made'.[68]

4.31. In other words, the same approach was taken to security for costs in arbitration as in litigation. The Court of Appeal expressed the same sentiment in 1980, saying that the same rule applied to arbitrations as to actions.[69]

International 303, 305; Simon Greenberg and Christopher Kee, 'Can You Seek Security for Costs in International Arbitration in Australia?' (2016) 109 *Australian Construction Law Newsletter* 44, 47.

59 *DAC Report* (n 51) [193]. See Chapter 1, *1.2.1.3 Disempowerment of states* for other criticism and support of the decision by Beechey (n 54); Andrews (n 59); Davenport (n 62); Jan Paulsson, 'The Unwelcome Atavism of Ken–Ren: The House of Lords Shows Its Meddle' (1994) 12(3) *ASA Bulletin* 439; Sophie Nappert, 'The House of Lords on Security for Costs and ICC Arbitration' (1994) 73(4) *Canadian Bar Review* 553; Jonathan Hill, 'Security For Costs In ICC Arbitration' (1995) 1 *Lloyd's Maritime and Commercial Law Quarterly* 19; Paul Mitchard, 'England', in 'International Guide to Commercial Arbitration' (1995) *International Financial Law Review* 15.

60 Paulsson (n 63) 439.

61 Ibid 440.

62 Ibid 441. See also David Branson, 'The Ken–Ren Case: It Is an Ado Where More Aid Is Less Help' (1994) 10(3) *Arbitration International* 313, 314.

63 *Coppée–Lavalin v Ken–Ren'* (n 53)72A. See also 45D–E; 66B–C.

64 Branson (n 72) 314.

65 (n 59) 593.

66 *Coppée–Lavalin v Ken–Ren'* (n 53) 69D–E.

67 Ibid 65B.

68 Ibid 66A–B.

69 *Ramsay International Ltd v Scientific Control Systems Iran Ltd* (Court of Appeal, Bridge, Cumming-Bruce and Brightman LJJ, 11 February 1980) 2 ('*Ramsay International*').

4.32. Lord Woolf also quoted Bingham LJ in *Bani v Korea Shipbuilding*[70] as saying:

> The arbitration is one which, however complex its peculiar facts, is of a very familiar kind. The application for security is of the most routine kind. The commercial judge will deal with several each week. But the argument will usually be short and relate to quantum only, and security will usually be given by agreement or not applied for. This is because practitioners have a very shrewd idea what to expect, so that expensive and time-consuming contests can be avoided.[71]

4.33. If those applications were all related to arbitration, it shows their prevalence. If they were related to arbitration and litigation, as seems more likely,[72] it shows the commonality of approach in both.

4.34. Later cases did not understand *Coppée–Lavalin v Ken–Ren* to have made exceptional circumstances the criterion for ordering security for costs in all international commercial arbitrations. Two decisions in the London Commercial Court, made within two days of each other in 1995, did not require exceptional circumstances. In the first, *Petromin SA v Secnav Marine Ltd*,[73] counsel appear not to have relied on *Coppée–Lavalin v Ken–Ren*, as there is no reference to it in the judgment despite both parties being foreign to the UK and the contract having no connection to the UK other than a London arbitration clause.[74]

4.35. In the second, *Regia Autonoma De Electricitate Renel v Gulf Petroleum International Ltd*,[75] Rix J distinguished *Coppée–Lavalin v Ken–Ren* by saying the arbitration clause with which he was dealing expressly referred to the *Arbitration Act 1950* (UK) and English procedural and substantive law, with the result that the invocation of English arbitration law was deliberate rather than consequential upon London being the seat.[76] In other words, that arbitration was not an unconnected ICC arbitration. Neither of those cases referred to any general practice before or after *Coppée–Lavalin v Ken–Ren* restricting the application of security for costs in international commercial arbitration generally to exceptional circumstances.

4.36. A review of court decisions from 1934 to 1997 confirms that the same approach was taken in international commercial arbitration as in litigation in UK courts.[77] In *Bank Mellat* in 1984, Kerr LJ said 'if the respondent is English and the claimant is foreign, and there is no agreement that any particular rules are to apply, then an order for security is likely to be the norm, in the same way as in actions'.[78] This is clearly demonstrated by

70 (n 59) 448.

71 *Coppée–Lavalin v Ken–Ren* (n 53) 69H–70A.

72 In 2021, the Court of Appeal noted 'the very large number of applications for security for costs which regularly come before the courts of the Queen's Bench and Chancery Divisions': *Rowe v Ingenious Media Holdings plcs* [2021] EWCA Civ 29 [28].

73 [1995] 1 Lloyd's Rep 603.

74 Ibid 606.

75 [1996] 1 Lloyd's Rep 67.

76 Ibid 71.

77 *Bani v Korea Shipbuilding* (n 59); *Hudson v Bentley* (n 59); *Bilcon Ltd v Fegmay Investments Ltd* [1966] 2 QB 221; *Lindsay Parkinson* (n 56); *Mavani v Ralli Bros Ltd* [1973] 1 WLR 468; *Pearson v Naydler* (n 31); *Ramsay International* (n 79); *Hitachi Shipbuilding & Engineering Co Ltd v Viafiel Compania Naviera SA* [1981] 2 Lloyd's Rep 498 (CA); *Flender Werft* (n 31).

78 (n 50) 303C.

decisions relating to litigation and arbitration drawing applicable principles and examples from each other without distinction or comment.[79]

4.37. An early draft of the Bill that became the *Arbitration Act 1996* contained wording to the effect that tribunals could order security for costs 'wherever the court would have power' and 'on the same principles as the court', but the Departmental Advisory Committee received a significant number of criticisms from foreign arbitration specialists and institutions.[80] They were concerned that such a provision would require either access to and detailed knowledge of the White Book, or instructing English lawyers for the purpose of a security for costs application.

4.38. Other concerns were expressed that there were no principles or guidelines for the exercise of this power in the draft Bill.[81] The Committee considered enumerating the discretionary factors but decided it was impracticable, lengthy, and complicated to codify the case law that had been carefully worked out over many years.[82]

4.39. Instead of prescribing conditions for the granting of security, the Departmental Advisory Committee redrafted the Bill to state the grounds on which it could *not* be granted, namely if the only ground was the foreign residence or management and control of the claimant.[83]

LCIA statistics

4.40. LCIA does not publish decisions on security for costs but publishes statistics of applications and dispositions in its Annual Casework Report.[84] LCIA's statistics on the number of applications for security for costs, including the number that fail and succeed, suggest that LCIA tribunals apply a more liberal test to the facility than ICC tribunals. There are a number of unknowns preventing that suggestion being taken further, although it may be buttressed by plausible speculation.

4.41. LCIA tribunals typically deal with more applications for security for costs each year than have been published by the ICC in its 100-year history. The only meaningful difference between ICC and LCIA arbitrations that can be gleaned from the available information is the greater number of arbitrators on LCIA tribunals from common law costs-shifting jurisdictions. A plausible but unverifiable speculation is that there is also a greater number of counsel from common law costs-shifting jurisdictions acting in LCIA arbitrations. Those propositions are explored later to help determine if the statistics support the suggestion that tribunals do not require exceptional circumstances.

79 For example, in *Keary Developments Ltd v Tarmac Construction Ltd* [1995] 3 All ER 534 (CA), a case relating to security for costs in litigation, the court drew principles from *Lindsay Parkinson* (n 56), *Pearson v Naydler* (n 31), and *Flender Werft* (n 31) without questioning their relevance to arbitration. See also Greenberg and Kee (n 62) 50–1.

80 *DAC Report* (n 51) [366].

81 Ibid [364].

82 Ibid [365].

83 *DAC Report* (n 51) [367].

84 LCIA, 'Reports' (Web Page, undated) <https://www.lcia.org/lcia/reports.aspx>.

4.42. From the inception of the ICC International Court of Arbitration in 1923[85] to 2020, the ICC has published 23 tribunal decisions on security for costs,[86] with a 24th and 25th yet to be published at the time of writing.[87] Five of those applications were successful,[88] yielding a success rate of 17%.[89] In 2019 alone, tribunals in LCIA arbitrations dealt with 31 applications, ten of which were successful,[90] giving a success rate over 32%. Before courts in the United Kingdom were precluded from granting security for costs in 1997, the House of Lords noted in 1993 that judges were dealing with several applications each week.[91]

4.43. Three sets of figures are relevant to the question of whether the ICC decisions are representative of decisions more generally – the number of arbitrations administered by the institution, the number of applications made and the number successful. Table 4.3 shows those figures for 2017, 2018, 2019, and 2020 for ICC and LCIA arbitrations. The year 2017 was chosen as the commencement year as the LCIA did not publish the numbers of applications for security for costs before that year,[92] and ICC arbitrations had no applications in the 11-year period 2009 to 2019.[93]

4.44. The ratio of applications to administered arbitrations is much higher in LCIA arbitrations than in ICC arbitrations, 5% compared to 0% for the period 2009–2019 and then 2% for 2020. Lower figures are obtained if the number of applications over the history of ICC is compared to the number of arbitrations in that period. In 2019 ICC announced its 25,000th case.[94] Twenty-four applications in 25,000 cases is 0.1%, and four awards of security are 0.016%. This is indicative only and assumes there were no applications or awards between 1923 and 1994.

4.45. The statistics cast doubt on the proposition that the 'exceptional nature of order for security for costs is not particular to ICC arbitration, but is applicable generally to international arbitrations'.[95]

85 'History' (Web Page, undated) <http://www.iccwbo.org/about-icc/history/>.

86 Haridi (n 1) It is evident from occasional references to apparently unpublished decisions that these are not the entirety of decisions of ICC tribunals regarding security for costs, for example, ICC Award No 4126 of 1984 and ICC Award No 6697 of 1990 referred to in FA 7489 (n 162) [9].

87 The writer was involved in both applications as counsel and has a copy of the decisions from which the ruling and reasons are extracted without identifying the parties. Security for costs was refused in the 24th and granted in the 25th, the first successful application in an ICC arbitration against a natural person claimant.

88 Including the yet-to-be-reported 25th application in 2021 in which the writer was involved.

89 This accords approximately with the estimate of a 20% success rate given in PO 14433 (n 179) [45].

90 LCIA, *2019 Annual Casework Report* (Report, 2020) ('2019') 70.

91 *Coppée–Lavalin v Ken–Ren* (n 53) 69H–70A.

92 See the Director General's Report for each of 2000 to 2011, the Registrar's Report for each of 2012 to 2015, and the report LCIA, *Facts and Figures – 2016: A Robust Caseload* (Report, 2016), all at <https://www.lcia.org/lcia/reports.aspx>.

93 Haridi (n 1) 94–5. Lest it be thought 2018 and 2019 were not representative of previous years, there was no published application for security for costs in an ICC arbitration in the 11 years 2009 to 2019.

94 ICC, *ICC Dispute Resolution 2019 Statistics* (Report, 2020) ('2019') 4 <www.iccwbo.org/dr-stat2019>.

95 ICCA-Queen Mary Task Force, Report on Third-Party Funding in International Arbitration (Report, ICCA and Queen Mary University of London, April 2018) *ICCA Report on Third-Party Funding* 166. See also Joseph and Foxton (n 5) 213 [6.2] making no distinction between arbitrations administered by different institutions.

Table 4.3 Arbitrations, applications for, and awards of, security for costs 2009–2020

Year	*Arbitrations*[96]		*Applications*		*Awards*	
	ICC	*LCIA*	*ICC*	*LCIA*	*ICC*	*LCIA*
2009–2016			0[97]	?	0	?
2017	1,578[98]	486[99]	0[100]	31[101]	0	10[102]
2018	1,603[103]	604[104]	0[105]	34[106]	0	10[107]
2019	1,694[108]	617[109]	0[110]	31[111]	0	10[112]
2020	1,833[113]	755[114]	6[115]	35[116]	1[117]	16[118]
TOTAL	**6,708**	**2,462**	**6**	**131**	**1**	**46**

4.46. LCIA is just one of what might be called the common law institutions, situated in common law jurisdictions accustomed to security for costs in litigation. SIAC and HKIAC are the second and third most preferred institutions in the world respectively

96 The number of pending arbitrations administered by the institution at the end of the year.

97 Haridi (n 1) 94.

98 (2018) 2 *ICC Dispute Resolution Bulletin* 52.

99 LCIA, *2017 Annual Casework Report* (Report, 2018) ('2017') 4 <https://www.lcia.org/lcia/reports.aspx>.

100 Ibid 94–5. Lest it be thought 2018 and 2019 were not representative of previous years, there was no published application for security for costs in an ICC arbitration in the 11 years 2009 to 2019.

101 Ibid 18.

102 Ibid.

103 ICC, *ICC Dispute Resolution 2018 Statistics* (Report, 2019) ('2018') 8 <www.iccwbo.org/dr-stat2018>.

104 This is an approximate figure since LCIA does not publish its total number of pending administered arbitrations each year. This figure is the total of new referrals to LCIA in 2017 and 2018, chosen on the basis of the median total duration of LCIA arbitrations being 16 months, with 70% of cases disputing USD 1 million or less being resolved in less than 12 months: LCIA, *Facts and Figures – Costs and Duration: 2013–2016* (Report, 2017) <https://www.lcia.org/lcia/reports.aspx>. Some cases from 2016 would have remained pending in 2018, and some cases commenced in 2017 and 2018 would have settled or been otherwise disposed of within those years. This approach enjoys some support from the remarkable similarity of the cases pending in ICC at the end of 2019 (1,694) with the total of new cases commenced in ICC in 2018 (842) and 2019 (851), 1,693: see the ICC 2018 (n 121) and ICC 2019 (n 106). The figure is for indicative purposes only and precision is not required.

105 Ibid.

106 LCIA, *2018 Annual Casework Report* (Report, 2019) ('2018') 18 <https://www.lcia.org/lcia/reports.aspx>.

107 Ibid.

108 ICC 2019 (n 106) 10.

109 The total of new referrals to LCIA in 2018 and 2019 on the same basis as the figure for 2018.

110 Ibid.

111 LCIA 2019 (n 102) 70.

112 Ibid.

113 ICC, *ICC Dispute Resolution 2020 Statistics* (Report, 2021) ('2020') 9.

114 The total of new referrals to LCIA under the LCIA Rules in 2019 (346) and 2020 (407) on the same basis as the figure for 2018: see LCIA 2019 (n 102) 5 and LCIA, *2020 Annual Casework Report* (Report, 2021) ('2020') 9, both available at <https://www.lcia.org/lcia/reports.aspx>. The number of referrals is taken from those under the LCIA Rules as the applications for security for costs are made under those rules and not under other rules administered by LCIA: see LCIA 2019 (n 102) 70 and LCIA 2020.

115 Ibid 94–7, together with the 24th decision mentioned earlier.

116 LCIA 2020 (n 126) 25.

117 Ibid 95, bearing out in one year the overall 17% success rate.

118 Ibid.

for international commercial arbitration, after ICC and followed by LCIA.[119] Both SIAC and HKIAC, like LCIA, contain express provision for security for costs in their arbitral rules.[120] London and Singapore are the equal most preferred seats for international commercial arbitration, followed closely by Hong Kong and distantly by Paris.[121] Legislation in Singapore[122] and Hong Kong[123] also contains express provision for security for costs, constituting the *lex arbitri* in arbitrations seated in those jurisdictions.

4.47. This significant difference in experience between the two institutions most popular with users[124] cannot be explained by the types of disputes they administer,[125] the law governing the arbitration,[126] the law governing the contract,[127] the nationality of the parties,[128] or the value of the disputes.[129] All of those features are either roughly equivalent or immaterial to the question of security for costs (such as the law governing the contract).[130] It may be partly explained by the seat of the arbitration being England and the express power to grant security in the *Arbitration Act 1996* (UK), with 81% of LCIA

---

119 QMUL 2021 10, Chart 6.

120 *SIAC Rules 2016*, r 27(j); *2018 HKIAC Administered Rules*, Art 24.

121 QMUL 2021 6, Chart 2.

122 *International Arbitration Act* (Singapore, cap 143A, 2002 rev ed), s 12(1)(a).

123 *Arbitration Ordinance* (Hong Kong) cap 609, s 56(1)(a).

124 In the Queen Mary Survey 2018, 77% of participants included ICC in their answer and 51% included LCIA, followed by SIAC at 36% and HKIAC at 27%: QMUL 2018 13, Chart 12.

125 The industry sectors the subject of the arbitrations in the ICC and LCIA were substantially similar in 2019. LCIA administered disputes in banking and finance (32%), energy and resources (22%), transport and commodities (15%), and 5% each for insurance, professional services, and construction and infrastructure: LCIA 2019 (n 102) 7. Very similar, if not identical, industries were the subject of ICC arbitrations in that period: ICC 2019 (n 106) 15.

126 English law was the law governing 81% of LCIA arbitrations in 2019 with the next most popular being Mexican at 3%: LCIA 2019 (n 102) 13. English law being the *lex arbitri* should not make a significant difference to the number of security for costs applications or orders even though the *Arbitration Act 1996* (UK) confers the power to make orders on the tribunal. There is no doubt that ICC tribunals also have the power, and the UK Act makes no reference to the approach, thus putting ICC and LCIA arbitrations on an equal footing in relation to security for costs (apart from, perhaps, the uncertain psychological encouragement given by the express conferral of power in the Act). The ICC does not state the governing law of its arbitrations, reporting only the governing law of the contract and the place of the arbitration. This may reflect the common assumption and experience that it means both, especially where the seat is also England: *Enka Insaat Ve Sanayi AS v OOO Insurance Company Chubb* [2020] UKSC 38 [39]–[40] (Lord Leggatt and Lord Hamblen SCJJ; Lord Kerr SCJ agreeing).

127 The language of the LCIA 2019 (n 102) 13 is ambiguous as to whether the 'applicable law' it refers to is the law governing the arbitration or the contract. That ambiguity may also reflect the common assumption referred to in n 138. English law was the most common law of the contract in ICC arbitrations, in 16% of cases, followed by Swiss law with 12% and the laws of a US state and of France with 10% each: ICC 2019 (n 106) 15.

128 In LCIA arbitrations in 2019, 23.8% of parties were from Western Europe, 18.6% from the UK, 13.1% from Middle East and North Africa, 10.2% from Africa, 10% from Asia, and 11.2% from CIS, and Northern, Central and Eastern Europe combined. The remainder of arbitrations came from other regions in single digits: LCIA 2019 (n 102) 11. While the reported regions were differently named, the nationality or origin of ICC parties were similar with 29.5% from North and West Europe, 19.4% from South and East Asia and the Pacific, 15.5% from Latin America and Caribbean, 10.8% from Central and West Asia, 9.1% from North America, 8.2% from Central and East Europe, 5.2% from Sub-Saharan Africa, and 2.3% from North Africa. Presumably the UK is included in the 29.5% for North and West Europe: ICC 2019 (n 106) 9.

129 In 2019, the value of LCIA arbitrations was USD 1 million or less (43%), USD 1–5 million (29%), USD 5–10 million (8%), USD 10–20 million (6%), USD 20–50 million (6%), USD 50–100 million (5%), over USD 100 million (4%): LCIA 2019 (n 102) 15. The value of ICC cases was generally higher with 23.7% below USD 1 million, USD 1–5 million (27.2%), USD 5–10 million (10.1%), USD 10–30 million (13.7%), USD 30–50 million (5.6%), USD 50–80 million (3.5%), USD 80–100 million (1.5%), USD 100–500 million (6.1%), and over USD 500 million (2.1%). While larger, the difference does not account for a difference in numbers of orders for security for costs.

130 Security for costs, being a matter of procedure, being one for the *lex arbitri* or arbitral rules, absent party agreement: Waincymer (n 4) 1194 [15.2.1]; Born (n 4) 2495.

arbitrations seated in England compared to 17.1% of ICC arbitrations, yet London was the most popular seat for ICC arbitrations, suggesting that the success rate should be higher in ICC arbitrations if that is a factor.[131]

4.48. Further, the presence of an express power theoretically should make no difference as there has been no doubt since at least 1990 that ICC tribunals have the power to order security,[132] and the LCIA rules are silent as to the approach to be taken to the exercise of the power. It may be that the express conferral of a power in the LCIA rules encourages applications and orders, reflecting the psychology perceived by those drafting the 1998 ICC rules who are said to have been reluctant to refer expressly to security for costs for fear of encouraging a proliferation of applications.[133] The higher prevalence of applications in LCIA arbitrations is not fully explained by the inclusion in the LCIA rules of an express power to award security for costs.[134]

4.49. Two differences, one reported and another postulated, in arbitrations administered by the two institutions may account for the different statistics for security for costs. The reported difference is the nationality of the arbitrators, and the postulated difference is the nationality or training of counsel. In LCIA arbitrations in 2019, 51% of arbitrators were of British nationality. If arbitrators from jurisdictions familiar with common law security for costs in litigation are included,[135] that figure increases to 67.8% of arbitrators familiar with the facility.[136] The arbitrations were decided roughly equally by three-member tribunals (54%) and by sole arbitrators (46%).[137] On the reasonable assumption that Commonwealth arbitrators were appointed, some as sole arbitrators[138] and some on tribunals where one or more of the members were Commonwealth arbitrators,[139] some 40%–60% of LCIA arbitrations would likely have had a tribunal member familiar with security for costs. Where that person was sole arbitrator or presiding arbitrator of a three-member tribunal, their influence over the arbitral procedure would have been absolute or considerable, respectively.[140]

131 'England' (presumably meaning a city in England, as a city is usually the seat of arbitrations) was the seat in 89% of LCIA arbitrations in 2019: LCIA 2019 (n 102) 13. London was the also the most popular seat ('place') in ICC arbitrations at 17.1% followed by Paris at 15.9%, Geneva at 8%, and Singapore at 4.8%: ICC 2019 (n 106) 14, 28, Table 08.

132 *ICC Case No 6697* (1990) *Societe Casa v Societe Cambior* 1992 Rev Arb 135. See also *Coppée–Lavalin v Ken–Ren* (n 68) 54E-F; Robert B Kovacs, 'A Transnational Approach to the Arbitrability of Insolvency Proceedings in International Arbitration' (2012) 21(5) *Journal of Bankruptcy Law and Practice* 521, noting the tribunal in ICC Case No 6632 of 1993 seated in Brussels entertaining an application for security for costs, citing Gaillard and Savage (n 6) 356.

133 *ICCA Report on Third-Party Funding* (n 108) 165, citing Derains and Schwartz (n 6) 297.

134 Rule 25.2 of the *LCIA Arbitration Rules 2020*.

135 Canada (5.1%), Australia (3.1%), Ireland (2.6%), South Africa (2.4%), Singapore (1.4%), New Zealand (0.8%), India (0.7%), Nigeria (0.7%) (together with British arbitrators, 'Commonwealth arbitrators'). As to Nigeria, see AO Rhodes-Vivour, 'Security for the Respondent's Costs of Arbitral Proceedings with Particular Reference to the Arbitration and Conciliation Act Cap 19, 1990 Laws of Nigeria' (2005) (2/1) *News Journal of the Chartered Institute of Arbitration Nigerian Branch* 1 <https://drvlawplace.com/wp-content/uploads/2020/06/Security-for-costs.pdf>.

136 LCIA 2019 (n 102) 14.

137 Ibid.

138 Given that only some 19% of parties were British, it is reasonable to assume that not every sole arbitrator was a Commonwealth arbitrator.

139 It could be expected that some three-member tribunals would have no Commonwealth arbitrator and others would have one or more Commonwealth arbitrators.

140 Rule 14.7 of the *LCIA Arbitration Rules 2020* vests the power to make procedural decisions alone in the presiding arbitrator, with the consent of the other members and the parties; Rule 26.5 entitles the presiding arbitrator to decide any deadlock.

4.50. ICC arbitrations provide a stark contrast, with only 17.5% of British arbitrators even though they accounted for the most from any one nation (258 compared to the next largest of 147 (10% Swiss).[141] Adding the numbers of Commonwealth arbitrators from other countries (10.36%)[142] does not lift their total number in ICC arbitrations (27.86%) remotely close to those in LCIA arbitrations (67.8%). As with LCIA arbitrations, ICC arbitrations were split roughly equally between sole arbitrators (41%) and three-member tribunals (59%).[143]

4.51. Applying similar assumptions as to LCIA arbitrations, only some 10%–20% of ICC arbitrations are likely to have had a Commonwealth arbitrator as a member. This is a significant difference in influence on the tribunal and may go far towards explaining the difference in numbers of applications and orders for security for costs. It and the following factor are the only real differences between ICC arbitrations and LCIA arbitrations apparently relevant to security for costs, apart from the published decisions of ICC tribunals requiring exceptional circumstances.

4.52. The postulated factor is the origin or training of party counsel. This is not reported in ICC or LCIA statistics, but it is reasonable to assume counsel with UK origins or training may advise parties, in one capacity or another,[144] where the seat is in England (89% of LCIA arbitrations)[145] or where the applicable law is English (81% of LCIA arbitrations).[146] Myburgh and Paniagua stated in 2016 that disputes based on New York or English law tend to use lawyers who specialise in that law and are typically located in New York or London respectively.[147] Counsel from or trained in the UK will be alert to the possibility of an application for security for costs and may be more comfortable making an application. A combination of counsel familiar with applications, and tribunals comfortable with making orders, may account for their higher incidence in LCIA arbitrations.[148]

4.53. Finally, there is the considerable effect of publication only of ICC and ASA decisions on security for costs to consider. Those decisions and the commentary on them generally require exceptional circumstances before ordering security for costs. ICC tribunals are faced with this authority on any properly opposed application and observably feel constrained not to break with decades of practice.[149] LCIA tribunals, while possibly influenced by ICC decisions to an extent, need not feel so constrained, and can distinguish those statements on the basis of their having been made in ICC arbitrations where there is no express provision for security for costs and where they are known for their antipathy to the facility.

141 ICC 2019 (n 106) 13.

142 Canada (2.71%), Australia (2.57%), India (2.3%), Singapore (1.76%), Ireland (1.02%): ICC 2019 (n 106) 13.

143 Ibid 13, 24, Table 05.

144 Either as counsel on the record or consulting to those counsel as an academic, solicitor, or barrister.

145 See (n 143).

146 See (n 138).

147 Andrew Myburgh and Jordi Paniagua, 'Does International Commercial Arbitration Promote Foreign Direct Investment?' (2016) 59(3) *Journal of Law and Economics* 597, 602.

148 Redfern and O'Leary (n 8) 400.

149 Procedural Order No 4, ICC, April 2009, (2010) 28(1) ASA Bulletin 59, where previous decisions were followed to the effect that insolvency was insufficient to warrant an order for security.

ANNEXURE 4A

ICC and Swiss tribunals' security for costs decisions

Table 4A.1 ICC tribunal decisions on security for costs

Decision
Final Award in Case No 7489 (1993) ('FA 7489')[150]
Final Award in Case No 7047 (1994) ('FA 7047')[151]
Interim Award in Case No 11399 (2001) ('IA 11399')[152]
Interim Award in Case No 11405 (2002) ('IA 11405')[153]
Procedural Order of 6 June 2003 in ICC Case No 12035 ('PO 12035')[154]
Procedural Order of 11 June 2003 in ICC Case No 12228 ('PO 12228')[155]
Procedural Order of 30 July 2003 in ICC Case No 12393 ('PO 12393')[156]
Procedural Order of January 2006 in ICC Case No 12732 ('PO 12732')[157]
Procedural Order of December 2003 in ICC Case No 12853 ('PO 12853')[158]
Procedural Order of February 2006 in ICC Case No 13359 ('PO 13359')[159]
Procedural Order of May 2006 in ICC Case No 13620 ('PO 13620')[160]
Procedural Order of November 2006 in ICC Case No 14020 ('PO 14020')[161]
Procedural Order of January 2007 in ICC Case No 14355 ('PO 14355')[162]
Procedural Order of December 2007 in ICC Case No 14993 ('PO 14993')[163]
Procedural Order of December 2007 in ICC Case No 14661 ('PO1 14661')[164]

(Continued)

150 Reported in (1999) 8(2) *ICC International Court of Arbitration Bulletin* 68.
151 Reported in (1997) 8(1) *ICC International Court of Arbitration Bulletin* 61.
152 Reported in ICC, *Special Supplement 2011: Interim, Conservatory and Emergency Measures in ICC Arbitration* 36.
153 Reported in (2006) 17(2) *ICC International Court of Arbitration Bulletin* 96.
154 Reported in ICC, *Special Supplement 2010: Decisions on ICC Arbitration Procedure: A Selection of Procedural Orders Issue by Arbitral Tribunals Acting Under the ICC Rules of Arbitration (2003–2004)* (ICC, 2010).
155 Ibid.
156 Ibid.
157 Reported in ICC, *Special Supplement 2014: Procedural Decisions in ICC Arbitration* 62 (ICC, 2014).
158 (n 154).
159 Reported in ICC, *Special Supplement 2014: Procedural Decisions in ICC Arbitration* 63 (ICC, 2014).
160 Reported in ICC, *Special Supplement 2014: Procedural Decisions in ICC Arbitration* 65 (ICC, 2014).
161 Reported in ICC, *Special Supplement 2014: Procedural Decisions in ICC Arbitration* 67 (ICC, 2014).
162 Reported in ICC, *Special Supplement 2014: Procedural Decisions in ICC Arbitration* 70 (ICC, 2014).
163 Reported in ICC, *Special Supplement 2014: Procedural Decisions in ICC Arbitration* 77 (ICC, 2014).
164 Reported in ICC, *Special Supplement 2014: Procedural Decisions in ICC Arbitration* 74 (ICC, 2014).

Table 4A.1 (Continued)

Decision
Procedural Order of December 2008 in ICC Case No 14661 ('PO2 14661')[165]
Procedural Order of July 2008 in ICC Case No 15218 ('PO 15218')[166]
Procedural Order of October 2008 in ICC Case No 14433 ('PO 14433')[167]
Procedural order ICC-PO-2020–224 ('PO 224')[168]
Procedural order ICC-PO2–2020–225 ('PO 225')[169]
Procedural Order ICC-PO6–2020–226 ('PO 226')[170]
Procedural Order ICC-PO3–2020–227 ('PO 227')[171]
Procedural Order ICC-PO3–2020–228 ('PO 228')[172]

Table 4A.2 Swiss tribunal decisions on security for costs

Decision
Order of 12 November 1991 ('ZCC 1991')[173]
X Panama v Une personne physique domiciliée à Genève, Award, 1995 ('ZCC 1995')[174]
XY International v Company Z, Procedural Decision in ICC Arbitration No. . . . 1995 ('*XY International v Company Z*')[175]
A SpA (Italy) v B AG (Germany), Decision, 25 September 1997. ('*A SpA v B AG*')[176]
Award of 21 December 1998 (Neuchâtel, ad hoc) ('*Award 1998*')[177]
Swiss entity v Dutch entity, Award, HKZ Case No. 415, 20 November 2001 ('HKZ 415')[178]
ABC AG v Mr X, Procedural Order, 27 November 2002 ('*ABC AG v Mr X*')[179]
Mr X v Mrs Y, Decision, 2003 ('*Mr X v Mrs Y*')[180]
X SA v A B and others, Commerce/Industry/and Chamber of Commerce of the Canton of Ticino, Ccia-Ti No 103/00, 25 July 2003 ('*X SA v A B*')[181]
Parties Not Indicated, Procedural Order, ICC Case No 12542/EC, 19 December 2003 ('ICC 12542')[182]

(Continued)

165 Reported in ICC, *Special Supplement 2014: Procedural Decisions in ICC Arbitration* 76 (ICC, 2014).
166 Reported in ICC, *Special Supplement 2014: Procedural Decisions in ICC Arbitration* 79 (ICC, 2014).
167 Reported in ICC, *Special Supplement 2014: Procedural Decisions in ICC Arbitration* 73 (ICC, 2014).
168 Extracted in Haridi (n 1) 98.
169 Ibid 100.
170 Ibid 105.
171 Ibid 106.
172 Ibid 109.
173 Reported in (1995) 13(1) *ASA Bulletin* 84.
174 Reported in (1995) 13(3) *ASA Bulletin* 529.
175 Reported in (1997) 15(2) *ASA Bulletin* 363.
176 Reported in (2001) 19(4) *ASA Bulletin* 745.
177 Reported in (1998) 17(1) *ASA Bulletin* 59.
178 Reported in (2002) 20(3) *ASA Bulletin* 467.
179 Reported in (2005) 23(1) *ASA Bulletin* 108.
180 Reported in (2010) 28(1) *ASA Bulletin* 15.
181 Reported in (2010) 28(1) *ASA Bulletin* 28.
182 Reported in (2005) 23(4) *ASA Bulletin* 685.

Table 4A.2 (Continued)

Decision
Claimants 1–2 v Respondents 1–16, Order No 1, 2008 ('*Claimants 1–2 v Respondents 1–16*')[183]
XXX Inc v YYY SA, Procedural Order No 2, 2009 in ICC Case 15951 ('*XXX Inc v YYY SA*')[184]
Procedural Order No 4, 2009 ('PO 4')[185]
Procedural Order No 7, SCAI Case No. 300273–2013, 4 September 2014 ('SCAI 300273')[186]
Procedural Order No. 4, LCIA Case No. 132551, 2014 ('LCIA 132551')[187]

183 Reported in (2010) 28(1) *ASA Bulletin* 47.
184 Reported in (2010) 28(1) *ASA Bulletin* 71.
185 Reported in (2010) 28(1) *ASA Bulletin* 59.
186 Reported in (2018) 36(3) *ASA Bulletin* 661.
187 Reported in (2018) 36(3) *ASA Bulletin* 664.

CHAPTER 5

Total circumstances factors

Introduction

5.1. Factors influencing the granting of security for costs taking into account the total circumstances have evolved over 230 years[1] from the single determinant of the claimant's foreign residence to factors that are logically probative of the claimant's ability and willingness to pay an adverse costs order, and whether ordering security is just in all the circumstances.[2] Because it involves the exercise of a discretion, the factors are not fixed or closed.[3] It is reasonable to assume that LCIA tribunals take these factors into account, following the approach of the UK courts when they had the power from 1934 to 1997, and given the relatively high number of applications and their success in LCIA arbitrations.

5.2. Considerations that have been taken into account in favour of granting security for costs may be divided into three categories – those going to the financial condition of the claimant, the likelihood of a costs order being made, and the conduct of the parties.[4] They are considered here as the financial factors, the liability factors, and the conduct factors, before turning to the fairness factors generally considered to be against ordering security.

5.3. All factors are subject to the terms of the source of power to grant security for costs which, in arbitration, may be the *lex arbitri*, institutional rules, general or inherent case management rules or (unusually) party agreement.[5] Regard must first be had to the relevant source to determine any preconditions or limitations on the power.

5.4. Facts determine cases.[6] Not every factor will be relevant in every case, and the factors present may have different strength and effect depending on the circumstances.[7]

---

1 Since at least *Fitzgerald v Whitmore* (1786) 1 TR 362.

2 Alan Redfern and Sam O'Leary, 'Why It Is Time for International Arbitration to Embrace Security for Costs' (2016) 32 *Arbitration International* 397, 410–11; Malaysia: *Lina Soo (F) v Ngu Chu Chiong & Ngu Choo Chiong* [1999] 1 LNS 76; [1999] MLJU 442; *Goldquest International Ltd v Teh Leong Kiat* [2003] AMEJ 0021; [2003] 2 CLJ 402; *Luminous Crossroads Sdn Bhd v Lim Kong Huat Construction* [2001] 4 AMR 4861; [2002] 5 CLJ 100; [2001] MLJU 475.

3 Australia: *Trility Pty Ltd v Ancon Drilling Pty Ltd* [2013] VSC 577 [11]–[13] ('*Trility*'); *Westonia Earthmoving Pty Ltd v Cliffs Asia Pacific Iron Ore Pty Ltd* [2013] WASC 57 [6] ('*Westonia*'). Malaysia: *Faridah Begum bte Abdullah v Dato' Michael Chong* [1995] 2 AMR 1191 ('*Faridah Begum*'); [1995] 2 MLJ 404; *Chen Siew Lee v Tan Bak Lee* [2018] AMEJ 0540; [2018] 11 MLJ 34. India: *Kassiopi Maritime Co. Ltd. v MTAL Layyah* [2014] 5 Bom CR 566.

4 Reference in this chapter is naturally primarily to court decisions as they have developed the criteria for granting security for costs. Many references are to Australian decisions because of the number of courts in the federation and the number of written decisions they publish.

5 See [3.1].

6 *Merribee Pastoral Industries v Australia and New Zealand Banking Group Ltd* (1998) 193 CLR 502 ('*Merribee*') [26].

7 *Westonia* (n 3).

DOI: 10.4324/9781003479628-5

A factor may be wholly irrelevant in one set of facts but almost determinative in another. Those considered here arising from the litigation context will be relevant in arbitration by analogy, to a greater or lesser extent, depending on the terms of the power and the arguments discussed in Chapters 7 and 8.

Financial factors in favour of security for costs

5.5. *Foreign residence.*[8] One of the original grounds for granting security for costs in litigation was that the claimant resided abroad, making it difficult or impossible to enforce an order for costs. With the increasing ability to enforce orders abroad through conventions[9] and reciprocal arrangements,[10] this ground has diminished in significance.[11] It will have greater applicability when combined with another factor[12] such as the claimant's impecuniosity.[13]

5.6. *Impecuniousity.* Claimant's present impecuniosity is a significant factor[14] as an indicator that the claimant may be unable to pay an adverse costs order in the future but 'something more' is usually required[15] whether the claimant is a natural person or a corporation.[16] The additional factor must be weightier to warrant an order against a natural person than against a corporation, illustrating the traditional reluctance to make orders for security against natural persons.[17]

5.7. Factors additional to the impecuniosity of natural persons that have justified an order for security for costs have been their:

- History of failure to comply with costs orders, the transfer of money to an overseas account, and prevarication and lack of frankness in evidence on that subject;[18]
- Foreign residence;[19]

8 Malaysia: *Adarsh Pandit v Viking Engineering Sdn Bhd* [1998] 2 AMR 1009. India: *Organizing Committee Commonwealth Games v Nussli (Switzerland) Ltd.* [2014] SCC OnLine Del 883.

9 Hague Conference on Private International Law, *Convention on Choice of Court Agreements,* opened for signature 30 June 2005 (entered into force 1 October 2015) ('*Choice of Court Convention*').

10 For example, s 12 of the Foreign Proceedings (Excess of Jurisdiction) Act 1984 (Cth); *Reciprocal Enforcement of Commonwealth Judgments Act* (Singapore, cap 264, rev ed 1985) and *Reciprocal Enforcement of Foreign Judgments Act* (Singapore, cap 265, rev ed 2001).

11 The UK rules of court include a prohibition against ordering security against a resident of a state bound by the 2005 *Hague Convention*: *Civil Procedure Rules 2005* (UK) r 25.13(2)(a)(ii).

12 *Lo Surdo v Public Trustee* [2003] NSWSC 837 [26]; *Re Estate Condon; Battenberg v Phillips* [2017] NSWSC 1813 [121].

13 *Barton v Minister for Foreign Affairs* (1984) 2 FCR 463, 594; *Loque v Hansen Technologies Ltd* [2003] FCA 81.

14 *Sir Lindsay Parkinson & Company Ltd v Triplan Ltd* [1973] QB 609, 626A-D, 627D-F and 628H–629A ('*Lindsay Parkinson*').

15 *Knight v Beyond Properties Pty Ltd* [2005] FCA 764 [32] ('*Knight*'); *Rowe v Andrews* [2021] TASSC 34 [7] ('*Rowe v Andrews*'), citing *Bryan E Fencot & Associates Pty Ltd v Eretta Pty Ltd* (1987) 16 FCR 497, 509 [57]–[59] ('*Fencot*').

16 Malaysia: *Faridah Begum binti Abdullah v Dato Michael Chong* [1995] 2 MLJ 404; *Doree Industries (M) Sdn Bhd v Sri Ram & Co* [2007] 1 MLJ 722; *Rodwin v Bahadur v CIMB Bank Berhad* [2018] 6 AMR 803; Malaysia, UK: *Cowell v Taylor* (1885) 31 ChD 34; *Le Mesurier v Ferguson* (1903) 20 TLR 32. Trinidad and Tobago: *Marjorie Ilma Knox v John Vere Evelyn Deane* [2011] CCJ Appeal No. 8 ('*Marjorie Ilma Knox*').

17 *Mr D v Ms P* [2020] NSWCA 174 [31]–[39]; *Mohareb v Harbour Radio Pty Ltd* [2020] NSWCA 231 [15] ('*Mohareb appeal*').

18 *Mohareb v Fairfax Media Publications Pty Limited* [2019] NSWSC 1685 ('*Mohareb*') [54].

19 *Barton v Minister for Foreign Affairs* (1984) 2 FCR 463, 594 (Morling J); *Loque v Hansen Technologies Ltd* [2003] FCA 81.

- Claiming for the benefit of others;[20]
- Lack of prospects of success;[21]
- Amount of security not being oppressive or stifling, and a lack of security materially damaging the respondent, in open standing litigation;[22]
- Low prospects of a contingent claim where security would not stifle the proceeding;[23]
- Impecuniosity being self-inflicted;[24]
- Self-denuding of assets before[25] or after[26] proceedings were commenced, or before they were contemplated to avoid costs orders in other proceedings;[27] and
- Funding by a third party.[28]

5.8. *Present or future means to pay.* Short of impecuniosity, a corporate claimant's likely inability to meet a costs order is a substantial or 'most significant' factor in favour of security.[29] A claimant may not be impecunious but may have such obligations and liabilities, including those arising from the proceedings, that it would be practically unable to pay a costs order when it is made in the amount estimated.

5.9. *Corporate claimant.* Security for costs is available against corporations under legislation or otherwise on the underlying principles that the corporation is suing for the benefit of others – its shareholders – and that the limited liability character of corporations could prejudice respondents.[30]

5.10. *Corporate liquidation.* Being in liquidation is a strong indicator of impecuniosity and of likely future inability to pay a costs order[31] and is not, of itself, a reason not to order security.[32] A distinction is drawn between cases in which the claimant is the liquidator personally and where it is as agent for the company. Security for costs will not be ordered where the liquidator personally is claimant, because she is exercising a

20 *Cunningham v Olliver* (Federal Court of Australia, Burchett J, 21 November 1994) (see *Knight v Beyond Properties Pty Ltd* [2005] FCA 764 [33].

21 *Chang v Comcare Australia* [1999] FCA 1677 [32] ('*Chang*'); *Morris v Hanley* [2000] NSWSC 957 ('*Morris*') [21], [38], [39], the latter also including large costs to the defendants.

22 *Melville v Craig Nowlan & Associates Pty Ltd* (2002) 54 NSWLR 82 ('*Melville*') [132].

23 *Liu v Resi Ventures Leakes Pty Ltd (No 2)* [2019] VSC 638 [62], [67].

24 *Mohareb appeal* (n 17) [45] where the plaintiff had not worked for ten years and his impecuniosity resulted from a long history of unsuccessful litigation instigated and pursued by him.

25 *Rajski v Computer Manufacture & Design Pty Ltd* [1982] 2 NSWLR 443 ('*Rajski*') (n 447–8, confirmed on appeal in [1983] 2 NSWLR 122 ('*Rajski appeal*') 128.

26 *Cherry v Read* (Full Court of the Federal Court of Australia, 21 November 1996), cited in *Mohareb* (n 18) [55].

27 *Mohareb* (n 18) [56].

28 *Augusta Ventures Limited v Mt Arthur Coal Pty Limited [2020] FCAFC 194* ('Augusta') [33].

29 *Pearson v Naydler* [1977] 1 WLR 899 ('*Pearson v Naydler*'); *Bank Mellat v Helliniki Techniki SA* [1984] 1 QB 291, 300G; *DSQ Property Co Ltd v Lotus Cars Ltd* [1987] 1 WLR 127 ('*DSQ Property*') 130.

30 *Pearson v Naydler* (n 29); *Green v CGU Insurance Ltd [2008] NSWCA 148 [72] ('Green appeal'), citing Buckley v Bennell Design and Constructions Pty Ltd* (1974) 1 ACLR 301 303–4. India: *Intertoll Ics Cecons. O & M Co. Pvt. Ltd. v National Highways Authority of India* [2013] 135 DRJ 160 ('*Intertoll*').

31 Malaysia, UK: *Northampton Coal, Iron, and Waggon Co v Midland Waggon Co* (1878) 7 ChD 500, CA (Eng); *Pure Spirit Co v Fowler* (1890) 25 QBD 235; *Northampton Coal, Iron, and Waggon Co v Midland Waggon Co* (1878) 7 Ch D 500, 503. Uganda: *G.M. Combined (U) Limited v A.K. Detergents (U) Limited* [1996] SCC OnLine UGSC 14.

32 *Hession v Century 21 South Pacific Limited (1992) 28 NSWLR 120, cited with approval in Green appeal* (n 30) [27].

statutory power vested in her personally. Where the company is claimant, security for costs may be ordered on usual principles, particularly if there is a statutory power to do so.[33]

5.11. *Nominal claimant.*[34] Security may be ordered where someone is standing behind a claimant who stands to benefit from the proceeding. The underlying concern is that those substantially interested in the outcome of the proceedings have retreated behind an impecunious individual so as to avoid putting their own resources at risk of an adverse costs order.[35]

5.12. *Quantum of likely costs.* Logically, the higher the ultimate costs order, the more difficult the claimant will have in paying. It also suggests that the claimant's own costs will be commensurately high, increasing the claimant's financial burden. The magnitude of the claimant's legal and other costs is relevant to show its financial commitments in addition to potential liability to pay the applicant's costs.[36]

5.13. *Counterclaim.* The existence of a counterclaim raises additional considerations for and against granting security for costs, and raises the possibility of security for costs being granted to the original claimant for its costs of defending the counterclaim.[37] Two security for costs orders theoretically may be made but rarely are – one to the respondent for the costs of defending the claim, and another to the claimant for the costs of defending the counterclaim.[38]

5.14. A respondent who raises a purely defensive counterclaim without raising additional matters may obtain security for its costs of defending the proceeding on the usual principles[39] and is unlikely to be required to give security for the claimant's costs of defending the counterclaim.[40]

5.15. Where the counterclaim arises out of essentially the same facts as the claim, security for the counterclaimant's costs of defending the claim might be refused[41] if the claim is likely to be stayed as a result of the claimant's inability to provide security, unless the counterclaimant gives an undertaking not to prosecute the counterclaim if the

---

33 *Green appeal* (n 30) [27], *citing Hession v Century 21 South Pacific Limited* (1992) 28 NSWLR 120.

34 UK: *Chuku v Chuku* [2017] EWHC 541 (Ch).

35 *Green appeal* (n 30) [74]; *Project 28 Pty Ltd v Barr* [2005] NSWCA 240 [114]–[115]; *Pearson* (n 29) *905; Fiduciary Ltd v Morningstar Research Pty Ltd* (2004) 208 ALR 564, 577 [53] ('*Morningstar*'); *Malaysia: Mechanalysis Sdn Bhd v Appraisal Property Management Sdn Bhd* [2016] AMEJ 1263; [2016] 11 MLJ 566; *UK: Jones v Gurney* [1913] WN72.

36 Trinidad and Tobago: *Marjorie Ilma Knox* (n 16).

37 Malaysia, UK: *Strong v Carlyle Press (No 2)* [1893] WN 51. India: *Intertoll* (n 30).

38 *Interwest Ltd v Tricontinental Corporation Ltd* (1991) 5 ACSR 621, 626; *Gobain RF Pty Ltd v Maax Spa Corporation Pty Ltd* [2004] VSC 335 [43]; *Grace Christian Chapel v Canaan Holdings Pty Ltd (Security for Costs)* [2019] VSC 5 [32].

39 UK: *Anglo Petroleum Ltd v TFB Mortgages Ltd* [2004] EWHC 1177 (Ch).

40 *Interwest* (n 38) 626, citing *Visco v Minter* [1969] 2 All ER 714, 716 ('*Visco*'); *Rad Drill Services Pty Ltd v Warrego Energy EP469 Pty Ltd* [2021] NSWSC 214 [39]; *Lima Orthopaedics Australia Pty Ltd v Proactive Ortho Pty Ltd* [2021] NSWSC 1014 [14]; *Bevwizz Group Pty Ltd v Transport Solutions Pty Ltd* [2008] NSWSC 1399 [18]; *New Fenix Compagnie Anonyme D'Assurances de Madrid v General Accident, Fire, and Life Assurance Corp Ltd* [1911] 2 KB 619, 625–6 ('*New Fenix*'); *Motakov Ltd v Commercial Hardware Suppliers Pty Ltd* (1952) 70 WN (NSW) 64; *Copson v DCM Coffee & Donuts Pty Ltd* (1996) ATPR 41–505; Malaysia, UK: *Neck v Taylor* [1893] 1 QB 560; UK: *Hutchison Telephone (UK) v Ultimate Response Ltd* [1993] BCLC 308, CA, 317d ('*Hutchison Telephone*').

41 UK: *BJ Crabtree (Insulation) Ltd v GPT Communications Systems* (1990) 59 BLR 43, CA.

claim is stayed.[42] It is considered unfair for the claimant to be unable to prosecute its claim but have to defend the same issues on the counterclaim.

5.16. If the respondent 'opens a counter attack on a different front',[43] or makes a counterclaim in excess of the amount of the claim, it is in danger of an order for security for costs,[44] at least in respect of the excess.[45] Where there is a counterclaim that is more than defensive, the amount awarded to a claimant or a respondent as security for the costs of defending the counterclaim or claim respectively, may be reduced,[46] or security may be refused,[47] to reflect any overlap in the work done on claim and counterclaim.[48]

5.17. Where a counterclaim is partly defensive and partly offensive, security for the claimant's costs of defending the counterclaim may be reduced by the amount of costs attributable to defending the defensive part of the counterclaim.[49] Security for the respondent's costs of defending the claim might also be refused where it has made a major counterclaim that is more than defensive, requiring the claimant to expend significant sums in defence.[50]

5.18. *Quantum of claim and counterclaim.*[51] Where a counterclaim is much larger or more complex than the claim, the claimant's potential liability on the counterclaim for damages and costs might significantly outweigh the amount it would receive on the claim, exposing it to increased financial uncertainty. This may provide an additional ground for granting security, or it may suggest it would be unfair to deprive the claimant of funds to defend the counterclaim by requiring it to provide security for the costs of defending its claim.[52]

5.19. *Outstanding costs orders or debts.* Non-payment of costs orders[53] or other debts to the applicant or others without proper excuse is a classic ground for granting security for cost.[54] It suggests the claimant is unable or unwilling to pay, and that it disregards

42 *Concrete Constructions v Dalma Formwork* [1999] NSWCA 16 [24]; *LPH Developments Pty Ltd v Jamieson Moore Pty Ltd* [2015] WASC 416 [19] ('*LPH Developments*'); *Colmax Glass Pty Ltd v Polytrade Pty Ltd* [2013] VSC 311 [20(d)] *Sydmar Pty Ltd v Statewise Developments Pty Ltd* (1987) 73 ALR 289, 300(H) ('*Sydmar*'); *Edenham Pty Ltd v Meares (No 2)* [2016] WASC 302 [20] ('*Edenham*'); UK: *Dumrul v Standard Chartered Bank* [2010] EWHC 2625 (although in this case, it concerns the dismissal of the claim).

43 *Visco* (n 40) 716; *Grace Christian* (n 38) [31]; Malaysia, UK: *Washoe Mining Co v Ferguson* (1866) LR 2 Eq 371; *New Fenix* (n 40); *City of Moscow Gas Co v International Financial Society* (1872) 7 Ch App 225; *Pure Spirit Co v Fowler* (1890) 25 QBD 235; *Firehold Land Co v Spargo* [1868] WN 94; UK: *Thistle Hotels Ltd v Gamma Four Ltd* [2004] EWHC 322; [2004] BCLC 174.

44 UK: *TC Developments (South East) Ltd v Investin Quay House Ltd* [2019] EWHC 1432 (TCC); [2019] Costs L 765.

45 *T Sloyan & Sons (Builders) Ltd and another v Brothers of Christian Instruction* [1974] 3 All ER 715, 721 ('*T Sloyan & Sons*').

46 *Grace Christian* (n 38) [53(c)]; *NZX Limited v Ralex Commodities Pty Limited* [2012] NZHC 1585 [30], [51]; *Mio Art Pty Ltd v Mango Boulevard Pty Ltd* [2018] QSC 31 [93]; *Sydmar* (n 42) 292, 297 (ln 30), 300(H), 302–3 ('*Sydmar*'); *Edenham* (n 42) [18]–[20], [24].

47 *LPH Developments* (n 42) [9].

48 Malaysia, UK: *T Sloyan & Sons* (n 45).

49 *ADS Advertising v Central West Business Park* [2005] VSC 265 [13].

50 *Sydmar* (n 42) 302–3.

51 UK: *Hutchison Telephone* (n 40) 314h, 317f-g.

52 Ibid.

53 Malaysia: *CNLT (Far East) Berhad v JCT Limited* [2018] 1 LNS 1127.

54 *Goldus Pty Ltd v Cummins (No 2)* [2020] FCA 971 [8] (failure to pay statutory charges and insurance premiums); *Ansa Enterprises Pty Ltd v Australian Finance Group Ltd* [2001] WASC 233, citing *Jebb v Superior Lawns Australia Pty Ltd* [2019] WASCA 208 [8], [31]; Mohareb appeal (n 17) [52]; *Nyoni v Pharmacy Board of Australia* [2018] FCA 1313 [36] ('*Nyoni*'); *Craven v Globe Valley Pty Ltd* [2018] QDC 155 [48(b)] ('*Craven*').

orders. These are indicators that the claimant may not pay an ultimate costs order. An alternative to ordering security for costs in those circumstances is to stay the proceeding until the costs are paid.[55]

5.20. *Non-compliance with interlocutory orders*. Non- or late compliance with interlocutory orders by the claimant can weigh in an applicant's favour as it indicates a disregard of orders and a claimant's potential not to pay costs voluntarily.[56]

5.21. *Dissipation of assets*. Dissipation of assets before or during the proceedings is highly relevant to the discretion,[57] indicating an intention to put assets beyond the reach of the applicant.[58] Even if that is not the intention, the fact of the dissipation may mean that the claimant will not be able to pay the applicant's costs or that the applicant will not be able to enforce a costs order.[59] The mere fact that a claimant converts real property assets into cash does not mean that those monies will no longer be available to satisfy any orders that might be made by the court,[60] and evidence or serious inference will be needed to prove dissipation to the appropriate standard.

5.22. It would also be relevant if it could be shown that the claimant is planning to dissipate assets before or after the award. It is more difficult to prove than past dissipation and would usually only be established inferentially unless agreements, statements, or intimations to that effect come to light.

5.23. *Third party funding*. The existence of a third party funder behind the claimant who stands to make a commercial profit from funding the litigation can be a ground for ordering security.[61] In litigation, this is on the basis that courts exist primarily for the vindication of rights rather than the making of profits, and those who fund for profit should not escape responsibility for costs.[62] Third party funders may be ordered to provide security in the proportion in which they share in the proceeds of the litigation, if that is disclosed. Otherwise, they may be required to pay the whole security.[63] The tribunal may

---

55 *Byrnes v John Fairfax Publications Pty Limited* [2006] NSWSC 251 [17]; *Ansa Enterprises Pty Ltd v Australian Finance Group Ltd* [2001] WASC 233; *Thames Investment & Securities plc v Benjamin* [1984] 1 WLR 1381, 1383; *Morton v Palmer* (1882) 9 QBD 89, 92; *Sinclair v British Telecommunications plc* [2000] 2 All ER 461, 467, 472g.

56 *Bhattacharya v Freedman* [2001] NSWSC 498 [27]; *Mbuzi v Hall* [2010] QSC 359 [68]. India: *Maharashtra State Electricity Board v Datar Switchgear Ltd.* [2003] 2 Bom CR 81 ('*Maharashtra SEB*').

57 UK: *Harris v Wallis* [2006] EWHC 630 (Ch) [24]–[25].

58 *Cheffick Ltd v JDM Associates* (1989) 43 BLR 52 (CA); *Shannon v ANZ Banking Group Ltd (No 2)* [1994] 2 Qd R 563; *Bhattacharya v Freedman* [2001] NSWSC 498 [27]; *Green appeal* (n 30) [45(3)]; *Mohareb appeal* (n 17) (transfer of money overseas without frank explanation). *Note the view that any person* is entitled to render themselves 'litigation proof' if they so choose: *Loque v Hansen Technologies Ltd* (2003) 125 FCR 590 [54] cited in *Kiefel v Victoria* [2014] FCA 604 [65]. UK: *Ackerman v Ackerman* [2011] EWHC 2183 (Ch); *Kolyada v Yurov* [2014] EWHC 2575 (Comm) [27]; *Al Jaber v Al Ibrahim* [2019] EWHC 1136 (Comm) [4]; *Re Tonstate Group Ltd* [2020] EWHC 328 (Ch) [11]. Kenya: *Muga Developers Limited v Njehu Gatabaki* [2017] SCC OnLine Ken 1164.

59 *Mohareb* (n 18), quoting *Cherry v Read* (Black CJ, Sackville and Finn JJ, Federal Court of Australia, 21 November 1996), affirmed in *Mohareb appeal* (n 17); UK: *Aoun v Bahri* [2002] EWHC 29 (Comm); [2002] CLC 776 [25]–[26].

60 *I J R Homes Pty Ltd v Toma (Building and Property)* [2016] VCAT 1626.

61 *Green appeal* (n 30) [85]; *Healy Air-conditioning Pty Ltd v Oracle Corporation Pty Ltd* (2003) 21 ACLC 866 [3]; *Global Finance Group Pty Ltd (in liq) v Marsden Partners* [2004] WASC 52 [59]–[60], [71]; *Maronis Holdings Ltd v Nippon Credit Australia Ltd* [2000] NSWSC 994 [11]–[12]; *Baygol Pty Ltd v Huntsman Chemical Co Australia Pty Ltd* [2004] FCA 1248 [37]–[39]; *Winnote Pty Ltd (in liq) v Page* (2005) 64 NSWLR 244 [23]; UK: *Re RBS (Rights Issue Litigation)* [2017] EWHC 1217 (Ch); [2017] 1 WLR 4635; *Bailey v Glaxosmithkline UK Ltd* [2017] EWHC 3195 (QB); [2018] 4 WLR 7. India: *Intertoll* (n 33).

62 *Green appeal* (n 30) [51].

63 Ibid [53].

accept an undertaking from a reputable, well-funded funder[64] or insurer,[65] rather than the posting of security. Because the overriding consideration in the discretion is what is just, a corporate funder will not be required to provide security if it is sufficiently capitalised and solvent that there is no reason to believe it will be unable to meet an adverse costs order, in the same way as obtains for a corporate claimant.[66]

5.24. *Enforcement difficulties.* Difficulty in enforcing costs orders against the claimant may be relevant if it arises from more than the mere fact of its foreign residence. Regard might be had to any particular difficulties with the jurisdiction where the assets are held, whether the claimant has placed them there deliberately to frustrate enforcement, the nature of the assets (for example if they are difficult to sell, are frequently sold below value, if the economy is depressed, or demand for those assets is low), or the assets are encumbered.

Liability factors in favour of security for costs

5.25. The purpose of security for costs orders is to ensure funds are available to satisfy an ultimate costs order in the applicant's favour.[67] If it is unlikely such an order will be made, there is no basis for an order for security.

5.26. *Agreement as to costs.* The parties may have agreed in the contract the subject of the proceedings to bear their own costs of a dispute. Arbitral tribunals generally uphold the parties' agreement on such issues unless required otherwise by the *lex arbtri* or the law of the arbitration agreement.[68] Such an agreement does not bind courts,[69] but the discretion will ordinarily be exercised so as to reflect that contractual right.[70]

---

64 In Australia, *Birbilis Bros Pty Ltd v Chubb Fire and Security Pty Ltd* [2018] QSC 3 [152]; *Traderight Pty Ltd v Bank of Queensland Ltd* [2010] NSWSC 1502 [93], [95]. In Canada, *David v Loblaw* 2018 ONSC 6469 [22]; *Printing Circles Inc v Compass Group Canada Ltd* (2007) 88 OR (3d) 685 [19]; *Borrelli v Chan* 2017 ONSC 1815 [50]; *SolarBlue LLC v Aus* 2013 ONSC 7638 [22]; *Telesis Technologies Inc v Sure Controls Systems Inc* 2010 ONSC 5288 [61]–[67].

65 *Nylex Corporation Pty Ltd v Basell Australia Pty Ltd* [2009] VSC 97 [58]–[62] ('*Nylex*'); *Versloot Dredging BV v HDI Gerling Industrie Vesicherung AG* [2013] EWHC 658 (Comm) ('*Versloot*'); *DIF III Global Co-Investment Fund LP v BBLP LLC* [2016] VSC 401 [49] ('*DIF III*').

66 *Rowe v Ingenious Media Holdings PLC* [2021] EWCA Civ 29 [26].

67 Ibid [66]; *Taurus Mining Finance Fund AIV LP v Sandfire Resources Ltd* [2021] WASC 52 [18]; *David Clarke Air Conditioning Pty Ltd v Quann [No 2]* [2016] WASC 176; *Enagic Co Ltd v Horizons (Asia) Pty Ltd (No 2)* [2020] FCA 1240 [39].

68 Nish Shetty, 'The Arbitration Agreement' in Sundaresh Menon (ed), *Arbitration in Singapore* (Sweet & Maxwell, 2014) 129, 167 [6.141], [6.144]; Colin YC Ong and Michel Patrick O'Reilly, *Costs in International Arbitration* (LexisNexis, 2013) 8 [1.4].

69 Unless it is pleaded as a separate claim arising out of the breach of contract sued upon substantively, in which case it is a debt claim crystallising on the making of the judgment on the substantive claim: *Abigroup Limited v Sandtara Pty Limited* [2002] NSWCA 45 [9]–[10]; *Testel Australia Pty Ltd v KRG Electrics Pty Ltd* [2013] SASC 91 [146]–[151], [155]; *Jana Pty Ltd v Ezistripdemo Pty Ltd* [2017] NSWSC 1286 [14]; *Manassen Holdings Pty Ltd v Commercial & General Corporation Pty Ltd (No 2)* [2019] SASC 183 [62]; *Cervo v Kingsley's Pty Ltd* [2018] ACTSC 179 [45]; *Chaplair Limited v Kumari* [2015] EWCA Civ 798 [45].

70 *Gomba Holdings (UK) Ltd v Minories Finance Ltd (No 2)* [1993] Ch 171, 187–8 (CA); *Chaplair Limited v Kumari* [2015] EWCA Civ 798 [34]; *Pacific Mirage Limited v Le Breton* [2014] FCAFC 46 [64]; *Stuart v Rabobank Australia Ltd (No 2)* [2021] FCA 1626 [14]; *Dymocks Franchise Systems (NSW) Pty Ltd v Chapter Three Pty Ltd* [2022] NSWSC 35 [29]; *Chen v Kevin McNamara & Son Pty Ltd* [2012] VSCA 229 [8]; *Lee v Australia and New Zealand Banking Group Ltd* [2013] QCA 284 [9]; *Platinum United II Pty Ltd v Mortgage Management Ltd (in liq)* [2011] QCA 229 [6]; *Manassen Holdings Pty Ltd v Commercial & General Corporation Pty Ltd (No 2)* [2019] SASC 183 [52]–[53]; *Choice Constructions Pty Ltd v Janceski* [2011] WASCA 358 [68]; *Cervo v Kingsley's Pty Ltd* [2018] ACTSC 179 [46]–[47]; *Indigenous Business Australia v Kani (No 2)* [2012] NTSC 37 [8]; *Bank of China (Hong Kong) Ltd v Twin Profit Ltd* [2011] 3 HKC 59 [6]–[8].

5.27. *No costs-shifting*. Security will not be ordered if there is no possibility of a costs order being made under the prevailing regime such as the institutional rules or the *lex arbitri*.[71] However, where it is merely the default position that each party bears its own costs but there is a discretion to order costs, consideration must be given to the likelihood that a costs order will be made.[72]

5.28. Respondents to an arbitration who are not legally represented may be entitled to security for their internal costs in defending the claim and for the costs of experts and the like, depending on the wording of the costs provisions and the reasonableness of the costs incurred.[73] Internal costs, properly incurred, would fall within provisions of rules permitting recovery of 'legal *and other*' costs, or similar.[74]

5.29. *The claim lacks merit or is baseless*. The claim's likelihood of success is relevant to the fundamental question of whether the claimant is likely to be ordered to pay the costs[75] where costs follow the event. The 'event' is the claimant's success.

5.30. The merits of a case are relevant at their extreme, with the enquiry being whether the substantive claim appears very strong or very weak.[76] In such cases, the merits will be a factor to be weighed with the other factors identified in the particular case. If the merits appear neither very strong nor very weak, they are neutral in the exercise of the discretion.[77]

5.31. A security for costs application should not be turned into a mini trial,[78] and the merits are not examined in detail.[79] The tribunal may conduct a preliminary evaluation of the prospects, provided, of course, it is made clear that any view is not concluded, is on the limited evidence and submissions available at that time, and is subject to further evidence and submissions in and after the hearing on the merits.

5.32. It is suggested that it is no less appropriate for tribunals to make overtly preliminary evaluations of the merits than it is for courts.[80] Space does not permit elaboration of the reasons, but in summary they are that the standard and test for independence and

71 Costs generally being considered a matter of procedure governed by the *lex arbitri*: Jeffrey Waincymer, *Procedure and Evidence in International Arbitration* (Kluwer, 2012) 1194 [15.2.1]; Gary B Born, *International Commercial Arbitration* (Kluwer, 2014) 2495.

72 *Hapisun Pty Ltd v Rikys & Moylan Pty Ltd* [2013] VSC 730 [43]; *Owners Corporation PS623721 v Shangri-La Construction Pty Ltd (Building and Property)* [2021] VCAT 581 [27].

73 Ong and O'Reilly (n 68) 108–10 [6.9].

74 For example, *Arbitration Act 1996* (UK) s 59(1)(c), LCIA Rules art 28(3), ICC Rules art 37(1) [emphasis added].

75 UK: *Keary Developments Ltd v Tarmac Construction Ltd* [1995] 3 All ER 534, 540, CA ('*Keary Developments*'); *Al-Koronky v Time-Life Entertainment Group Ltd* [2006] EWCA Civ 1123 ('*Al-Koronky*'). India: *Maharashtra SEB* (n 56).

76 *ACN 006 577 162 Pty Ltd v Beauville Pty Ltd* [2014] VSC 298 [8] ('*Beauville*'), citing *Porzelack KB v Porzelack (UK) Ltd* [1987] 1 All ER 1074, 1077 ('*Porzelack*').

77 *Cody v Live Board Holdings Ltd* [2015] NSWSC 1790 [109]; *Cody v Live Board Holdings Ltd* [2017] NSWSC 308 [64]; uncriticised on appeal in *Live Board Holdings Ltd v Cody Live Pty Ltd* [2017] NSWCA 302 [68]–[69]; *Whitelaw v Hookey* [2020] QCA 145 [13]; *Australian Battery Distributors Pty Ltd v Robert Bosch (Australia) Pty Ltd* [2015] FCA 1164 [32] ('*Battery Distributors*'); *Australian Equity Investors v Colliers International (NSW) Pty Limited* [2012] FCAFC 57 [15].

78 *Mohareb appeal* (n 17) [44].

79 *Omar Ali bin Mohd v Syed Jafaralsadeg bin Abdulkadir Alhadad* [1995] 3 SLR 388; *Frantonios Marine Services Pte Ltd v Kay Swee Tuan* [2008] 4 SLR 224; *Lynx Engineering Consultants Pty Ltd v The ANI Corporation Limited (No 3)* [2010] FCA 32 [7]; *Global Access Ltd v Educationdynamics LLC* [2009] QSC 373 [61].

80 Nigel Blackaby and Constantine Partasides, with Alan Redfern and Martin Hunter, *Redfern and Hunter on International Arbitration* (Oxford University Press, 6th ed, 2015) 276–7 [4.139]–[4.140].

impartiality is the same for courts and tribunals, merits are not considered in detail and are relevant only at the extremes, consideration of the merits is the same for courts and tribunals, the same judge may conduct the merits enquiry on a security for costs application as decides the dispute, enforcement of awards after an interlocutory merits enquiry is no more problematic than enforcement of judgments, and proper consideration of the merits ensures appropriate access to justice.

5.33. The principal relevant difference between arbitration and litigation is the absence of a right of appeal in most arbitrations[81] and consequently a lack of due process being the only realistic possibility of challenge to an award.[82] This can lead to tribunals being concerned not to give any basis for a challenge due, in the case of security for costs, to an apprehension the tribunal has prematurely formed a concluded view about the merits.[83] It is suggested that this concern need not materialise if the formation and expression of the preliminary evaluation are performed judiciously. Redfern and O'Leary say, in making the preliminary evaluation, 'there is no need for the tribunal to prejudge the outcome of the dispute and no reason why it should be thought to be doing so in making an order for security for costs'.[84]

5.34. *Abuse of process, etc.* A solid ground for awarding security for costs is if the proceeding is an abuse of process or vexatious.[85] Claims lacking bona fides, being brought for an ulterior purpose or being a duplication of other proceedings are examples of abuses of process or vexatious proceedings. It is becoming accepted that tribunals have power to prevent abuse of the arbitral process (or abuse of rights, as it is sometimes known).[86]

5.35. Where a claim is *prima facie* regular on its face and discloses a cause of action, in the absence of evidence to the contrary, the tribunal should proceed on the basis that the claim is with a reasonable prospect of success.[87] Evidence to the contrary to show lack of bona fides might be the claimant's motivation in bringing the claim (such as to harass),[88] vexatiousness evidenced by incessant and numerous applications,[89] and the surrounding circumstances relevant to the bona fides of the claim including whether it is trivial, whether the claimant's formulation of the claim has changed significantly over time, whether the remedy sought is within the tribunal's power, and how the parties behaved before the proceeding commenced.

---

81 Ibid 592 [10.67]. The UK is one of the few jurisdictions to permit an appeal, limited to a question of English law: *Arbitration Act 1996* (UK) s 69.

82 Sundaresh Menon, *International Commercial Courts: Towards a Transnational System of Dispute Resolution* (Speech, Dubai International Financial Centre Courts Lecture Series 2015, 22 January 2015) [48] <https://www.supremecourt.gov.sg/docs/default-source/default-document-library/media-room/opening-lecture-difc-lecture-series-2015.pdf>.

83 As a result, denying a party a full opportunity of presenting its case contrary to arts 18, 34(2)(a)(ii) and 36(1)(a)(ii) of the *Model Law*, and art V(b) of the *New York Convention*.

84 (n 2) 401.

85 *McHenry v Lewis* (1882) 22 Ch D 397, 408; *Morris v Hanley* [2000] NSWSC 957 ('*Morris v Hanley*'); *Melville* (n 22) [135]–[138]; *Green appeal* (n 30) [31].

86 Ahmed Al Far, *Abuse of Rights in International Arbitration* (Oxford University Press, 2020); Emmanuel Gaillard, 'Abuse of Process in International Arbitration' (2017) *ICSID Review* 1; John David Branson, 'The Abuse of Process Doctrine Extended: A Tool for Right Thinking People in International Arbitration' (2021) 38(2) *Journal of International Arbitration* 187; Günther J Horvath and Stephan Wilske (eds), *Guerilla Tactics in International Arbitration* (Kluwer, 2013).

87 *General Trade Industries Pty Ltd (in liquidation) v AGL Energy Limited (No 2)* [2023] FCA 556 [2–7].

88 *Bhagat v Murphy* [2000] NSWSC 892 [20]–[21] ('*Bhagat v Murphy*'); *Morris v Hanley* (n 85).

89 *Lall v 53–55 Hall Street Pty Ltd* [1978] 1 NSWLR 310, 313–14 ('*Lall*').

5.36. It can be an abuse of process for legal proceedings to be brought for an ulterior purpose – that is, for a principal purpose other than, or in addition to, the vindication of a bona fide legal right.[90] Such abuses can resound in costs orders against the party bringing the proceedings.[91] This principle may apply even in jurisdictions that have the default American rule of each party bearing its own costs, such that abusive conduct may result exceptionally in a costs order being made against that party.[92]

5.37. Duplication of an existing or previous claim made in proceedings may ground an order for security for costs, as may the bringing of numerous previous proceedings,[93] particularly if coupled with a failure to pay costs associated with those proceedings.[94] A careful analysis of the two claims may be necessary to reveal that they are the same so as to ensure the applicant is not being troubled twice for the same claim and the processes of the court are not being abused.

5.38. The claimant might be overly litigious or attempting to overwhelm the respondent with the number of proceedings, or might be a crusader litigant[95] with a genuine but misplaced sense of grievance.[96] Security for costs may be the appropriate response to this type of vexatious and harassing conduct[97] although it is not the purpose of security for costs to coerce a litigant into conducting a more efficient and focused proceeding, nor to operate as an assurance they are serious about the proceeding, nor to force them to think twice about continuing.[98]

Conduct factors in favour of security for costs

5.39. *Unreasonable conduct.* Costs are discretionary, with the conduct of the parties being relevant to the final order. Unreasonable or abusive conduct may resound in an adverse costs order and would be relevant to whether security for costs should be granted. Relevant conduct before the proceeding began could be unreasonable such as a refusal to negotiate or mediate (particularly if included in a multitiered dispute resolution clause), unreasonable refusal of an offer of compromise, inordinate unexplained delay in commencing proceedings, unreasonable behaviour or unexplained delay in following contractual dispute resolution processes, unreasonable lack of cooperation in the proceeding. These are simply illustrative examples, and any conduct that could properly be considered as unreasonable may be relevant to granting security.

90 *Williams v Spautz* (1992) 174 CLR 509, 522; *Flower & Hart v White Industries (Qld) Pty Limited* (1999) 87 FCR 134 [60]–[61], [64] ('*Flower & Hart*').

91 *Flower & Hart* (n 90).

92 Ong and O'Reilly (n 68) 16–17 [1.6], 67–70 [5.3], 75–83 [5.5].

93 *Nyoni* (n 54) [33], [37] where the plaintiff had brought proceedings resulting in 32 separate judgments of trial and appellate courts, most adverse to him.

94 *Mohareb appeal* (n 17) [45], [63].

95 In *Craven* (n 54) [48(a)] it was said that vexatious should be understood as meaning productive of serious and unjustified trouble and harassment. See also *Crocker v Toys 'R' Us (Australia) Pty Ltd (No 3)* [2015] FCA 728 [9] for an expanded meaning of 'vexatious'. India: *JS Ocean Liner LLC, Bur Dubai (UAE) v m.v. Golden Progress* [2007] 2 Bom CR 1.

96 *Lall* (n 89); *Sands v South Australia* [2013] SASC 105, [14]; *Mbuzi* (n 56) [87]; *Craven* (n 54) [29]–[31], [45(a)], [48(a)]; *Nyoni* (n 54) [37], [39] where the plaintiff had been mostly unsuccessful in six judgments of the Court of Appeal, 24 judgments by single judges, and two judgments of the Full Court: see [33].

97 *Mbuzi* (n 56) [85].

98 *Kiefel* (n 58) [87].

5.40. Unreasonable conduct by either party after proceedings are commenced is also relevant to the exercise of the discretion. Unexplained delay, unnecessary or excessive steps,[99] obstructive behaviour, repeatedly missed deadlines without justification, prolix or badly drafted documents, and unnecessary and burdensome requests of the other party are some examples of the type of conduct that would be relevant on an application for security. Again these are illustrative only and parties are not limited to these types.

5.41. *Prejudice from delay*. Delay in making an application is not, of itself, a bar to a grant of security for costs, the discretion depending 'entirely on the circumstances of each case'.[100] The ultimate issue is whether the claimant has been prejudiced by the delay. Four factors are highly relevant – (a) the applicant's explanation of any delay in making the application,[101] (b) the costs incurred to date, (c) the costs to be incurred in the future, and (d) any prejudice suffered by the claimant[102] as a result of an order. Security can be crafted to alleviate prejudice caused by delay by, for example, not awarding security for past costs or otherwise reducing the amount to achieve fairness.[103]

5.42. (a) Explanation of delay. An applicant should apply for security for costs promptly[104] after learning of the facts giving rise to the apprehension that the claimant will be unable to pay its costs.[105] 'Delay' in this context refers to the time between the applicant's learning of those facts and making the application.[106] What is prompt will depend on the circumstances, but there should be a credible explanation of the passage of time, such as the necessity to conduct confirming investigations, to obtain advice and instructions, or to marshal the facts.[107]

5.43. (b) Costs incurred. The greater the proportion of overall costs of the proceeding incurred at the time of the application, the more reluctant a tribunal will be to make an order.[108] This is for two reasons which can operate together or separately – the respondent has stood by and allowed the claimant to incur the costs, and the costs might be wasted if security is ordered and not provided. Prejudice by reason of delay may be proved or assumed where substantial costs have been incurred since the time the application should have been brought.[109]

---

99 *Nyoni* (n 54) [37], [39]; *Bhagat v Murphy* (n 88) [26]; *Mbuzi* (n 56) [85].

100 *Milfoil Pty Ltd v CBA* [2020] VSCA 223 [19]; *PPK Willoughby Pty Ltd v Baird* [2019] NSWCA 48 [11]; UK: *Everwarm Ltd v BN Rendering Ltd* [2019] EWHC 1985 (TCC), [15]–[16].

101 Malaysia: *Strukturmas (Selangor) Sdn Bhd v Majlis Perbandaran Petaling Jaya* [2001] AMEJ 0167; [2001] 3 MLJ 344.

102 Malaysia, UK: *Jenred Properties Ltd v Ente Nazionale Italiano per it Turismo* (1985) Financial Times, October 29, CA (Eng); UK: *RBIL v Ryhurst* [2011] EWHC 2209 (TCC); [2011] BLR 721; *Owners of the Panamax Alexander v Registered Owners of the NYK Falcon* [2022] EWHC 478 (Admlty).

103 *Re Oswal* [2016] VSC 52 [35], [36], [44] ('*Re Oswal*').

104 Malaysia: *Asian Shield Warehousing Sdn Bhd (dalam likuidasi) v Leopad Holdings Sdn Bhd* [2019] 1 AMR 456; *Yee Hua Holdings Sdn Bhd v Chin Yew Nam* [1999] 2 CLJ 63; *Co-operative Central Bank Ltd v YM Raja Tan Sri Aznam Raja Hj Ahmad* [2004] 5 CLJ 375, 377; *Kejuruteraan Taipan (M) Sdn Bhd v Loh & Loh Construction Sdn Bhd* [2006] AMEJ 0071; [2007] 1 MLJ 578, 580.

105 *Mohareb appeal* (n 17) [52]; *Morris v Hanley* (n 85) [30]; *Tim Barr Pty Ltd v Narui Gold Coast Pty Ltd* [2009] NSWSC 563 [27] ('*Tim Barr*'); *Idoport Pty Limited v National Australia Bank Limited* [2001] NSWSC 744 [68] ('*Idoport*').

106 *Mohareb appeal* (n 17) [16].

107 Ibid [55].

108 *Les & Zelda Investments Pty Ltd v Whitehaven Coal Ltd* [2020] NSWSC 1091 [24] ('*Les & Zelda*'); *Tim Barr* (n 105) [28]; *Precise Training Pty Ltd v Chief Commissioner of State Revenue* [2020] NSWSC 1202 [73] ('*Precise Training*').

109 *Green appeal* (n 30) [57]; *Re Oswal* (n 103) [36].

5.44. (c) Future costs. Security may be ordered despite delay where the costs yet to be incurred are high, particularly in comparison to the costs incurred to date, or where the plaintiff would have incurred the costs in any event.[110] The degree to which the proceedings have progressed during the delay is relevant.[111]

5.45. (d) Prejudice. A claimant may prove some prejudice other than the incurrence of costs that it would suffer because of the delay if security were ordered, and can rely on 'the assumed and presumed prejudice that inevitably arises out of such delay'.[112]

5.46. *As a condition of indulgence.* Security for costs may be ordered as a condition of granting an indulgence to either party such as amending pleadings,[113] adjourning a hearing,[114] granting an extension of time,[115] or obtaining documents from a non-party or a potential party.[116] Exceptionally, security may be ordered in litigation against a *respondent* in favour of a *claimant* as a condition of indulging the respondent, particularly if it would have the effect of increasing the claimant's costs.[117] Such a power may be within a tribunal's broad power to manage proceedings, akin to but not as extensive as the court's inherent jurisdiction.[118]

Fairness factors against security for costs

5.47. *Claimant is really the respondent.* In some cases the claimant initiates the claim because it is forced by the form of action or by the nature of the claim, but in reality it should be seen as the respondent.[119] Examples are a claimant suing the government for return of property wrongfully seized,[120] a stockholder suing to prevent compulsory acquisition of his stock,[121] a lessee suing to resist the forfeiture of the lease,[122] resisting 'self-help' measures available to the respondent under a contract,[123] defending one's property or rights,[124] where the other party should have commenced proceedings had they acted appropriately,[125] and where a cross-claim arises out of the same facts.[126]

---

110 *Precise Training* (n 108) [75].

111 *Fencot* (n 15) 514; *Chapel Road Pty Ltd v Australian Securities & Investments Commission (No 2)* [2012] NSWSC 511 [24]; *Tim Barr* (n 105); *Liberty Grove (Concord) Pty Ltd v Mirvac Projects Pty Ltd* [2008] NSWSC 48 [7]; *Re Oswal* (n 103) [36]; UK: *Warren v Marsden* [2014] EWHC 4410 (Comm).

112 *Re Oswal* (n 103) [34], [59]–[60].

113 *Burrows v Houda (No. 2)* [2021] NSWDC 127 [67]–[68].

114 *Michael Wilson & Partners Limited v Emmott* [2020] NSWCA 139 [23]: *'the price of the adjournment'*.

115 *Levi v Swaab* [2020] NSWSC 1119 [47] *('Levi'); Frigger v Banning (No 11)* [2020] FCA 1257 [3].

116 *Levi* (n 115) [100].

117 *Kelly, re Halifax Investment Services Pty Ltd (in liq) (No 10)* [2020] FCA 1146.

118 See Keith Mason, 'The Inherent Jurisdiction of the Court' (1983) 57 *Australian Law Journal* 449.

119 *Sun Asia Group Pty Ltd ATF v Invigor Group Ltd* [2021] NSWSC 1082 [121] ('*Sun Asia*') [121], citing *Willey v Synan* (1935) 54 CLR 175, 184 ('*Willey v Synan*').

120 *Willey v Synan* (n 119).

121 *Re Travelodge Australia Ltd* (1978) 21 ACTR 17.

122 *Dee-Tech Pty Ltd v Neddam Holdings Pty Ltd* [2009] NSWSC 1095 [13]–[15].

123 *Heller Factors Pty Ltd v John Arnold's Surf Shop Pty Ltd (in Liq)* (1979) 4 ACLR 492, 498.

124 *Classic Ceramic Importers Pty Ltd v Ceramic Antiga SA* (1994) 13 ACSR 263 267; Malaysia, UK (Ireland): *Watteen v Billam* (1841) 3 DG & Sm 516.

125 Ibid.

126 *Public Transport Ticketing Corporation v Integrated Transit Solutions Ltd* [2009] NSWSC 54 [45] ('*Public Transport Ticketing*'); Malaysia, UK: *Sykes v Sacerdoti* (1885) 15 QBD 42.

5.48. The reality of the situation is determinative rather than how the parties are formally arranged on the record.[127] The legal relationships involved in the disputes are not analysed minutely;[128] the nature of the claim will be examined to determine whether it is truly defensive.[129] Consideration of the application may be deferred if the situation is unclear at the time of the application.[130]

5.49. *Respondent has contributed to the claimant's financial situation.*[131] A frequent response by a claimant to an application for security for costs is that its financial condition is due to the actions of the respondent the subject of the proceeding.[132] For that argument to defeat an application, there should be 'clear unambiguous evidence that there is a probability or at least a reasonable chance, that the impecuniosity is attributable' to the respondent's conduct.[133] There must be a real causal connection between the conduct and impecuniosity that would make it unjust to require security. It must be established that the respondent has been guilty of some form of misconduct or unacceptable business dealings which caused the claimant's impecuniosity. Mere general assertions, not supported by evidence, will not suffice. To hold to the contrary would be to defeat the purpose of the rule.[134]

5.50. To succeed in that defence, a claimant 'would have to show two things: first, that it previously had financial resources; and, second, that the respondent's actions caused or at least materially contributed to an inability to meet an order for security'.[135]

5.51. All aspects of the claimant's financial position are examined including the position before the events complained of, the type of business, and any unusual events to the company or the economy generally.

5.52. The force of this factor is significantly reduced where the substantive claim is for loss of profits rather than a loss of pre-existing assets[136] because the claim is really that the respondent failed to make the claimant's position *better*, not that it made it *worse*.[137]

5.53. *Respondent assumed the risk.* An application for security for costs may be defeated where the grounds of the application were, or should have been, known to the claimant at the time of the transaction out of which the proceedings arise.[138] The philosophy is that

127 *Public Transport Ticketing* (n 126) [42]; *Maatschappij voor Fondsenbezit v Shell Transport and Trading Co* [1923] 2 KB 166, 177; *Willey v Synan* (n 119) 178–9; 184–5; UK: *Hutchison Telephone* (n 40) 317e.

128 *Madgwick v Kelly* [2013] FCAFC 61 [16].

129 *Battery Distributors* (n 77) [48]–[51].

130 *Sun Asia* (n 119) [128].

131 UK: *Sir Lindsay Parkinson* (n 14) 626; *Spy Academy Ltd v Sakar International Inc* [2009] EWCA Civ 985 [14].

132 *Melunu Pty Ltd v Claron Constructions Pty Ltd* [2004] NSWSC 1064 [31]; *Westonia* (n 3) [45]; Malaysia: *Quality Tractors (M) Sdn Bhd v United Asian Bank Bhd* [1980] 1 MLJ 95.

133 JH Hames, *Security for Costs: Extent of Discretion* (1976) 120 SJ 479.

134 *Dalma Formwork Pty Limited v Concrete Constructions Group Ltd* [1998] NSWSC 472; *Melunu Pty Ltd v Claron Constructions Pty Ltd* [2004] NSWSC 1064 [31]; *Westonia* (n 3) [45].

135 *Del Bosco v Outtrim* [2008] NSWSC 105 [26]; *Jazabas Pty Ltd v Haddad* [2007] NSWCA 291 [94]; *Battery Distributors* (n 77) [41]; *M A Productions Pty Ltd v Austarama Television Pty Ltd* (1982) 7 ACLR 97, 100; *Morningstar* (n 35) [88]; *Pioneer Park (in liq) v ANZ* [2005] NSWSC 832 [14]; *Sharjade v Darwinia Estate* [2006] NSWSC 708 [17]–[20].

136 *Wollongong City Council v Legal Business Centre Pty Ltd* [2012] NSWCA 245 [33]; *Battery Distributors* (n 77) [42].

137 *Battery Distributors* (n 77) [40]; *Fat-sel Pty Limited v Brambles Holdings Limited* (1985) 3 ACLC 312.

138 *Beauville* (n 76) [22]; *Battery Distributors* (n 77) [28]; *Salex NSW Pty Ltd v Congredior Pty Ltd* [2021] NSWSC 732 [32] ('*Salex*').

the applicant assumed the risk of dealing with the impecunious claimant or should have investigated the claimant's financial condition at the time and either not dealt with it or factored the poor finances into the deal.[139] In those cases, it can be said that a change in circumstances from the time of the transaction is required before security will be ordered.

5.54. For this to operate as a defence to an application, the risk that eventuated should be the same risk that was known or knowable at the time of the transaction, and the history of the transaction should support both the contention and the allegations in the claim.[140] It has been suggested by an appellate court that a respondent's acceptance of the risk of a claimant's non-performance or breach of a contract is not to be equated with an acceptance of the risk of being sued by the claimant, particularly where the rules of potential proceedings permit security for costs.[141]

5.55. *Security is oppressive.* Security for costs may be denied if an order would be oppressive to the claimant.[142] Oppression may take different forms. One common argument is that an application is being brought for the purpose of stultifying (stifling) a reasonably arguable claim[143] or that ordering security would be oppressive in having that effect.[144]

5.56. Although a powerful consideration, the probability of the claim being stifled by an order for security is not determinative. Application of the stifling principle involves weighing all factors in the balance.[145] Security may be ordered despite the probability of its stifling a claim where the claim has poor prospects,[146] where there is an element of vexation or abuse in its nature or manner of prosecution,[147] or where those who stand to benefit from the claim unreasonably decline to provide security.[148] The ability of the respondent to absorb the costs is not, of itself, a relevant consideration, but may raise the possibility of inferring that the application is being brought for the purpose of stifling the claim rather than to protect the applicant's interests.[149]

5.57. While the onus of proof in a security for costs application rests, from first to last, on the applicant, there is an evidential burden on the claimant to adduce evidence of matters that establish reasons why security should not be granted, including that ordering security would stifle the claim.[150] The *onus probandi* of those matters lies on the claim-

---

139 Chris Parker et al., 'A Global Perspective on Availability of Security for Cost and Claim in International Arbitration – Mirage or Oasis?', in *Herbert Smith Freehills* (Web Page, 1 February 2017) <https://www.herbertsmithfreehills.com/latest-thinking/a-global-perspective-on-availability-of-security-for-costs-and-claim-in>.

140 *Battery Distributors* (n 77) [45].

141 *Coca-Cola Amatil Victoria Ltd v P A A Enterprises Pty Ltd* [2003] VSCA 135 [12].

142 Malaysia: *Haidakota (M) Sdn Bhd v Tan Tiam Chai* [2009] 1 CLJ 699, 702 ('*Haidakota*'); [2008] MLJU 654, CA.

143 Parker et al. (n 139); *Westonia* (n 3) [30]; Malaysia, UK: *Sir Lindsay Parkinson* (n 14).

144 *Keary Developments* (n 75) 539h; Malaysia: *Haidakota* (n 142); [2008] MLJU 654; *Gateway Kand Pte Ltd v Turner (East Asia) Pte Ltd* [1988] 1 MLJ 416 UK; *Goldtrail Travel Ltd v Aydin* [2017] UKSC 57 ('*Goldtrail Travel*').

145 *Ninan v Westpac Banking Corporation* [2015] WASCA 94 [22]; *Nyoni* (n 54) [22], [39].

146 *Sax* (n 182) [25]–[27].

147 Ibid; *Mbuzi* (n 56) [95]; *Craven* (n 54) [48](c)]; UK: *Sarayiah v Williams* [2019] EWCA Civ 1387.

148 *Trility* (n 3) [18]–[21]; *Andrews v Zuccubarr Pty Ltd* [2020] VSC 675 [103] ('Zuccubarr'); *LRSM Enterprise Pty Ltd v Zurich Australian Insurance Limited* [2014] NSWCA 88 [43] ('*LRSM*').

149 *Westonia* (n 3).

150 *Battery Distributors* (n 77) [25]; *Concrete Mining Structures Pty Ltd v Cellcrete Australia Pty Ltd (No 2)* [2018] SASC 27 [12]; *Stuart v Mordialloc Sporting Club Inc* [2020] VSC 658 [85] ('*Stuart*'); *Re Metal Storm Limited (in liquidation)* [2018] NSWSC 900 [10]; *Salex* (n 138) [16]; UK: *Al-Koronky* (n 75).

ant, being matters peculiarly within its knowledge[151] and giving rise to a defence to the application.[152]

5.58. As a result, a claimant will not attract the stifling principle if it can only show there is a substantial risk of its being unable to raise the security. That the claim will be stifled must be established on the balance of probabilities,[153] and the claimant must show, by evidence,[154] the efforts it has made to obtain finance from those who stand behind it, from financiers (including third party funders)[155] and others[156] and that they are unable (not merely unwilling)[157] to provide the amount of security[158] or to offer to charge available assets.[159] The proportionality between the costs and the fruits of a successful judgment is relevant to the reasonableness of others' unwillingness to provide security.[160] Alternatively, an unwillingness may indicate that the proceeding should not continue.[161] The offer of an undertaking of personal liability by persons who stand behind the company may be effective to resist an order for security,[162] depending on the value of the undertaking and the means of the person giving it.[163]

5.59. If ordering security in a lump sum would be oppressive, it may be ordered in stages such as the close of submissions, after document disclosure, and so on.[164] This has the advantages of reducing the immediate burden on the claimant and providing a measure of security for the respondent.

5.60. Staged security is not always an answer to the stultification argument, and there are times when security is not granted for that reason. This is especially the case if other factors exist suggesting security should not be given such as the proceeding involving a matter of public importance,[165] or the respondent being responsible for the claimant's financial position.[166]

---

151 *King v Burdett* (1820) 4 B & Ald 140; James B Thayer, 'The Burden of Proof' (1890) 4(2) *Harvard Law Review Association* 45, 51.

152 *Stuart* (n 150) [73]; Procedural Order No 7, Swiss Chambers' Arbitration Institution, Case No 300273–2103 (4 September 2014) reported in (2018) 36(3) *ASA Bulletin* 661 [10]; *Thayer* (n 151) 45.

153 UK: *Goldtrail Travel* (n 144).

154 *Grocon Group Holdings Pty Limited v Infrastructure NSW* [2020] NSWSC 1194 [120] ('*Grocon*'); *Adelaide (SA Pools and Spa) Manufacturing and Installation Pty Limited v Westcourt General Insurance Brokers Pty Limited* [2016] SASC 60 [53]; *Hardingham v RP Data Pty Limited* [2020] FCA 1062; *Green appeal* (n 30) [27], [45]; *Battery Distributors* (n 77) [54]

155 *Idoport* (n 105) [40(d)]; UK: *Goldtrail Travel* (n 144); *Keary Developments* (n 75) 540 [6].

156 *Flender Werft AG v Aegean Maritime Ltd* [1990] 2 Lloyd's Rep 27, 29; *Petromin SA v Secnav Marine Ltd* [1995] 1 Lloyd's Rep 603, 608–9.

157 *Zuccubarr* (n 148) [103]; *Grocon* (n 154) [113]; *LRSM* (n 148) [36].

158 *Trility* (n 3) [18]–[21]; *Grocon* (n 154) [113]; *Treloar Constructions Pty Limited v McMillan* [2016] NSWCA 302 [15]; *Dennis v Joukhador* [2021] NSWSC 870 [49]; *Sinclair v British Telecommunications plc* [2000] 2 All ER 461, 469h.

159 *Battery Distributors* (n 77) [60].

160 *Mohareb* (n 59) [64]. A rational, practical, and reasonable unwillingness of those who stand behind a nominal plaintiff to provide funding may be sufficient to resist an order for security: *LRSM* (n 148) [43]; *Ariss v Express Interiors Pty Limited (In Liq)* [1996] 2 VR 507, 513) ('*Ariss*').

161 *Ariss* (n 160) 513.

162 *Westonia* (n 3) [41].

163 Ibid.

164 *Mohareb appeal* (n 17) [64]; *Les & Zelda* (n 108) [20], [89]; *Ballard v Brookfield Australia Investments Ltd* [2012] NSWCA 434 [53].

165 See [5.62].

166 See [5.49].

5.61. Another form of oppression alleged is that the 'use of the power would shut out a small company from making a genuine claim against a large company',[167] but it does not become oppressive by the mere prospect that an order for security for costs might shut out the smaller company from litigation. Something more must exist.[168]

5.62. *Public importance*. This factor has much less application in arbitration than in litigation where a consideration against ordering security is that there is an issue of genuine public interest, importance, or public policy in the proceeding.[169] Issues such as the interpretation of a problematic statute or standard form contract, resolution of a different approach between jurisdictions, or elucidation of the meaning of a common term, or a conviction for contempt,[170] are examples. The principle is that such proceedings are not merely for the benefit of the parties but are constituting something of a public service.

5.63. Many arbitral awards are not published and, in any case, do not have precedential effect.[171] This factor may have some room for application where the parties are in a form of long-term relationship and the issue is likely to arise again. In such a case, determination of the issue in the current arbitration may be said to serve purposes beyond the instant dispute by preventing future disputes from arising and stabilising the relationship.

5.64. *Offers or admissions*. Admissions of liability or indebtedness by the respondent made in the proceeding, in correspondence or elsewhere,[172] and offers of compromise,[173] may operate as a reason not to grant security.[174] They indicate that the claimant is likely to be successful on at least part of its claim and will probably not be ordered to pay all of the respondent's costs of defending.

5.65. *Special relationship*. A special relationship between the parties during the course of the transaction may make it unfair or improper to require security, such as where the parties had common directorships and one used the equipment of the other.[175] The length of the relationship may also be relevant.[176] The respondent may already hold some form of security as a result of the transaction or otherwise, making it unnecessary or unfair to grant what would be additional security.[177]

5.66. *Mixed corporate and natural claimants*. A corporate claimant will not be ordered to give security where a natural co-claimant would not be so ordered.[178] This is not an

167 *Equity Access Ltd v Westpac Banking Corporation* [1989] ATPR 40–972, 50,635; *Battery Distributors* (n 77) [36].

168 *Battery Distributors* (n 77) [37].

169 *Melville* (n 22) [99]–[102]; *Façade Treatment Engineering Pty Ltd (in liq) v Brookfield Multiplex Constructions Pty Ltd* [2015] VSCA 169 [14]; *Bruder Expedition Pty Ltd v Leigh* [2020] QCA 67 ('*Bruder*').

170 *Bruder* (n 169).

171 Cameron Ford, 'The Lost Precedents of Arbitration' (2022) 39(1) *Journal of International Arbitration* 29, 30.

172 Malaysia, UK: *Sir Lindsay Parkinson* (n 14).

173 Ibid.

174 *Westonia* (n 3) [60]; Malaysia, UK: *Hogan v Hogan (No 2)* [1924] 2 IR 14.

175 *Westralian Gold Mines Ltd v Westralian Mineral & Drilling Pty Ltd (In Liq)* (1986) 4 ACLC 167.

176 *J & M O'Brien Enterprises Pty Ltd v Shell Company of Australia Ltd* (1983) 70 FLR 261.

177 For example, *Westonia* (n 3) [61] where the respondent's holding of $440,000 security from the plaintiff was a deciding factor in refusing security.

178 'The view was taken that the defendant's position should not be improved by the mere circumstance that there was an additional plaintiff. In other words, as the defendant would not have been able to get an order for security against the impecunious plaintiff in the jurisdiction, it should be no better off by reason of the circumstance that a plaintiff outside the jurisdiction was also joined': *Street v Luna Park Sydney Pty Ltd* [2006] NSWSC 1317 [27] ('*Luna Park*'), citing *Sykes v Sykes* (1869) LR 4 CP 645; *D'Hormusgee & Co v Grey* (1882) 10 QBD 13;

absolute rule, and security may be ordered against one or more mixed co-claimants where their claims have different elements and aspects, so that they will not all necessarily succeed or fail together.[179] The existence of natural claimants is a factor that diminishes the respondent's claim to be entitled to security against the corporate claimant but does not extinguish it.[180] Where the degree of overlap between the claim of the mixed claimants is comparatively small, such that separate orders for costs might be made in respect of each of the plaintiffs, it is usually appropriate that an order for security be made.[181] This factor may have some relevance in arbitration where arbitrations with different claimants are consolidated.

5.67. *Respondent holds security.* Security for costs might be refused if a respondent already holds some form of security from which it can recover its costs such as parent company guarantees, performance bonds, and the like.[182] A question will be whether the terms of the security make it available for recovery of the respondent's costs of the arbitration.

5.68. '*Unclean hands*'. The argument that the respondent applying for security for costs comes with unclean hands is rarely successful[183] and is an equitable response to a common law or statutory remedy.[184] Nevertheless, security for costs being a discretionary remedy based in fairness and justice, conduct of the respondent that might otherwise engage traditional equitable barriers to relief may be relevant to the wide discretion whether to grant or refuse security.[185]

Pearson (n 29); *Interwest* (n 38) 635; *Morningstar* (n 35); *Maples v Hughes* [2002] NSWSC 617; UK: *Hello Quo the Movie Ltd v Duroc Media* [2014] EWHC (Ch) 4622.

179 *John Bishop (Caterers) Ltd v The National Union Bank Ltd* [1973] 1 All ER 707, 709–10; *Morningstar* (n 35); *Luna Park* (n 177) [28]; *Sun Asia* (n 119) [133].

180 *Interwest* (n 38) 635.

181 *Luna Park* (n 178) [27]; *Morningstar* (n 35) [33]–[36]; Malaysia, UK: *Slazengers Ltd v Seaspeed Ferries Ltd; The Seaspeed Dora* [1998] 1 WLR 221; [1987] 3 All ER 967, CA (Eng).

182 (n 177).

183 For example, in *Craven* (n 54) [45(d)]; *Martin v State of New South Wales* [2011] NSWLEC 20 [58]; *Sax v Campbell* [2020] NZHC 1297 [10], [22] ('*Sax*'). It may be relevant that allegations of unclean hands against the applicant in each of these cases was made by a self-represented plaintiff, both as to the making of the assertions and their outcome. India: *Wizdoms Naik International Limited v DSV Gerimal* [2020] SCC OnLine Bom 7646.

184 *Chapman v Michaelson* [1908] 2 Ch 612, affirmed [1909] 1 Ch 238; *Ansford v Plymouth Finance Co Ltd* [1933] NLR 209; *Mayfair Trading Co Pty Ltd v Dreyer* (1958) 101 CLR 428, 450–6; *Tito v Waddell (No 2)* [1977] Ch 106, 259; *AWB Limited v Cole (No 2)* [2006] FCA 913 [46]; JD Heydon, MJ Leeming and PG Turner, *Meagher, Gummow and Lehane's Equity Doctrines and Remedies* (LexisNexis, 5th ed, 2015) (n 183) 644 [19–315].

185 In Australia, see Heydon, Leeming and Turner (n 184) 644 [19–315]. Equitable defences are available to common law actions in the UK by virtue of s 38 of the *Judicature Act 1925* (UK): *Palermo Seafoods Pty Ltd v Lunapas* [2014] NSWSC 792 [173]–[174]. India: *Intertoll* (n 30).

CHAPTER 6

The mechanics

Applications

6.1. Applications for security for costs should be made without delay after it is discovered or suspected that the claimant may be unable to satisfy a costs order. This is to avoid the claimant incurring costs or other prejudice that would make it unfair to order security.[1]

6.2. Steps in making an application include establishing the claimant's financial condition and compliance attitude, estimating costs, seeking security from the claimant and the claimant responding to the request, and then making and responding to the application.

Establishing the financial and compliance condition

6.3. A respondent should conduct searches of the claimant as soon as it is reasonably suspected that arbitration might be commenced, to ascertain its financial condition and its apparent attitude to compliance with awards. These results go to show its ability and willingness to pay any eventual costs order. Searches include property held, tax paid, returns filed, statements made, disputes involved in, the state of the claimant's business, and any other factors that shed light on its ability or willingness to pay.

Estimating costs

6.4. An estimate of costs is prepared as the basis of the request for security. It is widely recognised that estimating costs is an inexact science and that, in any case, a broad-brush approach is taken to assessing the quantum of security.[2] The estimate should enable the tribunal to assess the probability of the future course of the arbitration and the reasonableness of the costs claimed. One way of doing this is to set out the steps expected to be taken in the arbitration, the approximate time estimated for each step, the lawyers involved in doing the work and their experience, and basis of charge. A claimant is likely to challenge each of those elements to reduce the costs estimate.

6.5. It is usually not necessary to engage professional costs assessors to prepare this estimate because of the many uncertainties involved and the broad-brush approach to fixing quantum.[3]

---

1 See [5.41].
2 See [6.18] and following.
3 See [6.19].

DOI: 10.4324/9781003479628-6

Seeking security from the claimant

6.6. An application for security for costs is customarily preceded by a request from the respondent for evidence from the claimant that it is able to meet an adverse costs order, or for the provision of security if satisfactory evidence is not provided.[4] A respondent should write to the claimant before making an application for a number of reasons. Most interlocutory applications should be preceded by a request, to avoid unnecessary cost and delay; the request gives the claimant an opportunity of demonstrating the strength of its case and its ability and willingness to pay costs; the claimant's response will show whether or not an application is needed and may give an indication of its prospects of success; and a request and the response can be relevant on the question of costs of the application.

Claimant's response to request

6.7. For its own benefit, a claimant should reply to a request for security for costs unless there are strong countervailing reasons. The legal burden of proof is on the respondent to establish an entitlement to security, but once that burden is discharged *prima facie*, an evidential burden may be placed on the claimant.[5] In practical terms that means that, once the respondent has established, *prima facie*, that the claimant is likely to be unable or unwilling to pay a costs order, the claimant should show why it can and will, or why the merits are so strong that an ultimate adverse costs order is unlikely.

6.8. A claimant failing to reply to a reasonable request for security gives the respondent an opportunity of suggesting, and the tribunal a reason for suspecting, that the claimant does not have an adequate answer. And a reply without providing some details of property or finances can raise the suggestion and suspicion of an insufficiency to satisfy a costs order. The claimant aims to strike a balance between giving enough information to show that an order is unwarranted, and not disclosing information that might eventually harm itself.

Making the application

6.9. Application to the tribunal is usually made by letter supported by the correspondence about security and the documents said to justify the order, and sometimes also by statements if necessary such as by accounting, finance, or market experts. Applications should not be a mini-trial and should be conducted in a way to discharge the respective burdens economically.[6] They should address the factors discussed in Chapter 5 that are applicable to the case.

Responding to the application

6.10. A claimant needs to respond to the application with sufficient material and arguments to discharge its evidential burden. It might, for example, raise arguments discussed

---

4 *Precise Training Pty Ltd v Chief Commissioner of State Revenue* [2020] NSWSC 1202 [71] ('*Precise Training*'); Stephen E Colbran, *Security for Costs* (Longman, 1993) 273 [15.2]; Roger Quick and Liz Harris, *Quick on Costs* (Thomson Reuters, 2017) [4.9580].

5 See [5.57], but this does not expressly occur in ICC arbitrations: see [4.14].

6 See [5.31].

in Chapters 7 and 8 to contend that exceptional circumstances are required but do not exist in the present case to justify an order. It might also raise any of the factors discussed in Chapter 5, particularly those against ordering security.

Orders

6.11. An order for security for costs should specify the form and amount of security to be provided, and the stages if ordered to be given in that way. The arbitration may be stayed pending provision of the security.[7] An order might be in the following form for security in a lump sum:

(1) The claimant provide security for the respondent's costs of defending the claims in the sum of [*amount*] by [*form*] within [*number*] days of this order.
(2) The arbitration is stayed until the claimant satisfies order 1.
(3) [*costs of the application*].

6.12. The first paragraphs of an order for staged security might be:[8]

(1) The claimant provide security for the respondent's costs of defending the claims by [*form*] in the following manner:
  (a) [*amount*] on or before [*date/event*];
  (b) [*amount*] on or before [*date/event*];
  (c) *etc.*

OR:

(1) The claimant provide security for the respondent's costs of defending the claims by [*form*] in an initial sum of [*amount*] on or before [*date/event*];
(2) The respondent have liberty to apply for further security for costs after [*date/event*];

with the remaining orders as in [6.11].

Costs of applications

6.13. Costs of applications for security for costs may be dealt with either by ordering the unsuccessful party to pay the successful party's costs,[9] or that costs be reserved to be decided in the final costs award,[10] or that costs follow the event of the final award, or that there be no order as to costs.

6.14. A nuance to the first of those options is that a claimant successfully resisting an application might be awarded costs of the application but that one of the other orders might be made where the respondent is successful in obtaining an order. This is on the basis that security for costs is an interim measure, the ultimate propriety of which depends on the final outcome of the arbitration (that is, the award of costs). A claimant defeating

7 See [8.59] et seq.

8 For example, see the approach in *Precise Training* (n 4).

9 Note that the presumptive rules for interlocutory costs in litigation may differ from those in arbitration where there is often no express rule: *Precise Training* (n 4) [101]; *Payne v Australian Pacific Airports (Melbourne) Pty Ltd* [2020] VCC 1458; *Neo Modular Pty Ltd v Enderby Apartments Pty Ltd (No 2)* [2020] WASC 375 [12]–[13].

10 Colin YC Ong and Michel Patrick O'Reilly, *Costs in International Arbitration* (LexisNexis, 2013) 168 [9.8].

an application *suggests* that the application should not have been brought, entitling the claimant to costs, whereas a respondent succeeding remains subject to the final outcome. Security is only necessary if a costs order is ultimately made in the respondent's favour. If it is not, that also suggests that the application was unnecessary and the respondent should not have its costs. However this might be affected by the parties' conduct leading up to and in the application, for example if the claimant acted unreasonably in not responding to the respondent's pre-application correspondence.

6.15. Factors influencing the discretion as to costs of an application will include the usual factors relevant to costs – the conduct of the parties, the necessity for the application, the reasonableness of the costs, the outcome of the application, the amount of security ordered compared with the amount sought or offered,[11] the prevailing legal and procedural regimes,[12] and perhaps the costs traditions in the parties' home jurisdictions.[13]

6.16. The amount of the costs of the application may be included in the amount awarded for security[14] but often this will make little difference to that amount because of the broad-brush approach and the discounting for contingencies.[15]

Cross-undertakings

6.17. In rare and exceptional cases, a defendant seeking security for costs in litigation may be required to give an undertaking to compensate the plaintiff for any damage caused by the plaintiff providing security, if it eventuates that security was not required.[16] Such a condition theoretically may be imposed on a respondent seeking security for costs in arbitration in jurisdictions with the equivalent of Arts 17 E and G of the *Model Law* – security for interim measures and liability for costs and damages caused by them.

Quantum

6.18. The amount can either be a lump sum, or the amount and timing of the first or more in a series of tranches where staged security is ordered.

6.19. The assessment of the quantum of security is a broad-brush exercise, not akin to a taxation of costs, but is not an abstract process and must have an evidentiary basis;[17] it involves the exercise of an unfettered discretion to award the amount considered to be fit in all the circumstances, according to the 'feel' of the case.[18] Estimating the costs to

11 *Precise Training* (n 4) [101].

12 For example, the *lex arbitri, lex causaue*, and *lex executionis* for guidance on conditions, and even to the *lex fori* for 'information' on the appropriate approach: Procedural Order No. 4, ICC, April 2009 (2010) 28(1) ASA Bulletin 59 [67], [161]. Berger points out, though, that the consensus is that international arbitration should be largely detached from domestic laws and procedural traditions, with the seat being nothing but an abstract legal nexus to the *lex loci arbitri*, without grounding them in the general procedural law and should not be trapped in the straitjacket of mandatory rules of domestic procedural law: Klaus Peter Berger, 'Common Law v Civil Law in International Arbitration: The Beginning or the End?' (2019) 36(3) *Journal of International Arbitration* 295, 297.

13 Jeffrey Waincymer, *Procedure and Evidence in International Arbitration* (Kluwer, 2012) 1199 [15.2.6] referring to the 1999 Final Award in *Himpurna California Energy Ptd and Pt (Persero) Perusahaan Listruik Negara.*

14 *Precise Training* (n 4) [98].

15 See [6.19] and [6.25].

16 *Rowe v Ingenious Media Holdings PLC* [2021] EWCA Civ 2 ('*Rowe v Ingenious*').

17 *Resilium Pty Ltd v Nest Insurance Consult Pty Ltd* [2021] NSWSC 974 [15].

18 *Trailer Trash Franchise Systems Pty Ltd v Fascia* [2017] VSCA 293 [64]–[65].

be incurred in defending proceedings is an inexact science and, frequently, estimates of costs prepared by experienced practitioners ultimately turn out to be inadequate.[19]

6.20. The amount should be just and reasonable having regard to all of the circumstances of the case. The tribunal is not obliged to give security in the amount sought, nor is it bound by the estimates of the parties.[20] The amount must not be so low that it fails to provide any real protection to the respondent, nor so high that it is oppressive to the claimant.[21]

6.21. The amount is determined by reference to the estimated costs the respondent could be expected to recover ultimately.[22] As a general rule in arbitration, all costs incurred reasonably and proportionately to the dispute are recoverable,[23] including costs incurred before commencement that contributed to the proceeding,[24] client's internal costs,[25] and interest on costs.[26]

6.22. The tribunal is not determining how much will ultimately be payable by way of costs. All it is doing is fixing an amount of security to be applied against whatever costs the respondent will recover if successful. If ultimately the costs are less than the amount of security provided, the claimant will get its money back.[27]

6.23. In principle, the amount of security could include an amount in respect of the respondent's contribution to the fees and expenses of the tribunal and institution as that amount would be included in an award of costs in the respondent's favour.[28]

6.24. Factors relevant to the question of whether security should be granted are also relevant in assessing quantum.[29] A factor weighing against the granting of security may not be sufficiently strong in the particular case to warrant refusing security, but it might operate to reduce the amount granted. Delay,[30] the merits,[31] the possibility of stifling a claim,[32] and a funder's profit from the arbitration[33] are examples of factors having this dual operation, depending on their strength.

6.25. The amount may be discounted to take account of the possibility of settlement or vicissitudes.[34] The discount may be greater at early stages in the proceeding where the prospect of the matter continuing to a hearing is less certain. There is little justification for discounting on this basis when security is ordered in tranches or for security for costs to the date of the order.[35]

---

19 *Rock JV Pty Ltd v Thiess Pty Ltd* [2020] WASC 324 [29].

20 See [5.41].

21 (n 17).

22 *Les & Zelda Investments Pty Ltd v Whitehaven Coal Ltd* [2020] NSWSC 1091 ('*Les & Zelda*').

23 Ong and O'Reilly (n 10) 101 [6.4].

24 Ibid 98 [6.3].

25 Ibid 108 [6.9].

26 Ibid 31 [2.7].

27 *Les & Zelda* (n 22) [144].

28 Ibid 166 [9.6], citing *Dermajaya Properties Sdn Bhd v Permium Properties Sdn Bhd and another* [2002] SGHC 53.

29 *National Bank of New Zealand Ltd v Donald Export Trading Ltd* [1980] 1 NZLR 97, 103; *Sabaza Pty Ltd v AMP Society* (1981) 6 ACLR 194, 199; *Bruce Pie & Sons Pty Ltd v R H Mainwaring, English & Peldan* [1985] 1 Qd R 401, 404.

30 *Milfoil Pty Ltd v CBA* [2020] VSCA 223 [16] ('*Milfoil*'); *Grocon Group Holding Pty Limited v Infrastructure NSW* [2020] NSWSC 1194 [139]; *Re Oswal* [2016] VSC 52 [34].

31 *Coonwarra Pty Ltd v Cornonero Pty Ltd* [2018] VSC 333 [77(b)].

32 Ibid [77(c)]; *Precise Training* (n 4) [85].

33 *Green v CGU Insurance Ltd* [2008] NSWCA 148 [6].

34 Cameron Ford, 'General Discounting of Security for Costs Discounted' (2021) *Northern Territory law Journal* <https:www//ntlj.com.au/article/812817>.

35 *Les & Zelda* (n 22) [84]–[85].

6.26. The amount of costs incurred before the application may be included in the amount of security if it is fair. It might be unfair if the application was late, no forewarning was given, or the amount would be stifling.[36]

6.27. An amount may be included in security in respect of costs incurred before the arbitration was commenced if those costs contributed to the arbitration, for example, obtaining legal advice or expert opinions on the claim.[37]

6.28. If the justice of the case requires the claimant to provide security, the prejudice to the claimant (or funder) in fixing the level of security too high is only the marginal financing cost.[38]

6.29. Security may be ordered in tranches for stages of the proceedings rather than in a lump sum for its entirety. An amount may be fixed for the costs of the next stage or stages such as submissions, disclosure, expert evidence, and the like. Tranches are appropriate where the future costs or procedural steps are uncertain[39] or where a payment of a lump sum would be oppressive or would stifle the proceeding.[40] However, if ordering security in tranches would merely lead the parties to a point beyond which the claimant could not continue financially, there would be no point in doing so. Multiple applications are also not the most efficient means of conducting an arbitration.[41] Where tranches are ordered, the parties are usually afforded the opportunity to have the amount of security adjusted, as the case goes on so as to reflect the actual level of expenditure and the more precise estimates that may be possible as the case proceeds.[42]

Form of security

6.30. There is a broad discretion in setting the form of security.[43] It is usually provided in the form of a bank or third party guarantee (such as parent company guarantee), letter of credit, an undertaking from a reputable funder,[44] or cash deposit into a stakeholder account. Security is not limited to any particular form. The question is how justice is best served in the particular circumstances of the case.[45]

6.31. Care must be taken to ensure that the security cannot be considered to be the property of either party in case of a liquidation, with the result of the other party being left merely to prove in the winding up.[46]

---

36 *Australian Battery Distributors Pty Ltd v Robert Bosch (Australia) Pty Ltd* [2015] FCA 1164 [63] ('*Battery Distributors*'); *Mohareb v Harbour Radio Pty Ltd* [2020] NSWCA 231 [54]; *Precise Training* (n 4) [85]; *Milfoil* (n 30) [16]; *Lima Orthopaedics Australia Pty Ltd v Proactive Ortho Pty Ltd* [2021] NSWSC 1014 [22].

37 *Pathway Investments Pty Ltd v National Australia Bank Limited* [2012] VSC 97 [8]–[9], citing *Lobster Group Ltd v Heidelberg Graphic Equipment Ltd* [2008] EWHC 413 (TCC).

38 *Les & Zelda* (n 22) [145].

39 Ibid [19]. *Kupang Resources Ltd v Elias* [2018] NSWSC 1553 [21].

40 *Battery Distributors* (n 36) [63(4)].

41 Ibid [63(5)].

42 *Les & Zelda* (n 22) [145].

43 *Yara Australia Pty Ltd v Oswal* (2013) 41 VR 245, 249 [10] ('*Yara*').

44 UK: *Omni Bridgeway (Fund 5) Cayman Invt. Ltd v Bugsby Property LLC* [2023] EWHC 2755 (Comm); *Rowe v Ingenious* (n 16) [26]. Australia: *Birbilis Bros Pty Ltd v Chubb Fire and Security Pty Ltd* [2018] QSC 3 [152]; *Traderight Pty Ltd v Bank of Queensland Ltd* [2010] NSWSC 1502 [93], [95]. Canada: *David v Loblaw* 2018 ONSC 6469 [22]; *Printing Circles Inc v Compass Group Canada Ltd* (2007) 88 OR (3d) 685 [19]; *Borrelli v Chan* 2017 ONSC 1815 [50]; *SolarBlue LLC v Aus* 2013 ONSC 7638 [22]; *Telesis Technologies Inc v Sure Controls Systems Inc* 2010 ONSC 5288 [61]–[67].

45 *DIF III Global Co-Investment Fund LP v BBLP LLC* [2016] VSC 401 [40(4)] ('*DIF III*').

46 *Dalian Huarui Heavy Industry International Company Ltd v Clyde & Co Australia* [2020] WASC 132.

6.32. Care must also be taken in jurisdictions providing for the loss of unregistered security interests, to ensure that either the interest created by the security is registered, or is structured so as to fall outside the legislation.[47]

6.33. The claimant is entitled to propose security in a form least disadvantageous to it,[48] but the true issue remains whether the form of security ordered is adequate to protect the respondent.[49]

6.34. The claimant bears a 'practical onus' of establishing that the proposed security is adequate and does not impose an 'unacceptable disadvantage' on the respondent.[50]

6.35. The form of a fund or asset will be immaterial so long as it is adequate to achieve its object as a security.[51]

6.36. The degree of likelihood of the respondent being unable to pay the costs, along with all the circumstances, actual and possible, may be taken into account in the exercise of discretion.[52]

6.37. To be adequate, the proposed security must satisfy the protective object of a security for costs order, namely, to provide a fund or asset against which a successful respondent can readily enforce an order for costs against the claimant.[53]

6.38. The fact the security may not be 'immediately available and accessible' when a costs order is made against a plaintiff is not a decisive factor which requires the security to be rejected.[54]

6.39. There may be countervailing circumstances in a particular case which point to the justice of the case not requiring that a fund in the jurisdiction be established,[55] such as substantial assets out of the jurisdiction against which a costs order may be enforced with relative ease pursuant to procedures which are well defined and known.[56] In such cases, security may be ordered for the costs of enforcement rather than for the potential adverse costs order.[57]

6.40. Depending on the terms of the insurance and the circumstances of the case, an 'After the Event' ('ATE') insurance policy may be capable of providing adequate security. There may be provisions within the ATE insurance policy which a defendant can point to and say that, on the happening of certain events, those provisions may reduce or obliterate the security otherwise provided. The court should approach such objections with care: In order to amount to a valid objection that an ATE policy does not provide appropriate security, the defendant's concern must be realistic, not theoretical or fanciful.[58]

---

47 Ibid, concerning the effect of the Australian *Personal Property Securities Act 2009* (Cth).

48 *Rosengrens Limited v Safe Deposit Centres Limited* [1984] 3 All ER 198, 200–1 ('*Rosengrens*').

49 *Blue Oil Energy Pty Limited v Tan* [2014] NSWCA 81 [22] ('*Blue Oil*').

50 *PS Chellaram* (1991) 102 ALR 321, 323; *Maxim's Caterers Limited v Magnona Pty Ltd (No 1)* [2010] FCA 450 [6] ('*Maxim's Caterers*'); *Berry v Innovia* [2014] FCA 357 [34]; *DIF III* (n 45) [39].

51 *Yara* (n 43) 249 [10]; *Rosengrens* (n 48) 200–1; *Blue Oil* (n 49) [22]. ('*Berry v Innovial*').

52 *Yara* (n 43) 249 [10].

53 *Maxim's Caterers* (n 50) [6]; *DIF III* (n 45) [23].

54 *Yara* (n 42) 250 [12].

55 *DIF III* (n 45) [16], [37].

56 (n 53).

57 *Berry v Innovia* (n 50) [40]; *Dense Medium Separation Powders Pty Ltd v Gondwana Chemicals Pty Ltd* [2011] NSWCA 84 [32]–[33]

58 *Harlequin Property (SVG) ltd v Wilkins Kennedy* [2015] EWCA 1122 (TCC).

CHAPTER 7

Party consent and security for costs

7.1. Arguments in favour of restricting the operation of security for costs in international commercial arbitration can be seen to have their foundations in the concepts of party consent, party autonomy, procedural fairness, and the nature of arbitration. Those rooted in party consent are discussed in this chapter, and the remainder in the next.

7.2. Security for costs is said to undermine party consent in that:

- The parties have agreed to submit to arbitration and should not be permitted to raise further barriers such as security for costs;[1]
- Rules requiring advance provision of institution and tribunal fees and costs are the proper exposition of the parties' intent on the question of financial conditions to arbitration;[2] and
- The respondent has knowingly agreed to deal with the claimant in its situation and should be taken to have assumed the risks of being sued by the claimant in that situation.[3] This is the predominant reason given for requiring exceptional circumstances before granting security for costs in international commercial arbitration.[4]

7.3. These and the other arguments are sometimes given as policy reasons for excluding security for costs from international commercial arbitration, or for limiting its application.[5] Another approach would be to consider them as factors in the exercise of the discretion when raised on the facts of an application.[6]

7.4. Party consent is indispensable to the existence of international commercial arbitration.[7] It is the basis of arbitrators' jurisdiction and powers,[8] unlike courts which rely on the jurisdiction of the state regardless of consent. The concept of party consent is said to have evolved to embrace forms of consent not traditionally included, due in part

---

1 Jeffrey Waincymer, *Procedure and Evidence in International Arbitration* (Kluwer, 2012) 636 [8.2.10.6].

2 Ibid.

3 Michael Hwang and Rajesh C Muttath, 'The Role of Courts in the Course of Arbitral Proceedings: Singapore and Other Asian Perspectives' (2002) 68 *Arbitration* 223.

4 See [5.53].

5 Hwang and Muttath (n 3) 236; Waincymer (n 1) 644 [8.3.1].

6 *S A Coppée–Lavalin NV v Ken–Ren Chemicals and Fertilizers Ltd (In liq)* [1995] 1 AC 38, 62F–G ('*Coppée–Lavalin v Ken–Ren*'); *Green v CGU Insurance Ltd* [2008] NSWCA 148 [27], [42].

7 Andrea Marco Steingruber, *Consent in International Arbitration* (Oxford University Press, 2012) 2 [1.05]. The law does not uphold arbitration agreements where consent has been vitiated: Jan Paulsson, *The Idea of Arbitration* (Oxford University Press, 2013) 108 [4.3].

8 Steingruber (n 7) 11 [2.01], 13 [2.10].

DOI: 10.4324/9781003479628-7

to the tendency of arbitration to expansionism,[9] and to the increasing detail in arbitral rules and procedures[10] as a result of the competitive institutionalisation of arbitration[11] and of the competition between litigation and arbitration manifested in courts modernising, refining case management,[12] specialising, and creating international commercial courts[13] to re-establish their pre-eminence in cross-border dispute resolution,[14] and institutions adopting aspects of litigation requested by users of arbitration.[15]

7.5. Party consent is said to have become marginalised by the growth of arbitration and parties in certain situations having little choice but to agree. Until 1899, consent to arbitrate was only manifest by an agreement after a dispute had arisen. Pre-dispute arbitration agreements are now the norm and a party may be subjected to arbitration where it must consent if it wishes to enter the international marketplace, or purchases a product, enters employment, participates in a sport, joins an organisation prescribing arbitration in its articles of association, where legislation mandates arbitration, and where arbitral rules subject it to joinder to an arbitration.[16] Party consent is also eroded in commercial transactions where a party has relatively less bargaining power.[17]

No further barriers to arbitration and fees exhaust the issue

7.6. The arguments as to no further barriers to arbitration and that fees exhaust the financial issue are based on the premise that when a party consents to arbitration, it is only consenting – or taken to be consenting – to arbitration as opposed to litigation and to the payment of tribunal and institutional fees. The arguments may have some currency in an *ad hoc* arbitration or before it was generally accepted that tribunals had power to grant security for costs. Parties are now taken to have consented to the procedures

9 Ibid 17 [2.23], 21 [2.38], 22–4 [2.43]–[2.52], 71 [5.08]–[5.09], 166–9 [10.04]–[10.17].

10 In publications of institutions explaining and effectively adding to the procedures available in its rules, such as the ICC *Note to Parties and Arbitral Tribunals on the Conduct of the Arbitration under the ICC Rules of Arbitration* (ICC, 2021).

11 With institutions mimicking developments in one another's rules: IBA, *The Current state and Future of International Arbitration: Regional Perspectives* (IBA, September 2015) 8, 11, 14, 68; Yves Dezalay and Bryant G Garth, *Dealing in Virtue: International Commercial Arbitration and the Construction of Transnational Legal Order* (Chicago University Press, 1996) 44. See also Sam Luttrell, *Bias Challenges in International Arbitration: The Need for a 'Real Danger' Test* (Kluwer, 2009) 10.

12 Clyde Croft, 'Aon and Its Implications for the Commercial Court' [2010] *Victorian Judicial Scholarship* 57; David Spencer, 'The Decline of the Trial in Australia' (October 2011) *Arbitrator and Mediator* 1, 6.

13 In Singapore, Frankfurt, Paris, the Netherlands, and China, and discussions for the creation of one in Australia.

14 IBA, *The Current State and Future of International Arbitration: Regional Perspectives* (IBA, September 2015) 10.

15 *QMUL 2018, International Arbitration Survey: The Evolution of International Arbitration ('QMUL 2018')* 30–1. Under modern rules, for example, in addition to consolidation and joinder mentioned earlier, the institution may appoint an emergency arbitrator (eg, SIAC-2016 Sch 1), order an expedited procedure (eg, SIAC-2016 r 5), appoint the tribunal if the appointment process is unfair (eg, ICC-2021, art 12(9)); the tribunal may order the disclosure of third party funding (eg, ICC-2021, art 11(7)), exclude a party's chosen counsel (eg, ICC Rules 2021 art 17(1) and (2)), direct the hearing be conducted virtually (eg, ICC-2021 art 26(1)), and deal with issues summarily (eg, SIAC-2016 r 28; ICC-2021 art 22).

16 Steingruber (n 7) 17 [2.23], 21 [2.38], 22–4 [2.43]–[2.52], 71 [5.08]–[5.09], 166–9 [10.04]–[10.17].

17 *Ferris v Plaister* (1994) 34 NSWLR 474, 491G, agreeing with *Prima Paint Corp v Flood & Conklin Mfg Co* 388 US 395, 414 (1967). See also Fleming James Jr, 'Assumption of Risk' (1952) 61(2) *Yale Law Journal* 141, 164–5.

available in agreed procedural rules,[18] in the *lex arbitri*,[19] or in the tribunal's procedural control over the proceeding.[20]

7.7. Security for costs is now regarded as an interim measure within tribunals' power whether under an express provision,[21] a general interim measures power,[22] or implied in the tribunal's procedural control[23] under the very few sets of arbitral rules[24] or *lex arbitri*[25] that contain neither an express power for security for costs nor for interim measures granted by the tribunal.

7.8. The result is a marginalisation of consent[26] and a decline in the consensual character of arbitration.[27] In essence, the international arbitration community – states,[28] institutions,[29]

---

18 *Model Law* art 2(e) stating that 'where a provision of this Law refers to the fact that the parties have agreed or that they may agree or in any other way refers to an agreement of the parties, such agreement includes any arbitration rules referred to in that agreement'. See also Benjamin Hayward, *Conflict of Laws and Arbitral Discretion* (Oxford University Press, 2017) 56 [2.16].

19 *Hudson Strumpffabrik GMBH v Bentley Engineering Co Ltd* [1962] 2 QB 587, 592. Examples of *lex arbitri* including security for costs are the *International Arbitration Act 1974* (Cth) s 23K; *Arbitration Act 2005* (Malaysia) s 11(1)(a) and 19(10(a); *Arbitration Amendment Act 2007* (New Zealand, SR 2007/94) sch 1 art 17; *International Arbitration Act* (Singapore, cap 143A, rev ed 2007) s 12(1)(a) and (4); *Arbitration Act 1996* (UK) ss 38(3) and 39(2)(b).

20 A choice conveyed impliedly is just as much a choice entitled to respect in accordance with the principle of party autonomy as a choice stated expressly: *Enka Insaat Ve Sanayi AS v OOO Insurance Company Chubb* [2020] UKSC 38 [129].

21 For example, AMINZ Arbitration Rules art 66(1) incorporating *Arbitration Act 1996* (New Zealand, SR 1996/99) s 17B; ACICA Arbitration Rules r 37.2(e); ACICA Expedited Arbitration Rules r 25.2(e); art 27(1) CEPANI Arbitration Rules art 27(1); DIFC Arbitration Rules art 25.2; HKIAC Administered Arbitration Rules art 24; IAC Arbitration and Mediation Rules art 23.1(10); LCIA Arbitration Rules art 25.2; SIAC Rules r 27j; SCC Arbitration Rules art 38; SCC Rules for Expedited Arbitrations art 39; THAC Arbitration Rules art 66(5); VIAC Rules art 33(6).

22 Jason Fry et al., *The Secretariat's Guide to Arbitration* (ICC Services, 2012) [3–1035], cited in ICCA–Queen Mary Task Force, *Report on Third-Party Funding in International Arbitration* (Report, ICCA and QMUL, April 2018) 166 ('*ICCA Report on Third-Party Funding*').

23 Laurence Craig, William Park and Jan Paulsson, *International Chamber of Commerce Arbitration* (Oxford University Press, 2001) 467; cf Colin YC Ong and Michael Patrick O'Reilly, *Costs in International Arbitration* (LexisNexis, 2013) 153–4 who argue that a power to order security for costs cannot be implied in arbitration but that it must be found in the arbitration agreement, citing *Union Stearinerie Lanza v Wiener* [1917] 2 KB 558 and *Inforica Inc v CGI Information Systems and Management Consultants Inc* 2008 CanLII 60706 [30].

24 Of the 34 sets of institutional rules surveyed, only four had no express provision for either security for costs or interim measures to be granted by the tribunal: BANI-2018, BAC-2015, CIETAC-2015 and SHIAC-2015. The latter three are explicable by the fact that institutions based in the People's Republic of China leave the granting of interim measures to the courts. The omission of an express power in the BANI-2018 rules is partly ameliorated by art 32(1) of the *Law on Arbitration and Alternative Dispute Resolution* (Indonesia, No 30 of 1999), BANI being situated in Indonesia and with the probability that arbitrations conducted under those rules will be subject to the *lex arbitri* of Indonesia or another jurisdiction with an express power to grant either security for costs in particular or interim measures in general. Of the 25 jurisdictions surveyed (counting all Australian jurisdictions as one), only three did not have such an express power conferred on the tribunal – USA, Kazakshtan, and the People's Republic of China. The latter two confer jurisdiction on the courts to grant interim measures in arbitration: art 25(1) of the *Law of the Republic of Kazakshtan on International Commercial Arbitration* (Kazakhstan) 28 December 2004, No. 23-III ZRK, permitting application to a competent court for a measure to secure the claim; art 28 of the *Arbitration Law of the People's Republic of China* requiring the arbitration commission to forward to the People's Court a request for putting property under custody where the award cannot or is hard to be executed (English translation at <http://english.mofcom.gov.cn/article/policyrelease/Businessregulations/201312/20131200432698.shtml>).

25 USA, Kazakshtan and the People's Republic of China – (n 24).

26 Steingruber (n 7) 15 [2.17].

27 Ibid 21 [2.39].

28 In legislating for mandatory arbitration such as in the *Ted Stevens Olympic and Amateur Sports Act* (US), in particular at s 220509 of the United States Code: Steingruber (n 7) 24 [2.51].

29 In enacting rules permitting joinder of parties to the arbitration who are not signatories of the arbitration agreement, and consolidation of two or more arbitrations: ibid 166–9 [10.04]–[10.17].

parties,[30] arbitrators[31] – have decided, incrementally and often separately, that aspects of arbitration serve their purpose, and as a result, they mandate,[32] force,[33] or persuade[34] counterparties to 'agree' to, or be subject to,[35] arbitration. It may be seen as inconsistent to isolate security for costs as undermining party consent when significant other provisions arguably more intrusive have been introduced into international commercial arbitration.

Assumption of the risk

7.9. The analysis of ICC and Swiss decisions on security for costs in Chapter 4 shows that the most common reason given by tribunals for requiring exceptional circumstances before granting security for costs is grounded in the respondent's assumption of the risk in dealing with the claimant. A fundamental change in the claimant's condition from the time the transaction was formed has been identified as the common denominator of the majority of arbitral decisions rejecting applications for security[36] and is the necessary consequence of a respondent being taken to have assumed the risk.[37] Because the respondent assumed the risk, a fundamental change in circumstances is said to be required to justify security for costs.[38] This is seen as a function of party consent as the respondent consented to both the transaction and to arbitration.

7.10. Possible responses to the argument are:

(1) It is not supported by the juridical basis of the facility;
(2) It is grounded in an outdated notion of freedom of contract;
(3) It assumes consent to the transaction includes acceptance of the risk of being sued;
(4) It assumes knowledge unlikely to held;
(5) It involves a non sequitur in assuming the claimant will not pay costs;
(6) It assumes that funding from a third party is not available;
(7) It is inconsistent with the assumption of good faith;
(8) It assumes there are higher risks in international trade than domestic;
(9) It assumes parties have freedom of choice;
(10) It does not correlate risks and consequences;
(11) It illogically applies to only one aspect of the relationship;
(12) It undermines the purpose of security for costs;
(13) It does not take account of the subtleties of each situation; and
(14) It presents an unnecessarily binary choice.

Those potential responses are considered briefly next.

---

30 In prescribing arbitration in contracts of adhesion or where they have greater bargaining power.

31 In applying rules of institutions and entertaining arbitrations where less than free, direct, unequivocal consent is present.

32 Steingruber (n 7) 23–4 [2.48]–[2.52].

33 Ibid 21 [2.38].

34 Ibid 17 [2.23].

35 Through joinder rules in institutional rules: ibid 166–9 [10.04]–[10.17].

36 Procedural Order of December 2007 in ICC Case No. 14993, 4, citing Eric Schwartz and Yves Derains, *Guide to the ICC Rules of Arbitration* (Kluwer, 2nd ed, 2005) 297. See also Alastair Henderson, 'Security for Costs in Arbitration in Singapore' (2011) 7 *Asian International Arbitration Journal* 54, 69 who notes that these considerations have been influential in arbitration circles.

37 Waincymer (n 1) 650 [8.3.5].

38 Henderson (n 36) 69.

(1) Unsupported by the juridical basis

7.11. The juridical basis of security for costs is historically in the prevention of abuse of process and, contemporarily in the socio-economic goal of preventing the incurrence of unpayable debts.[39] It serves the public interest objective and the compensation purpose.[40] Both bases can then be seen to support the legitimacy of international commercial arbitration, said to be under threat.[41]

7.12. Security for costs is designed to protect the integrity of the process to ensure parties will continue to have confidence to choose international commercial arbitration, and to ensure the system can continue to perform its valuable social functions. Not only does international commercial arbitration serve the social function of resolving serious commercial disputes where courts would not be suitable, it also relieves the burden on courts, frees resources for other disputants, and reduces the cost to society of litigation.

7.13. When the jurisprudential basis of the facility is acknowledged to be that broader, valuable public interest rather than solely for the private rights of the parties, the mere entry of the respondent into the transaction knowing the claimant's financial condition should not frustrate that public interest. In other words, the actions of the parties are less relevant to that particular public interest in the integrity and legitimacy of the process, unless their actions are so extreme as to undermine the interest, for example, by not deserving condonation.

(2) Freedom of contract is no longer unconstrained

7.14. The notion that it is fair for respondents to bear the risk of not recovering costs by dealing with claimants and in entering transactions is rooted in the social and economic theories underlying freedom of contract, in '[t]he fundamental principle that in the ordering of our affairs we should make as much use as possible of the spontaneous forces of society, and resort as little as possible to coercion'.[42] An incident of those theories – and that freedom – was that parties are responsible for entering contracts and for their

39 See [2.12] to [2.21].

40 *Matthews v SPI Electricity Pty Ltd (No 9)* [2013] VSC 671 [174] ('*Matthews*').

41 Sundaresh Menon, 'Arbitration's Blade: International Arbitration and the Rule of Law' (2021) 38(1) *Journal of International Arbitration* 1, [7]–[8] ('Arbitration's Blade'); James Allsop, 'Commercial and Investor–State Arbitration: The Importance of Recognising Their Differences' [2018] *Federal Judicial Scholarship* 3 [26] ('Commercial and investor–state arbitration'); Neil Kaplan, 'Winter of Discontent' 34 *Journal of International Arbitration* 373, 374; Jonathan Mance, 'Arbitration: A Law Unto Itself?' (2016) 32 *Arbitration International* 223; Ahmed Al Far, *Abuse of Rights in International Arbitration* (Oxford University Press, 2020); Emmanuel Gaillard, 'Abuse of Process in International Arbitration' (2017) *ICSID Review* 1 ('Abuse of Process'); Sam Luttrell, *Bias Challenges in International Arbitration: The Need for a 'Real Danger' Test* (Kluwer, 2009); Klaus Sachs, 'Time and Money: Cost Control and Effective Case Management' in Loukas A Mistelis and Julian DM Lew (eds), *Pervasive Problems in International Arbitration* (Kluwer, 2006) 103 [5.45]; Horvath et al. (eds), *Guerilla Tactics in International Arbitration* (Kluwer, 2013); Sundaresh Menon, *Some Cautionary Notes for an Age of Opportunity* (Speech, CIArb International Arbitration Conference, 22 August 2013) <https://singaporeinternationalarbitration.files.wordpress.com/2013/08/130822-some-cautionary-notes-for-an-age-of-opportunity-1.pdf> ('Cautionary Notes'); Doak Bishop and Margrete Stevens, 'The Compelling Need for a Code of Ethics in International Arbitration: Transparency, Integrity and Legitimacy' 5 <https://www.josemigueljudice-arbitration.com/xms/files/02_TEXTOS_ARBITRAGEM/01_Doutrina_ScolarsTexts/ethics/ethics_in_int_arb_-_icca_2010_-_bishop.pdf>.

42 FA Hayek, *The Road to Serfdom* (Routledge Classics, 2001) 17. See also Milton Friedman, *Free to Choose* (Harcourt, 1990) 26 with his 'voluntary exchange, spontaneous cooperation'.

consequences.[43] While the expression of the theories has since been moderated in aspects of the law,[44] their legacy remains in the attribution to the respondent of the risk of costs.

7.15. The proposition that the respondent has assumed the risk of dealing with the claimant has echoes of notions of unrestrained freedom of contract. It fails to keep pace with developments in law and society recognising that that concept, and the concomitant unlimited responsibility for entering contracts, is no longer given free rein.[45]

7.16. Governments and courts now intervene to greater and lesser extents, depending on their persuasion and the issue, to regulate markets and behaviour.[46]

7.17. Corporate responsibility has changed in the half-century since Freidman famously said that 'there is one and only one social responsibility of business – to use its resources and engage in activities designed to increase its profits'.[47] Society's expectations of corporate, governmental, and even personal behaviour have evolved.[48] Friedman's shareholder model has been replaced in this context by Freeman's stakeholder model of creating value for all of the business's stakeholders.[49] The notion that a company bears all of the risk in dealing with another company is incongruent with 21st century corporate morality, and legal and economic theory.[50]

7.18. Strict enforcement of the doctrine of freedom to contract in its original form, including holding a party to have assumed certain risks of transacting with another, can work injustice; the sanctity of contracts – being a matter of substantive law – is not threatened by a discretionary procedural remedy such as security for costs.

---

43 For example, *Printing and Numerical Registering Co v Sampson* (1875) 19 Eq 462.

44 *George Mitchell (Chesterhall) Ltd v Finney Lock Seeds Ltd* [1983] QB 284, 297) affirmed on appeal in [1983] 2 AC 803.

45 Ibid.

46 For example, the *Supply of Goods (Implied Terms) Act 1973* (UK), *Trade Practices Act 1974* (Cth), amended and renamed the *Competition and Consumer Act 2010* (Cth), the *Unfair Contract Terms Act 1977* (UK) and the *Sale of Goods Act 1979* (UK). It is a subsidiary point, however the development of the law of negligence from *Donoghue v Stevenson* [1932] AC 562 might be seen as evidence of the courts' willingness to provide remedies not provided for by contract – in other words, a willingness to ameliorate the harshness of there being no contract, as a harbinger of a similar attitude to the harshness of a contract.

47 Milton Friedman, 'The Social Responsibility of Business. *The New York Times Magazine*, September 13th' in Milton Friedman (ed), *An Economist's Protest: Columns on Political Economy* (Glen Ridge/Thomas Horton & Daughters, 1972) 184.

48 For example, in 2020 the chief executive officer and other senior executives of a global mining company were forced to resign over the company's demolition of 46,000-year-old aboriginal caves, despite its having the legal right to do so: Laura He and Angus Watson, 'Rio Tinto CEO Resigns after Destruction of 46,000-Year-Old Sacred Indigenous Site' *CNN Business* (Web Page, 11 September 2020) <https://edition.cnn.com/2020/09/10/business/rio-tinto-ceo-intl-hnk/index.html>. In 2019 the Business Roundtable, a trade association of chief executives of leading American corporations, issued a 300-word 'Statement on the Purpose of a Corporation' that stressed 'a fundamental commitment to all of our stakeholders' and did not specifically mention 'shareholders' until the second-to-last paragraph: Brian R Cheffins, 'Stop Blaming Milton Friedman!' (2021) 98(6) *Washington University Law Review* 4, citing Business Roundtable, *Statement on the Purpose of a Corporation* (Web Page, 19 August 2019) <https://opportunity.businessroundtable.org/wp-content/uploads/2019/12/BRTStatement-on-the-Purpose-of-a-Corporation-with-Signatures.pdf>.

49 Ignacio Ferror, W Michael Hoffman and Robert E McNulty, 'Must Milton Friedman Embrace Stakeholder Theory?' (2014) 119(1) *Business and Society Review* 37 38; Edward Freeman, *Strategic Management: A Stakeholder Approach* (Pitman, 1984).

50 Steve Denning, 'The Origin of "The World's Dumbest Idea": Milton Friedman' *Forbes* (Web Page, 26 June 2013) <https://www.forbes.com/sites/stevedenning/2013/06/26/the-origin-of-the-worlds-dumbest-idea-milton-friedman/?sh=2696f631870e>.

(3) Consent to the transaction vs risk to being sued

7.19. Three types of consent are relevant – at the highest level, consent to the transaction with the counterparty; at the next level, consent to arbitration to resolve disputes in that transaction; at the lowest level, consent to the risk of being sued in the instant arbitration. Consent to the transaction, involving acceptance of the risk of a claimant's non-performance or breach of a contract, is not to be equated with an acceptance of the risk of being sued by the claimant.[51] If it is, the risk of being sued carries with it the ability to obtain security for costs from the claimant to ameliorate the risk.[52] It is arbitrary to exclude from consideration the methods of reducing the risk that the claimant consented to by consenting to arbitration and by commencing the arbitration.

7.20. The latter brings with it consent to the incidents of arbitration and does not provide a basis for avoiding security for costs.[53]

(4) It assumes knowledge unlikely to be held

7.21. The assumption of risk proposition assumes the respondent knew of, or had an opportunity of investigating, the claimant's financial position, knew of the practice that costs follow the event, had turned its mind to it in negotiations, and decided to continue regardless. There cannot logically be an assumption of the risk if a fact necessary to the occurrence of the risk is unknown. It is unlikely commercial parties negotiating contracts know or contemplate the possibility of costs being awarded in their favour if they are sued by their counterparty and succeed, given the uncertainty in that proposition in international commercial arbitration[54] and the improbability of parties addressing the costs of disputes in contractual negotiations.[55]

(5) It involves a non sequitur in assuming the claimant will not pay

7.22. Inherent in the assumption of risk argument is the assumption that the respondent knew or should have known, from the claimant's existing financial condition, that it might not be able to pay costs in the future if it commences and loses arbitration. Justice Saville (as he then was)[56] pointed out in 1990 that the proposition involves a *non sequitur* in that simply because the claimant is a shell company, it is not to be assumed that it is without financial backers or has no means.[57] The same may be said of companies in poor financial condition. He said that those who are in truth financially interested in a

51 *Coca-Cola Amatil Victoria Ltd v P A A Enterprises Pty Ltd* [2003] VSCA 135 [9] [12].

52 Ibid.

53 See [7.6].

54 Micha Bühler, 'Awarding Costs in International Commercial Arbitration: An Overview' (2004) 22(2) *ASA Bulletin* 249.

55 Waincymer (n 1) 645 [8.3.2]; Gary B Born, *International Commercial Arbitration* (Kluwer, 3rd ed, 2021) [17.02][A][6]; Gustavo Moser, *Rethinking Choice of Law in Cross-Border Sales* (Eleven International Publishing, 2018) 217.

56 Later elevated to the Court of Appeal, then to the House of Lords and the Supreme Court.

57 *Flender Werft AG v Aegean Maritime Ltd* [1990] 2 Lloyd's Rep 27, 30 *('Flender Werft')*.

transaction would be able to avoid demonstrating the courage of their conviction in their cause by interposing a shell company with no assets.[58]

7.23. Relieving such companies from exposure to security for costs would encourage parties to shelter behind empty shells, endangering not only recovery of costs against them where they are claimants but also of any substantive awards as respondents.[59]

7.24. The multifactorial approach to security for costs accommodates this concern by the stifling principle, that is, the discretionary consideration that security for costs will not be granted if the claimant can show that having to provide security would stifle a genuine claim.[60] That principle is engaged where the claimant is able to show that neither it nor those standing behind it and benefitting from the proceedings are able to provide security, and the company is not able to raise a loan[61] or obtain third party funding.[62] The law looks not only at the financial ability of the claimant, but also to its possible sources of funds.

7.25. If the law is able to take that ability into consideration at the time the application is entertained, why should the respondent only be taken to have assumed the risk of the claimant being unable to pay? If the finances of the backers are relevant at the time of the application, they ought also be relevant at the time of the transaction. And if the respondent is taken to have assumed the risk that the claimant could not pay, it should also be taken to have assumed the risk that the backers could not pay. This then opens an enquiry into the financial standing of the backers at the time of the transaction such that a respondent faced with this argument may adduce or seek evidence of their finances at that time.[63]

7.26. This approach breaks down when taken to its logical conclusion in the context of other discretionary factors. A party who – unexpected at the time of the transaction – ultimately becomes a respondent to proceedings, should be entitled to assume either that the company which becomes the claimant will be able to pay for proceedings it commences (or to put it another way, will not commence proceedings for which it cannot pay), or that it will be able to obtain funding from 'directors, shareholders or other backers or interested persons',[64] or from lenders[65] or funders.[66] It is inconsistent for the law to allow a court or tribunal at the time of the application to look to those means but not the respondent at the time of the transaction, when disputes – particularly suits against the respondent – are not only not in contemplation, but are contrary to intentions.

(6) It assumes third party funding is not available

7.27. Third party funding is 'very much an integral part of the future of the global arbitration and litigation markets'.[67] The argument that the respondent has assumed the risk

58 Ibid.

59 *Pearson v Naydler* [1977] 1 WLR 899, 905B ('*Pearson v Naydler*').

60 *Flender Werft* (n 57) 29.

61 Ibid; *Petromin SA v Secnav Marine Ltd* [1995] 1 Lloyd's Rep 603, 609–11 *('Petromin')* 608–9.

62 *Idoport Pty Limited v National Australia Bank Limited* [2001] NSWSC 744 [40(d)] ('*Idoport*').

63 *Trident International v Manchester Ship Canal* [1990] BCLC 263, cited for that proposition in *Petromin* (n 61) 609.

64 *Keary Developments v Tarmac Construction Ltd* (Court of Appeal, Peter Gibson LJ, 13 April 1994), cited in *Petromin* (n 61) 609.

65 *Flender Werft* (n 57) 29; *Petromin* (n 61) 608–9.

66 *Idoport* (n 62) [40(d)].

67 *ICCA Report on Third-Party Funding* (n 22) 17, 19.

of not recovering costs simply by transacting with the claimant assumes that third party funding would not be available to the claimant for the present claim. To put it another way, the argument involves the proposition that it was unreasonable for the respondent to proceed with the transaction thinking that third party funding would be available to the claimant.

7.28. Principal factors in a decision to provide funding to a claimant are, in order, the return on investment and the merits of the case.[68] Funders usually only recover their investment if the claim succeeds so have an interest in the merits.[69] If a respondent entering a transaction is taken to have anticipated its own failure in the transaction, being sued by the claimant, and not recovering its costs, it is logical, or at least fair, that it also be taken to have anticipated that the claimant would obtain funding for a meritorious claim of appreciable value where costs are proportionate to the claim.[70]

(7) It is inconsistent with the assumption of good faith

7.29. The assumption of risk proposition is inconsistent with an early argument used by a tribunal against granting security for costs, namely that by submitting to ICC arbitration, the claimant has undertaken to carry out the award.[71] Submission to arbitration occurs at the time the arbitration agreement is entered into.[72] The party who becomes the respondent should be considered to be relying on that undertaking and not assuming any risk that the other party will not honour an adverse costs award. It is better, though, that both fictions – that the claimant has undertaken to honour the award and that the respondent assumed the risk of transacting with the claimant – be abandoned for the purposes of security for costs.

(8) It assumes higher risks of international trade

7.30. It is said in a number of ICC decisions on security for costs that respondents should be taken to have assumed the risks of *international* trade, which are higher than *domestic* trade.[73] Leaving aside the truth of that assumption, security for costs is a mechanism to reduce those risks. It is not logical to draw a line before the door of the tribunal and to say that all risks on the other side of the line are to be borne by the parties, or one of them, when the tribunal has in its hands a facility to alleviate the risk before it eventuates.

7.31. This argument is similar to that of Lord Mustill in saying, after outlining the defendant's potential difficulty in recovering costs, that 'an uncorrectable miscarriage of

68 Ibid 25, 71–4. Other factors considered are the value of the claim, the amount to be advanced, jurisdictional obstacles, defences, nature and length of the proceeding, possibility of settlement, creditworthiness of parties, counsel and their compensation structure, and additional obligations of the funded party: ibid 25.

69 Ibid 26–7.

70 Ibid 26, 74–8.

71 Final Award, ICC, Case No 7489, 1994 reported in (1999) 8(2) *ICC International Court of Arbitration Bulletin* 68 [12].

72 Steingruber (n 7) 13 [2.10].

73 Procedural Order, ICC, Case No 14355, January 2007 reported in (2014) *Special Supplement 2014: Procedural Decisions in ICC Arbitration* 70; Procedural Order, ICC, PO3–2020–228 reported in Samaa AF Haridi, 'Security for Costs and Claim under the ICC Rules of Arbitration – Rare, But Possible' (2020) 2 *ICC Dispute Resolution Bulletin* 77, 109.

justice is something which parties risk by agreeing to entrust their disputes to a private dispute resolution system which has very few internal resources to deal with someone who will not play fair'.[74] The answer is that, in the security for costs power, courts and tribunals have at their disposal a tool that prevents that uncorrectable miscarriage of justice (ie, the inability of a successful defendant to recover costs)[75] and to devise a rule that secures a just and sensible conclusion.[76]

(9) It assumes freedom of choice

7.32. The assumption of risk argument assumes the respondent has complete freedom in entering the transaction and is able to negotiate terms to suit itself. Rarely is a party in such a dominant position. Constraints act upon the respondent to limit pure freedom at a number of levels – at the most basic level, there is the question of *whether* to contract, followed by the question of with *whom* to contract, the price, specifications, and the many different terms to be negotiated and compromised. Even the apparently strongest companies can be in a position where the need for the product and its availability and price effectively limits freedom to one or two counterparties and reduces real negotiating power.[77] The 'choices' for a party can simply be to pay a lower price for lower quality, take higher risk and higher profit, to pay a higher price for higher quality, lower risk and lower profit, or not to buy and to cease production. While theoretically having a choice, the purchaser is driven to one of those options by its internal and external imperatives, and by its relative bargaining power with its counterparty.[78]

7.33. Twin effects of this phenomenon are that freedom of contract is limited, and that entering transactions is not wholly voluntary. There are occasions when a party has little choice but to enter a particular transaction if it wishes to remain in business, or in profitable business. Those qualifications undermine the degree to which the party has voluntarily assumed the risk of not recovering costs if sued by the other.

(10) The risk is unidentified, unquantified, un-correlated

7.34. The proposition that the respondent has assumed the risk of dealing with the claimant does not properly identify and quantify the risk said to be assumed, nor correlate it with the entitlement to costs. The consenting conduct of the respondent said to give rise to the disentitlement to costs is entering the transaction knowing the financial condition of the claimant. By doing so, the respondent is said to have assumed the risk of not recovering costs if sued by the claimant. There is little logical or practical correlation between the consenting conduct and the consequences.

74 *Coppée–Lavalin v Ken–Ren* (n 6) 65D-E.

75 Ibid 65C.

76 *Ferris v Plaister* (n 17) 490A–B.

77 For example, where anti-dumping measures are implemented against imports, such as in Australian Anti-Dumping Commission, *Consideration Report No. 473* (Report, 12 June 2018) <https://www.industry.gov.au/regulations-and-standards/anti-dumping-and-countervailing-system/anti-dumping-commission-archive-cases/473>.

78 *Ferris v Plaister* (n 17) 490A–B.

7.35. It is possible to identify three typical levels of enquiry parties make of each other before entering a transaction. The first level is as to the ability of the other to perform the contract – to deliver the widgets on time according to specifications, or to pay for the widgets. The second level is as to recourse if the other party does not perform – matters such as reputation, financial standing, warranties, insurance, and security. A third level of enquiry might be investigating the other's attitude to disputes by searching court registers and arbitration awards, and by asking for details of previous disputes.

7.36. These first three levels of enquiry are conducted from the point of view of the enquirer being the claimant, to determine whether the other party will perform the contract or meet an award in favour of the claimant if the claimant sues and succeeds. They are not usually conducted from the perspective of the enquirer being a respondent, defending proceedings brought by the other party, as that requires an assumption that the enquirer will default on the contract, or be perceived by the other party to have defaulted. While theoretically a possibility, parties normally do not enter transactions on such an assumption. If there is a risk of actual or perceived default, parties will or should address that in negotiations and in the terms of the contract (overtly if it can be discussed with the other party, or covertly if it cannot), rather than by merely attempting to divine the other's attitude.

7.37. Beyond those enquiries and on the enquirer's assumption that it will default or be perceived to have defaulted and will be sued by the other party, a fourth level of enquiry might be into the other's ability to fund disputes and to pay orders for costs. This does not reflect parties' attitudes or practices in entering transactions and is a counsel of perfection few would follow. It assumes commercial parties, with limited freedom, will act as disinterested lawyers with limitless resources and choices.

7.38. Framing these enquiries in the context of the risks they are intended to mitigate, the risks are:

(1) The other party is not able to perform the contract;
(2) The other party will not perform the contract;
(3) The other party will not compensate for non-performance;
(4) The other party will need to be sued to obtain compensation for non-performance;
(5) The enquirer will not perform the contract;
(6) The enquirer will not compensate for non-performance;
(7) The enquirer will be sued for non-performance;
(8) The enquirer will not wish or be able to settle the dispute;
(9) The enquirer will succeed in the dispute; and
(10) The other party will not be able to pay the enquirer's costs.

7.39. The first four of those risks are linear in that they all relate to the other party's ability to perform and to compensate for non-performance. They are all from the perception of the enquirer as claimant. The remaining six risks reverse that perception to being that of the enquirer as respondent, and involve decreasing levels of risk, some of which may be able to be mitigated further by the enquirer during the conduct of the dispute (e.g., by an offer of compromise or *Calderbank* letter).[79] It is commercially unrealistic to attribute such an exercise to a respondent, or expect it to be undertaken.

---

79 Referring to a letter offering to settle and reserving the right to bring the letter to the attention of the court or tribunal on the question of costs in accordance with *Calderbank v Calderbank* [1975] 3 All ER 333 (CA). If the

(11) It applies only one aspect of the legal relationship

7.40. The proposition under consideration, ironically in the context of fairness, singles out the risk of costs as the only risk the respondent is taken to have assumed in dealing with the particular claimant. In no other contractual cause of action, defence, remedy, or interim measure is a party's assumption of the risk that eventuated relevant. It is no defence to a claim of non-conformance with specifications that the claimant knew the respondent generally produced poor products, or in a claim for late delivery that the respondent knew the claimant was usually tardy.[80] The defence of *volenti non fit injuria* is not available to causes of action based on contract, being limited to breaches of delictual duties.[81] Damages in contract are not reduced for contributory negligence[82] (for example, by the claimant not taking sufficient care in vetting the ultimately under-performing respondent).

7.41. Neither are interim measures declined or reduced on the basis the applicant has assumed the risk of the apprehended conduct, even where fairness and justice are overt elements in the calculus for granting the measure. For example, an interlocutory injunction may be granted where the applicant is able to show it has a *prima facie* case, that damages are inadequate, and that the harm to the other party does not outweigh the harm to the applicant.[83] Striking the balance between those harms requires considering the fairness or justice of the situation. Yet at no point does the claimant's acceptance of the risk of the event it wishes to enjoin become relevant. It would not be accepted, for example, that the claimant should not have a freezing order because it assumed the risk of the respondent transferring assets out of the jurisdiction, knowing when it entered the transaction that the respondent company had a foreign parent and no other business in the jurisdiction.

(12) It undermines the purpose of security for costs

7.42. Security for costs' purpose against corporations is to prevent the privilege of limited liability from being used in an oppressive and unfair way by those with means behind them indulging in fail-safe litigation, with no risk of bearing the respondent's costs, and unjustly leaving successful respondent with no recourse.[84] It is an important purpose, serving both the compensation purpose and the public interest objective.[85] Security for costs supports the compensation purpose by ensuring the respondent's success is not pyrrhic and the award is able to be satisfied.[86] It supports the public interest objective in

offeror achieves an equal or better result on judgment, the court or tribunal may exercise its discretion to award costs, or indemnity costs (depending on whether the offeror is the plaintiff or defendant) from the time the offer should reasonably have been accepted.

80 For example, Art 35(3) of the *United Nations Convention on Contracts for the International Sale of Goods* does not relieve a seller from liability for non-conformance with express specifications even if the buyer knew or should have known the specifications would not be complied with.

81 *Rogers v Interpacific Resorts (Australia) Pty Ltd* [2007] QSC 239 [26]; *Owens v Midway Amusements Pty Ltd* [1986] ACTSC 64 [12].

82 Sirko Harder, 'Contributory Negligence in Contract and Equity' (2014) 13 *Otago Law Review* 307, 308; *Astley v Austrust Ltd* (1999) 197 CLR 1 [53].

83 For example, Model Law art 17A (1).

84 *Pearson v Naydler* (n 59) 904–5; *Flender Werft* (n 57) 30–1.

85 *Matthews* (n 40)[174].

86 Ibid. Yves Fortier, an internationally renowned arbitrator, has written that interim measures such as security for costs are critical to a party's ability to secure meaningful relief, consistent with the parties' original arbitration

being necessary for the due administration of justice and preventing an abuse of rights or of process, being the fundamental juridical basis of the facility.[87]

7.43. That purpose would be frustrated if respondents were taken to have assumed the risk of dealing with those companies. There is a strong and important similarity in that sense between security for costs and *Mareva* injunctions. The juridical basis of both is to prevent an abuse of process by ensuring there will be assets against which an award may be enforced,[88] and the respondent's acceptance of the risk in dealing with the claimant should be no more relevant to security for costs than it is to *Mareva* injunctions.

(13) It fails to take account of the subtleties of each situation

7.44. Arguing that the respondent assumes the risk ignores subtleties within individual situations that may make it unfair or illogical to deny a respondent security for costs simply because of entering into the transaction. Circumstances such as a trading relationship pre-existing the subject transaction and the risk allegedly accepted,[89] the reasons for entering the transaction,[90] any pre-contractual representations and conduct by the claimant,[91] the financial standing of those behind the future claimant,[92] and the nature, size, and structure of the corporate claimant,[93] may expand the focus beyond merely whether the claimant was financially sound at the time of the agreement. When considering the respondent's acceptance of the risk in entering the particular transaction, all aspects of the acceptance of that risk should be considered, not merely the single feature of the claimant's financial condition. It is the essence of the exercise of a judicial discretion to treat every situation on its own merits[94] and balance all relevant interests.[95]

(14) It presents an unnecessarily binary choice

7.45. The effect of finding the respondent to have assumed the risk of transacting with the claimant is to deny respondents security for costs completely. This is an unnecessarily binary choice between receiving and not receiving security. Instead, the assumption

---

agreement: Yves Fortier, 'Interim Measures' in Arthur W Rovine (ed), *Contemporary Issues in International Arbitration and Mediation: The Fordham Papers 2008* (Martinus Nijhoff, 2009) 52.

87 *Rajski v Computer Manufacture & Design Pty Limited* [1982] 2 NSWLR 443 [447]–[448]; *Morris v Hanley* [2000] NSWSC 957 [11]–[14]; *Melville v Craig Nowlan and Associates Pty Limited* [2002] NSWCA 32, 54 NSWLR 82 [135]–[138]; *Green v CGU Insurance Ltd* [2008] NSWCA 148 [7], [31].

88 The basis of the *Mareva* injunction being that 'the circumstances are such that there is a danger of (the defendant's) absconding, or a danger of the assets being removed out of the jurisdiction or disposed of within the jurisdiction, or otherwise dealt with so that there is a danger that the plaintiff, if he gets judgment, will not be able to get it satisfied': *Rahman (Prince Abdul) v Abu-Taha* (1980) 3 All ER 409, 412 (Lord Denning MR) quoted with approval in *Jackson v Sterling Industries Ltd* (1987) 162 CLR 612 (Deane J; Mason CJ, Wilson, Dawson, and Brennan JJ agreeing; Toohey and Gaudron JJ agreeing in substance).

89 *Australian Battery Distributors Pty Ltd v Robert Bosch (Australia) Pty Ltd* [2015] FCA 1164 [43]–[45] ('*Battery Distributors*').

90 For example, as suggested earlier at section 'The risk is unidentified, unquantified, un-corelated'.

91 *Battery Distributors* (n 89) [43]–[45].

92 *Flender Werft* (n 57) 29; *Petromin* (n 61) 608–9.

93 *Salex NSW Pty Ltd v Congredior Pty Ltd* [2021] NSWSC 732 [35]–[36] ('*Salex*') [35]–[36].

94 *Trility Pty Ltd v Ancon Drilling Pty Ltd* [2013] VSC 577 [10]–[13].

95 *Han v Cho* 2008 BCSC 1229 [26].

of risk could operate as a factor in the exercise of the discretion,[96] and the amount of security granted could be discounted to reflect the degree to which acceptance of the risk is relevant in the overall consideration of factors, including a consideration of the subtleties of the situation discussed immediately above.

7.46. Awards of security for costs are routinely discounted from the full amount the respondent claims to arrive at a figure fair in all the circumstances. Three types of discounts may be identified in the common law cases, which may be referred to as the recoverability discount, the specific discount, and the general discount.[97] Factors relevant to the question of whether security should be granted are also relevant in assessing quantum.[98]

96 *Coca-Cola* (n 51) [13]; *Southbank Liquor Stores Vic Pty Ltd, Re* [2021] VSC 404 [42]–[45]; *Salex* (n 93) [38]; *Mecrus Pty Ltd v Industrial Energy Pty Ltd* (2015) 327 ALR 523 [74]; *Battery Distributors* (n 89) [26], [45].

97 Cameron Ford, 'General Discounting of Security for Costs Discounted' (2021) *Northern Territory Law Journal* 7 <https:www.ntlj.com.au/article/812817>.

98 See [6.18] et seq.

CHAPTER 8

Party autonomy, procedural fairness, and the nature of arbitration

Introduction

8.1. Arguments have been made in favour of restricting the operation of security for costs in international commercial arbitration on the grounds that the facility:

(1) Infringes party autonomy;
(2) Denies the claimant procedural fairness;
(3) Is contrary to the international nature of international commercial arbitration;
(4) Is contrary to the general nature of arbitration; and
(5) Is unfair to creditors of the claimant.

These contentions and possible responses to them are considered next.

(1) Party autonomy

8.2. Party autonomy is considered to be the first,[1] or the guiding,[2] principle of international commercial arbitration. It is the liberty states grant to parties to agree aspects of their contract that would otherwise be stipulated by the state. In granting parties autonomy to do so, states permit them to agree, among other things, for their contract to be governed by a law other than the law of the state (or the law the state would specify),[3] and to resolve their disputes by private means rather than through courts of the state (or the courts the state would specify).[4] Despite its centrality to the arbitral system, perceptions of its significance have fluctuated, with Lord Cooke, for example, referring in 1999 – 40 years after party autonomy found its expression in the *New York Convention* – to the 'new-found emphasis on party autonomy'.[5]

8.3. International commercial arbitration depends upon party autonomy for its existence. Without this autonomy, parties would not be free to avoid state courts and to choose international commercial arbitration. It is the principle animating the *New York Convention*

1 *S A Coppée-Lavalin NV v Ken-Ren Chemicals and Fertilizers Ltd (In liq)* [1995] 1 AC 38, 51H (Lord Mustill) ('*Coppée-Lavalin v Ken-Ren*').

2 Nigel Blackaby and Constantine Partasides with Alan Redfern and Martin Hunter, *Redfern and Hunter on International Arbitration* (Oxford University Press, 6th ed, 2015) 645 [8.3.2]. See also Karl-Heinz Böckstiegel, 'The Role of Party Autonomy in International Arbitration' in *ICDR Handbook on International Arbitration & ADR* (ICDR, 2017) 105–6.

3 Through the state's choice of law rules.

4 Through the state's jurisdictional rules.

5 Lord Cooke, 'Party Autonomy' (1999) 30(1) *Victoria University of Wellington Law Review* 257, 258.

DOI: 10.4324/9781003479628-8

that recognises parties' choice of international commercial arbitration[6] and provides an international framework for enforcement of awards rendered as a result of that choice.[7] With the *New York Convention* being said to form the bedrock of modern international commercial arbitration[8] constituting the most successful treaty in private international law,[9] having been acceded to by 172 states,[10] it can be said that party autonomy has been implicitly acknowledged by each of those states.

8.4. The *Model Law* also gives voice to party autonomy generally in its provisions for enforcement of arbitration agreements[11] and recognition and enforcement of arbitral awards,[12] and specifically in its placement of the agreement of the parties above the discretion of the tribunal in relation to arbitral procedure.[13] One hundred and seventeen jurisdictions, including 84 states, have enacted legislation based on the *Model Law*,[14] and states with legislation not based on the *Model Law* acknowledge party autonomy.[15]

8.5. It is this liberty which is said to be infringed by the unexpected imposition of security for costs after the transaction and the arbitration agreement are entered into and after the arbitration is commenced. The imposition of an alien process not addressed or contemplated by the parties at the time of the transaction is said to encroach impermissibly on party autonomy. Four responses may be given to that proposition:

(a) The parties are bound to the consequences of their choices;
(b) The law chooses when the parties do not;
(c) Party autonomy is the right to agree, not the right to veto; and
(d) Party autonomy has limitations.

(1a) Choices have consequences

8.6. It is generally accepted that parties are taken to have accepted the consequences of their choice of seat, *lex arbitri*, and institutional rules.[16] The latter is recognised by

---

6 Article II(1) of the *New York Convention*.

7 Article III of the *New York Convention*.

8 *Kabab-Ji SAL v Kout Food Group* [2021] UKSC 48 [10] ('*Kabab-Ji*').

9 'New York Arbitration Convention' (Web Page, undated) <http://www.newyorkconvention.org/in+brief>.

10 Ibid. See United Nations, 'Convention on the Recognition and Enforcement of Foreign Arbitral Awards' *United Nations Treaty Series* (Web Page, undated) <https://treaties.un.org/Pages/showDetails.aspx?objid=080000028002a36b&clang=_en>.

11 Article 8(1) of the *Model Law*.

12 Article 35 of the *Model Law*.

13 Articles 19(1) and 34(1) of the *Model Law*.

14 See 'UNCITRAL Status' in *UNCITRAL Model Law on International Commercial Arbitration* (Web Page, undated) <https://uncitral.un.org/en/texts/arbitration/modellaw/commercial_arbitration/status>.

15 For example, the UK in s 1(b) of the *Arbitration Act 1996* (UK) stating that 'the parties should be free to agree how their disputes are resolved, subject only to such safeguards as are necessary in the public interest'; Indonesia in art 3 of the *Law on Arbitration and Alternative Dispute Resolution* (Indonesia, No 30 of 1999) removing disputes subject to arbitration from the jurisdiction of the District Court, and art 4(1) empowering arbitrators to determine such a dispute; and in art 5 of 国际商事法庭 [Arbitration Law of the People's Republic of China] (People's Republic of China) National People's Congress, Order No 31, 31 August 1994 ('*PRC Arbitration Law*') forbidding a court from accepting a dispute that is subject to a valid arbitration agreement.

16 Benjamin Hayward, *Conflict of Laws and Arbitral Discretion* (Oxford University Press, 2017) 56 [2.16]; Blackaby and Partasides (n 2) 307 [5.10]; Jeffrey Waincymer, *Procedure and Evidence in International Arbitration* (Kluwer, 2012) 645 [8.3.4]; Gary B Born, *International Commercial Arbitration* (Kluwer, 3rd ed, 2021) 2300 [15.02][C], 2302 [15.02][D]; Andrea Marco Steingruber, *Consent in International Arbitration* (Oxford University Press, 2012) 166 [10.04], 171 [10.26], 173–4 [10.34]–[10.35], 184 [10.73]; Andrea Carlevaris, 'Limits to Party Autonomy and Institutional Rules' in Franco Ferrari (ed), *Limits to Party Autonomy in International Commercial*

the *Model Law* stating in Article 2(e) that 'where a provision of this Law refers to the fact that the parties have agreed or that they may agree or in any other way refers to an agreement of the parties, such agreement includes any arbitration rules referred to in that agreement'. It is also recognised through the *New York Convention's* and the *Model Law's* territorial application of the law of the seat as the *lex arbitri*.[17] In the words of Lord Mustill, 'parties choose arbitration for better or for worse'.[18]

8.7. Party autonomy is honoured in recognising the consequences of a joint choice by the parties.[19] The UK Supreme Court confirmed in 2020 that, 'a choice conveyed impliedly is just as much a choice entitled to respect in accordance with the principle of party autonomy as a choice stated expressly'.[20] In the US, a five-member Supreme Judicial Court of Massachusetts held to similar effect that incorporation of arbitral rules by reference in a contract subjected parties to those rules.[21]

8.8. The French Cour de Cassation has taken a different view, holding that the guarantee of access to justice contained in art 6(1) of the *European Convention for the Protection of Human Rights and Fundamental Freedoms*[22] prevails over the provisions of agreed institutional rules.[23] English courts adopt the position, said to be in conformity with that of the European Court of Human Rights, that the guarantee applies to both claimant applicant and respondent,[24] and that the state may regulate access to its courts proportionately between the aims and means, and so as not to impair the essence of the right.[25] This difference in approaches presages a similar difference in approaches to security for costs, with the French attitude indicating it would not be receptive to security for costs on the basis that the agreed institutional rules provided for the facility.

8.9. The French decision has been criticised as abandoning the court's former preferable stance of 'accept[ing] the binding force of institutional arbitration rules which the parties have adhered to prior to the commencement of their dispute'.[26] It has been explained as an illustration of the 'tendency in France to discard arbitration rules in favour of the fundamental principles of fair trial'.[27]

Arbitration (JurisNet, 2016) 1, 2; Diego P Fernández Arroyo, 'Arbitrator's Procedural Powers: The Last Frontier of Party Autonomy?' in Franco Ferrari (ed), *Limits to Party Autonomy in International Commercial Arbitration* (JurisNet, 2016) 199, 200, 201.

17 *New York Convention* arts V(1)(a), (d) and (e); *Model Law* art 1(2).

18 *Coppée–Lavalin v Ken–Ren* (n 1) 65D-E.

19 Carlevaris (n 16) 35.

20 *Enka Insaat Ve Sanayi AS v OOO Insurance Company Chubb* [2020] UKSC 38 [129] ('*Enka v Chubb*').

21 *Charles Construction v Deriderian*, 412 Mass 14 (1992) 16.

22 *European Convention for the Protection of Human Rights and Fundamental Freedoms*, opened for signature 4 November 1950, ETS 5 (entered into force 3 September 1953) ('*European Convention of Human Rights*').

23 *Société Pirelli & Cie Spa v Société Licensing Projects et autres, Supreme Court of Cassation of France, First Civil Law Chamber, Arrêt no. 392 FS-P+B+I, pourvoi no. N 11–27.770, 28 March 2013*, Revue de l'Arbitrage 746 (No 3, 2013), holding that it is permissible to consider an impecunious respondent's counterclaim withdrawn for non-payment of advances on institutional fees only if the counterclaim is separate from the claim. See Carlevaris (n 16) 10–13.

24 *Rowe v Ingenious Media Holdings plc* [2021] EWCA Civ 29 [86].

25 *Tolstoy Miloslavsky v United Kingdom* (1995) 20 EHRR 442 [59], as explained in *Al-Koronky v Time-Life Entertainment Group Ltd* [2007] 1 Costs LR 57 [30].

26 Detlev Kühner, 'The Impact of Party Impecuniosity on Arbitration Agreements: The Example of France and Germany' (2014) 31(6) *Journal of International Arbitration* 807, 811.

27 Ibid 811–12, quoting a French author's comments translated as: 'Arbitration is no longer the last bastion of the binding nature of contracts. The latter loses ground against the power of the fundamental principles of fair trial'.

8.10. Power to order security for costs in international commercial arbitration may be found in one or more of four sources, namely in the arbitration agreement,[28] institutional rules,[29] *lex arbitri*,[30] and the tribunal's general power to control proceedings or to preserve the integrity of the proceeding[31] under the very few sets of arbitral rules[32] or *lex arbitri*[33] that contain neither an express power for security for costs nor for interim measures granted by the tribunal.

8.11. Where those rules or *lex arbitri* are chosen, the parties may be taken as having accepted the availability of security for costs.[34]

(1b) The law chooses when the parties do not

8.12. If parties do not expressly state a choice for a matter in their agreement, the law frequently makes the choice for them without impinging on the doctrine of party autonomy. Classic examples in the arbitration sphere are the law prescribing the law governing the contract,[35] the law governing the substance of the dispute,[36] the law governing the arbitration agreement,[37] the seat of the arbitration,[38] the *lex arbitri*,[39] the method of appointment of the tribunal,[40] and the relevant choice of law rule[41] where the parties are silent.

8.13. Those are not mere matters of detail or procedure but have the potential to affect substantive party rights and obligations.[42] For example, selection of the governing law of the contract could have the consequence that a party has lost the case before it has begun[43] or is unable to present and argue its case.[44] Selection of the seat creates the architecture supporting the arbitration comprised of the courts, laws, and procedures;[45] determines the standards to be applied on an application to remove an arbitrator[46] and to

---

28 See [5.2].

29 See [5.8].

30 See [5.3.

31 See [7.7] fn 23.

32 See [7.7] fn 24.

33 USA, Kazakshtan and the People's Republic of China.

34 *New York Convention* arts V(1)(a), (d) and (e); *Model Law* art 1(2); *Coppée–Lavalin v Ken–Ren* (n 1) 65D-E.

35 Hayward (n 16) Chapter 2, IV Potentially Applicable Rules 74–95.

36 Ibid 15–16 [1.28].

37 *BNA v BNB* [2020] 1 Lloyd's Rep 55 [44]; *Enka v Chubb* (n 20) [58]; *Kabab-Ji* (n 8) [28], [35]; *Sulamérica Cia Nacoinal de Seguros SA v Enesa Eugenharia SA* [2012] EWCA Civ 638.

38 Selected by the institution, the tribunal, or the court, depending on the existence and content of any applicable rules and the level of detail in the arbitration agreement: Waincymer (n 16) 170 [3.5.1].

39 *Enka v Chubb* (n 20) [1].

40 *KVC Rice Intertrade Co Ltd v Asian Mineral Resources Pte Ltd* [2017] SGHC 32 [71] which held that 'where there was truly no other way to prevent injustice to a would-be claimant, a Singapore court would be prepared to step in to directly appoint an arbitrator, provided the dispute had some connection with Singapore'.

41 Hayward (n 16) 59 [2.23].

42 Ibid 32 [1.63].

43 Peter Binder, *International Commercial Arbitration and Conciliation in UNCITRAL Model Law Jurisdictions* (Sweet & Maxwell, 3rd ed, 2010) 336 [6–011], cited in Hayward (n 16) 59 [1.63]. Hayward lists 19 non-exhaustive types of disputes where the choice of contract governing law may directly determine or have significant impact on the outcome: 33 [1.67].

44 Hayward (n 16) 35–8 [1.72]–[1.77].

45 Blackaby and Partasides (n 2) 183 [3.84] et seq. See also art 1(2) of the *Model Law* which states that it only applies if the place of arbitration is in the territory of the state: Hayward (n 16) 51 [2.04].

46 Sam Luttrell, *Bias Challenges* (Kluwer, 2009) 11–12; Blackaby and Partasides (n 2) 167 [3.42], citing *Smith Ltd v H International* [1991] 2 Lloyd's Rep 127, 130.

set aside the award;[47] imports the private international law provision;[48] and may be, or may determine, the law governing the arbitration agreement.[49]

8.14. It may be thought remarkable that parties and commentators are sanguine about the law choosing such fundamental aspects of arbitration yet resist a remedial procedural facility such as security for costs.

8.15. When the law chooses those matters for silent parties, it generally does so without being required to divine the intention – ie, the choice – of the parties, whether their objective or subjective intention. It does so by the application of sets of rules developed by private international law to resolve conflicts of laws. For example, the 'Rome I Regulation'[50] applicable to jurisdictions within the European Union (and potentially beyond)[51] contains a set of presumptions or *prima facie* rules for determining the law governing the contract,[52] with the law of the country most closely connected to the contract having pre-eminence.[53] None of those presumptions or rules refers to the intention of the parties, and in fact apply only when no choice has been 'made expressly or clearly demonstrated by the terms of the contract or the circumstances of the case'.[54]

8.16. Common law courts take a similar approach, with English law in the second half of the 20th century gradually replacing the enquiry into the presumed intention of the parties where they had not made a choice with a positive rule of law applying the law of the closest and most real connection.[55]

8.17. Neither of those supervening attributions of a contractual governing law attracts criticism that it erodes party autonomy or freedom of contract.[56] To the contrary, it is seen as honouring freedom to contract in providing what is needed to make the contract work[57] and for '[t]he proper functioning of the internal [EU] market' in creating certainty of contract.[58]

8.18. A principle to be extracted from those approaches is that the law overrides or supplements the parties' exercise of their autonomy on details of the arbitration agreement or the broader contract where necessary to uphold that agreement or contract and to give effect to the submission to arbitration. It does so without regard to the parties' intent. Taking a similar approach to security for costs will not undermine party autonomy to any greater degree than does the law choosing these matters for the parties.

---

47 Redfern and Hunter (n 2) 570 [10.04].

48 Hayward (n 16) 51 [2.04].

49 Blackaby and Partasides (n 2) 159 [3.15]; *Enka v Chubb* (n 20) [170]; *Kabab-Ji* (n 8) [28], [35].

50 *Regulation (EC) No 593/2008 of the European Parliament of the Council of 17 June 2008 on the law applicable to contractual obligations* [2008] OJ L 177/6 ('*Rome I Regulation*'): see *Enka v Chubb* (n 20) [25].

51 Hayward (n 16) 55 [2.14] noting that its predecessor, the *Rome Convention*, was applied in arbitration, and both are said to have universal application in that they may require the application of the law of any state, though not a member of the European Union.

52 Article 4(1) of the Rome I Regulation sets out a series of types of contracts and specifies the law applicable to each, for example, art 4(1)(a) prescribes that contracts for the sale of goods are governed by the law of the country where the seller has his habitual residence.

53 Articles 4(3) and 4(4) of the *Rome I Regulation.*

54 Articles 3(1) and 4(1) of the *Rome I Regulation.*

55 *Enka v Chubb* (n 20) [36].

56 Party autonomy being an expression of freedom of contract: Steingruber (n 16) 12 [2.05]–[2.06].

57 *Insigma Technology Co Ltd v Alstom Technology Ltd* [2009] 3 SLR 936 [31] which held that 'where the parties have evinced a clear intention to settle any dispute by arbitration, the court should give effect to such intention, even if certain aspects of the agreement may be ambiguous, inconsistent, incomplete or lacking in certain particulars'.

58 Recital (6) of the Rome I Regulation.

(1c) Right to agree, not to veto retrospectively

8.19. Party autonomy is not the right of each individual party to choose separately from the other. It is the right of the parties to agree, that is, to choose jointly. Lord Cooke said '[t]he autonomy is that of the parties acting together when they make their arbitration agreement. It is not of course that of a party later disenchanted'.[59] Party autonomy is honoured with respect to security for costs by the parties agreeing that the facility will or will not apply, and they are free to do so. Silence on the issue is as much a choice as an express agreement. Silence conveys that the parties are content to abide by the chosen arbitral rules (if any), the accepted arbitral practice and the discretion of the tribunal. Party autonomy does not require one party unilaterally to have the right to veto retrospectively a procedure available under the rules or accepted practice after the fact.

8.20. If security for costs were restricted on this basis to cases where the parties had agreed to its availability in the arbitration agreement, the same argument could be made against most other interim measures and interlocutory procedures such as injunctions, security for the claim, and disclosure of documents. Arbitration agreements rarely, if ever, prescribe the interim measures and interlocutory procedures available to the parties, and their failure to do so is not taken as excluding them.[60] Arbitration clauses are often in standard form contracts to which the parties probably give scant attention or had little or no power to negotiate.[61] Parties might also incorporate model clauses proffered by institutions which are typically very brief.[62] Neither is their imposition on the parties without the agreement of both considered to be an unacceptable encroachment on party autonomy. If it were, no injunction, for example, would ever be granted by a tribunal in international commercial arbitration as it is rare for arbitration agreements to confer such a power on the tribunal.[63] Interim measures are regarded as essential to the efficacy of the arbitral process and apply unless the parties jointly exclude them.[64]

(1d) Party autonomy has limits

8.21. While party autonomy is jealously guarded, it is not inviolate.[65] There are limits to parties' right to agree, imposed at different stages of the disputes process.[66] They have

---

59 Lord Cooke (n 5) 258.

60 Waincymer (n 16) 645 [8.3.2]; Born (n 16) [17.02][A][6]; Gustavo Moser, *Rethinking Choice of Law in Cross-Border Sales* (Eleven International Publishing, 2018) 217.

61 *Ferris v Plaister* (1994) 34 NSWLR 474, 491G (Kirby P), agreeing with *Prima Paint Corp v Flood & Conklin Mfg Co* 388 US 395, 414 (1967).

62 For example, the SIAC model clause at <https://siac.org.sg/model-clauses/siac-model-clause>; the HKIAC model clause at <https://www.hkiac.org/arbitration/model-clauses>; the LCIA recommended clauses at <https://www.lcia.org/dispute_resolution_services/lcia_recommended_clauses.aspx>.

63 It is not uncommon for a complex dispute resolution provision in a contract specifying arbitration as the final mechanism to include a reservation of the parties' ability to seek urgent, interim relief from nominated courts to whose jurisdiction the parties submit. See, eg, the advice of Bernado Cremades, *Multi-Tiered Dispute Resolution Clauses* 10 <https://fidic.org/sites/default/files/36%20cremades_2004.pdf>.

64 Stephen Benz, 'Strengthening Interim Measures in International Arbitration' (2018) 50 *Georgetown Journal of International Law* 143, 145.

65 Steingruber (n 16) 30 [2.73] noting that party autonomy requires very limited interference with a party's will, citing Julian Lew, Loukas Mistelis and Stefan Kröll, *Comparative International Commercial Arbitration* (Kluwer, 2003) [2.39].

66 See generally, Michael Pryles, 'Limits to Party Autonomy in Arbitral Procedure' (2007) 24(3) *Journal of International Arbitration* 327 who notes limitation on the form of the agreement (329), on unworkable changes

been described as the 'outer limits' and the 'inner limits' of party autonomy, with the outer limits being the mandatory laws applying to the arbitration, and the inner limits being the prescriptions of the procedural rules and arbitral discretion.[67] Outer limits include parties' preclusion, at the initial stage of choosing a dispute resolution mechanism, from agreeing to arbitrate disputes deemed by the law to be non-arbitrable.[68] For those disputes, parties are limited to mechanisms prescribed by the state.[69] Mandatory laws may dictate the substantive law to be applied to the contract and to the arbitration, despite the parties' agreement.[70]

8.22. At the stage of drafting an arbitration clause, outer limits are imposed by the formal requirements of the *New York Convention*[71] and of enactments based on the *Model Law*,[72] and by the law as to the essential elements of a valid arbitration agreement.[73] Parties are free to act contrary to those provisions at the risk of their arbitration agreement or the resultant award being held to be invalid or unenforceable.[74] Freedom of appointment of a party's arbitrator is constrained by the rules relating to bias,[75] conflicts of interest,[76] equal treatment of the parties,[77] nationality requirements,[78] capacity requirements,[79] loss of right to appoint,[80] the number of arbitrators,[81] personal and professional requirements,[82] and, potentially, religious requirements[83] and anti-discrimination legislation.[84] Parties have

---

to institutional rules (329), on changes to the arbitration agreement after the constitution of the tribunal (331), on agreeing extraordinarily long time limits (333) and hearing times and types (338).

67 Carlevaris (n 16) 3.

68 Blackaby and Partasides (n 2) 110–24 [2.124]–[2.160]. Arts II(I) and V(2)(a) of the *New York Convention* and arts 34(2)(b)(i) and 36(1)(b)(i) of the *Model Law* limit both to disputes that are 'capable of settlement by arbitration'. See Friedrich Rosenfeld, 'Limits to Party Autonomy to Protect Weaker Parties in International Arbitration' in Franco Ferrari (ed), *Limits to Party Autonomy in International Commercial Arbitration* (JurisNet, 2016) 419, 421–34; Francesca Ragno, 'Inarbitrability: A Ghost Hovering over Europe?' in Franco Ferrari (ed), *Limits to Party Autonomy in International Commercial Arbitration* (JurisNet, 2016) 127, 132–44, who suggests that while some consider arbitrability to be a solved issue or dead doctrine, it operates in Europe especially in areas characterised by the inequality of bargaining power, and where there is a risk of the disapplication of the mandatory rules of the *lex fori*.

69 Bernard Hanotiau, 'What Law Governs the Issue of Arbitrability?' (1996) 12(4) *Arbitration International* 391.

70 Inka Hanefeld, 'Limits to Party Autonomy Imposed by European Mandatory Law' in Franco Ferrari (ed), *Limits to Party Autonomy in International Commercial Arbitration* (JurisNet, 2016) 401, 402–13.

71 Article II(2) of the *New York Convention* defining an 'agreement in writing' for submission to arbitration to include a clause in a contract or an arbitration agreement, signed by the parties or in an exchange of letters or telegrams.

72 Article 7 of the *Model Law* requiring an arbitration to be in writing.

73 Blackaby and Partasides (n 2) 12–15 [1.40]–[1.48]; Benjamin G Davis, 'Pathological Clauses: Frédéric Eisemann's Still Vital Criteria' (1991) 7(4) *Arbitration International* 365, 366; *IBA Guidelines for Drafting International Arbitration Clauses* (IBA, 2010) [1].

74 Carlevaris (n 16) 5.

75 Luttrell (n 46) 2–3; Brian King, 'Party Autonomy, the "Right" to Appoint, and the Rise of Strategic Challenges' in Franco Ferrari (ed), *Limits to Party Autonomy in International Commercial Arbitration* (JurisNet, 2016) 37, 42–8; George A Bermann, 'Limits to Party Autonomy in the Composition of the Arbitral Panel' in Franco Ferrari (ed), *Limits to Party Autonomy in International Commercial Arbitration* (JurisNet, 2016) 83, 106–9.

76 *IBA Guidelines on Conflicts of Interest in International Arbitration* (IBA, 2014).

77 King (n 75) 48–50; Bermann (n 75) 89–96.

78 King (n 75) 50–1; Bermann (n 75) 97–8.

79 Bermann (n 75) 98–100.

80 King (n 75) 51–4.

81 Bermann (n 75) 87–9.

82 Ibid 102–6.

83 Ibid 100–2.

84 In *Jivraz v Hashwani* [2011] UKSC 40 [20] ('*Jivraz v Hashwani*'), anti-discrimination legislation would have prevented the appointment of the arbitrators with the characteristics specified in the arbitration agreement had the relationship between party and arbitrator been one of employment, as held by the Court of Appeal in *Jivraz v Hashwani* [2010] EWCA Civ 712.

limited ability to determine who decides the issue of the tribunal's jurisdiction and the basis of which standard[85] and there is 'a policy question of first-order importance in the law of civil procedure as to what extent private parties, invoking a private agreement', may have access to publicly funded courts for interlocutory assistance.[86] At the post-award stage, parties can be limited in their control over the nature and extent of review or challenge to the award.[87] Parties, for example, cannot contractually confer jurisdiction on a court to create an otherwise non-existent merits review.[88]

8.23. Inner limits include the constraint on freedom to order the arbitration proceedings by mandatory rules of the *lex arbitri* generally,[89] by the *Model Law* analogues,[90] by procedural rules,[91] by some tribunal discretion as to procedure,[92] acceptance of the positions and submissions of parties,[93] and the choice of laws,[94] and by principles of good faith if imported into the arbitration.[95] Emergency arbitrators dealing with urgent applications for interim measures before the tribunal is constituted are appointed by the institution rather than by the parties in accordance with their arbitration agreement.[96] And liberty to settle a claim or agree to a consent award may be circumscribed in certain circumstances,[97] particularly in public-related disputes.[98] Where the parties had the opportunity to agree but remained silent, they submitted themselves to the arbitral rules they chose, the accepted

85 Stefan Kröll, 'Party Autonomy in Relation to Competence-Competence' in Franco Ferrari (ed), *Limits to Party Autonomy in International Commercial Arbitration* (JurisNet, 2016) 165, 166, 175.

86 Kevin David, Helen Hershkoff and Nathan Yaffe, 'Private Preference, Public Process: US Discovery in Aid of Foreign and International Arbitration' in Franco Ferrari (ed), *Limits to Party Autonomy in International Commercial Arbitration* (JurisNet, 2016) 233, 234.

87 Maxi Scherer and Linda Silberman, 'Limits to Party Autonomy at the Post-Award Stage' in Franco Ferrari (ed), *Limits to Party Autonomy in International Commercial Arbitration* (JurisNet, 2016) 441, 491–2.

88 For Australia and the UK, see Cameron Ford, 'Court's Duty to Ascertain Jurisdiction' (2011) 2 *Northern Territory Law Journal* 13, 17–18. For India, see Naman Verma 'Exclusive Jurisdictional Clauses in Commercial Contracts' *Academike*, 30 January 2015 <https://www.lawctopus.com/academike/exclusive-jurisdictional-clause-commercial-contracts/>. For the USA, see *Daimler AG v Bauman* 571 U S 117 (2014).

89 Hanefeld (n 70) 413–17.

90 For example, the parties' right to agree on a procedure for appointing the tribunal in art 11(2) of the *Model Law* is subject to the provisions of paragraphs (4) and (5).

91 Rosenfeld (n 68) 434–40.

92 Michael Pryles, 'Limits to Party Autonomy in Arbitral Procedure' (2007) 24(3) *Journal of International Arbitration* 327; Diego P Fernandez Arroyo, 'Arbitrator's Procedural Powers: The Last Frontier of Party Autonomy' in Franco Ferrari (ed), *Limits to Party Autonomy in International Commercial Arbitration* (JurisNet, 2016) 199, 200, 225–31.

93 Giuditta Cordero-Moss, 'The Arbitral Tribunal's Power in Respect of the Parties' Pleadings as a Limit to Party Autonomy on *Jura Novit Curia* and Related Issues' in Franco Ferrari (ed), *Limits to Party Autonomy in International Commercial Arbitration* (JurisNet, 2016) 289, 289–92.

94 Hayward (n 16) 145 [4.01]; Filip de Ly, 'Limits to Party Autonomy. Good Faith, Fair Dealing and International Commercial Arbitration' in Franco Ferrari (ed), *Limits to Party Autonomy in International Commercial Arbitration* (JurisNet, 2016) 363, 371.

95 Filip de Ly and Laurent Lévy (eds), *Interest, Auxiliary and Alternative Remedies in International Arbitration* (Kluwer, 2008) 374–82.

96 For example, ICC Rules 2021, art 29; LCIA Rules 2020, art 9B; SIAC Rules 2016, r 30.2 and sch 1; HKIAC Rules 2018, art 23.1 and sch 4; SCC Rules 2017, art 37(4) and app II. Ostensibly supporting party autonomy, but diminishing the parties' rights, it has been held that English courts do not have the power to grant interim relief before the tribunal is constituted if there is an agreement to have recourse to an emergency arbitrator and there is time to do so: *Gerald Metals SA v Timis* [2016] EWHC 2327 (Ch).

97 Arguably, the tribunal has a right to refuse to recognise a settlement if the terms are in conflict with binding laws, public policy, fundamental notions of fairness and justice, or in a case of suspected fraud or illicit settlement: Waincymer (n 16) 1286 [16.3.8].

98 Domenico Di Pietro, 'Party Autonomy and Public Policy Awards by Consent' in Franco Ferrari (ed), *Limits to Party Autonomy in International Commercial Arbitration* (JurisNet, 2016) 383, 385, 397–9.

practices of arbitration they chose, and the discretion of the tribunal they chose over which they have little control once appointed (absent party agreement).[99]

8.24. Arbitration statutes, both those based on the *Model Law* and those not, place other considerations above party autonomy at times. Procedural fairness, for example, is elevated above party autonomy in the removal of a party's chosen arbitrator,[100] and by the mandatory requirements of equality of treatment,[101] tribunal independence,[102] giving the parties a reasonable opportunity of being heard,[103] and using appropriate procedures to resolve the dispute fairly.[104]

Summary of party autonomy

8.25. Party autonomy is not infringed by a tribunal granting security for costs in international commercial arbitration. In submitting to arbitration, the parties are taken to have accepted the incidents of that submission including the exercise of powers expressly, impliedly, or inherently conferred on the tribunal. This is consonant with the law's approach to other aspects of arbitration where a choice is made for the parties where they do not choose, or do so imperfectly. It comports with the nature of party autonomy which is not absolute and has inner and outer limits which might loosely be described respectively as those necessary to give effect to the submission to arbitration and those necessary in the interests of public policy.

(2) Security for costs and procedural fairness

8.26. It has been suggested that ordering a claimant to provide security for costs imperils the award[105] and its recognition and enforcement[106] by denying the claimant procedural fairness contrary to the requirements of the *New York Convention*, *Model Law*, and some *lex arbitri*, in that it:

(a) Denies the mandated equal treatment in imposing a financial burden on the claimant but not on the respondent, and thereby denies the claimant a full[107] or reasonable[108] opportunity of presenting its case;[109] and

---

99 *Jivraz v Hashwani* (n 84) [42], at least under the *Arbitration Act 1996* (UK) which is similar in this respect to the *Model Law*. The articles of the *Model Law* analogous to the sections or the Act referred to at [42] are: s 33-arts 12(1) and 18 (fairness and impartiality); s 34-art 19(2) (tribunal decides procedure); s 40-arts 17C(5) and 17H (compliance with orders of tribunal). See Waincymer (n 16) 388 [6.2.4] as to tribunals' residual discretion and their right or duty to decline procedures with which they disagree or believe are inappropriate.

100 For example, in the *Arbitration Ordinance* (Hong Kong) cap 609 s 26(1). See Luttrell (n 46) 175.

101 Article 18 of the *Model Law* and, for example, *Arbitration Ordinance* (Hong Kong) cap 609, s 46(2).

102 Article 12 of the *Model Law* and, for example, *Arbitration Ordinance* (Hong Kong) cap 609 s 46(3)(a).

103 Article 18 of the *Model Law* and, for example, *Arbitration Ordinance* (Hong Kong) cap 609 s 46(3)(b).

104 For example, *Arbitration Ordinance* (Hong Kong) cap 609 s 46(3)(c) and *Arbitration Act 1996* (UK) s 33(1)(b).

105 Article 34(2)(a)(ii) of the *Model Law*; s 24(b) of the *International Arbitration Act* (Singapore, cap 143A, 2002 rev ed) as a denial of natural justice.

106 Article V(b) of the *New York Convention* and Article 36(1)(a)(ii) of the *Model Law*.

107 Article 18 of the *Model Law*.

108 In enacting the *Model Law*, some jurisdictions have replaced a 'full' opportunity of a party presenting its case with a 'reasonable' opportunity, such as s 18 of the Australian *International Arbitration Act 1974* (Cth) and its Australian state and territories analogues.

109 Gu Weixia, 'Security for Costs in International Commercial Arbitration' (2005) 22(3) *Journal of International Arbitration* 177.

(b) Risks prejudging, or appearing to prejudge, the merits of the substantive claim as those merits are one of the considerations on an application for security for costs. A corollary of this argument is that, unless tribunals delve into the merits of the claim, they risk stifling valid claims by orders for security for costs.[110]

Possible responses to those two propositions are given as follows.

(2a) Equal treatment and proper opportunity

8.27. Awards are susceptible to being set aside at the seat or not recognised and enforced in the enforcing jurisdiction if procedural fairness has been denied.[111] This is the concern that has led to a strong focus on compliance with due process requirements – 'due process paranoia'[112] – with tribunals being perceived to give excessive opportunities to parties and lacking confidence to deal decisively with issues, behaviour,[113] and interim measures.[114] Menon suggests tribunals should be emboldened in their robust control of the proceedings, secure in the knowledge that very few awards are set aside, or refused recognition and enforcement, on the grounds of lack of procedural fairness.[115] After an extensive review of developments since 2010, Nottage concludes that there is increasing deference by courts to tribunals' procedural decisions, and suggests that this might increase in relation to awards obtained through institutional rather than ad hoc arbitration, which is declining.[116]

8.28. Setting aside an award on that basis is made more difficult when the tribunal has exercised an express power to order security for costs under the *lex arbitri* or the applicable institutional rules, or has made the order under the interim measures power which is accepted as encompassing an order for security for costs.[117] Due process is seen in the context of the arbitration as agreed,[118] and if the arbitration agreement admits of an acceptance of security for costs, express or implied,[119] it will not be a breach of due process to grant an agreed measure unless prevented by rules at the seat.[120]

110 Thomas Webster and Michael Bühler, *Handbook of ICC Arbitration* (Thomson Reuters, 4th ed, 2018) 455 [28.34].

111 Blackaby and Partasides (n 2) 581–2 [10.36]–[10.38], 586–9 [10.52]–[10.59].

112 Sundaresh Menon, 'Dispelling Due Process Paranoia: Fairness, Efficiency and the Rule of Law' (2021) 17(1) *Asian International Arbitration Journal* 1 [4]–[8] ('*Due process paranoia*').

113 Lucy Ferguson Reed, 'Sanctions Available for Arbitrators to Curtail Guerilla Tactics' in Horvath and Wilske (eds), *Guerilla Tactics in International Arbitration* (Kluwer, 2015) 95 [2.04][A][1] who says that '[t]he fulcrum between procedural due process and efficiency is where one finds the tribunal's tools for countering guerrilla tactics'.

114 Menon, 'Due Process Paranoia' (n 112) [4]–[6].

115 Ibid [37].

116 Luke Nottage, 'Deference of Seat or Foreign Courts to International Commercial Arbitration Tribunals Concerning Procedural Issues: Australia in Regional and Global Contexts' (Conference Paper, New York University conference on Deference: The Shared System of Control in Arbitration, 21 January 2022) 36 <https://ssrn.com/abstract=4013970>.

117 See Alastair Henderson and Vikas Mahendra, 'Interlocutory Applications' in Sundaresh Menon (ed), *Arbitration in Singapore* (Thomson Reuters, 2014) 275, 296 [11.082] (Stephen R Bond, *The Nature of Conservatory and Provisional Measures* in *Conservatory and Provisional Measures in International Arbitration* (ICC Special Supplement, 1993) 8, and Eric A Schwartz, *The Practices and Experience of the ICC Court Conservatory and Provisional Measures in International Arbitration* (ICC Special Supplement, 1993) 45, cited by Lord Mustill in *Coppée–Lavalin v Ken–Ren* (n 1) 54D.

118 Waincymer (n 16) 645 [8.3.4].

119 Henderson and Mahendra (n 117).

120 Waincymer (n 16) 645 [8.3.2].

8.29. A claimant may have grounds to challenge an award that stays or dismisses the claim for non-payment of security for costs if the tribunal disregarded the accepted principles for ordering security. It might be argued, not that the tribunal erred in law in making the order (which would not be reviewable in most jurisdictions), but that the tribunal exceeded the scope of its mandate. The argument might be that the parties consented to an arbitration including the availability of security for costs on the accepted principles and that, in departing from those principles, the tribunal exceeded the parties' consent, prevented the claimant from presenting its case, breached art V(1)(d) of the *New York Convention* in deviating impermissibly from the agreed procedure.

(2b) Prejudgment of the merits

8.30. The second ground given for security for costs potentially denying the claimant procedural fairness is that the tribunal would, or would be seen to, prejudge the substantive merits of the claim.[121] This apprehension appears as one of the principal reasons given for restricting the operation of security for costs in international commercial arbitration to exceptional circumstances.[122]

8.31. Concerns of prejudgment of the merits are negated by the nature of the merits enquiry on an application for security for costs, the considered requirement of the *Model Law* that merits be considered without prejudging the outcome, and a number of authoritative sources, each considered next.

The nature of the merits enquiry

8.32. Consideration of the substantive merits on an application for security for costs is deliberately superficial.[123] The merits are not gone into in detail and are a neutral factor[124] 'unless it can be clearly demonstrated one way or another that there is a high degree of probability of success or failure'.[125]

The requirements of the Model Law

8.33. After six years of consideration, the *Model Law* was amended in 2006 to require expressly in art 17A(1)(b) that when determining an application for interim measures, the tribunal will consider whether '[t]here is a reasonable possibility that the requesting party will succeed on the merits of the claim'. The article goes on to state that this determination 'shall not affect the discretion of the arbitral tribunal in making a subsequent determination'. In other words, those debating the amendments to the *Model Law*, and

121 See, for example, Waincymer (n 16) 649 [8.3.5]; Alan Redfern and Martin Hunter, *Redfern and Hunter on International Arbitration* (Oxford University Press, 4th ed, 2004) [7.40]–[7.41]. *Cf* Alan Redfern and Sam O'Leary, 'Why It Is Time for International Arbitration to Embrace Security for Costs' (2016) 32 *Arbitration International* 397, 400.

122 Samaa AF Haridi, 'Security for Costs and Claim Under the ICC Rules of Arbitration – Rare, But Possible' (2020) 2 *ICC Dispute Resolution Bulletin* 77.

123 *Keary Developments Ltd v Tarmac Construction Ltd* [1995] 3 All ER 534 (CA), 540d citing *Porzelack KG v Porzelack (UK) Ltd* [1987] 1 ALL ER 1074, 1077 ('*Porzelack*').

124 *Renel v Gulf Petroleum* [1996] 1 Lloyd's Rep 67, 69 ('*Renel*'); *Jazabas v Haddad* [2007] NSWCA 291 [84]; *Australian Equity Investors v Colliers International (NSW) Pty Limited* [2012] FCAFC 57 [15]; *Australian Battery Distributors Pty Ltd v Robert Bosch (Australia) Pty Ltd* [2015] FCA 1164 [32]; *Cody v Live Board Holdings Ltd* [2015] NSWSC 1790 [109]; *Cody v Live Board Holdings Ltd* [2017] NSWSC 308 [64].

125 *Porzelack* (n 123) 1077E; *Petromin SA v Secnav Marine Ltd* [1995] 1 Lloyd's Rep 603 608 ('*Petromin*'); *Renel* (n 124) 68–9; *Ramsay International Ltd v Scientific Control Systems Iran Ltd* [1980] WL 612943 3 (CA).

those states that have enacted it, have recognised that such a determination does not amount to a prejudgment.

The authoritative sources

8.34. The Departmental Advisory Committee of the UK Parliament considering the draft Bill that became the *Arbitration Act 1996* (UK) was of the deliberate view that tribunals would not be affected in the ultimate consideration of the merits by matters disclosed in an interlocutory application for security for costs.[126]

8.35. Born says that decisions on interim measures, by their nature provisional, alterable, and revocable,[127] should not, as a technical matter, prejudge or predetermine the final award. Any interim view of the merits is preliminary only, does not constitute *res judicata*, and should not actually prejudge the merits.[128] Webster and Bühler simply note that an application for interim measures should establish a *prima facie* basis of a valid claim on the merits and that there is a likelihood of success.[129] Redfern and O'Leary say that there is no need for the tribunal to prejudge the outcome and no reason it should be thought to be doing so.[130] Yeşilirmak says the *prima facie* test has gained substantial recognition but that the enquiry should be limited to an overall assessment of the merits to determine if it is sufficiently strong to merit interim protection.[131]

8.36. It is unlikely an award would be successfully challenged on the basis merely that the substantive outcome on the merits accorded with a preliminary view expressed on an application for an interim measure. More would likely be required, such as a view expressed so strongly it betokened a concluded view or a closed mind. After reviewing the empirical studies,[132] Menon says it is exceptional for courts to set aside arbitral awards on due process grounds.[133]

8.37. This completes the responses to the arguments categorised as security for costs denying a claimant procedural fairness. The next category of arguments considered is that security for costs is contrary to the *international* nature of international commercial arbitration. Again, there is no logical connection between the two

126 Departmental Advisory Committee, Parliament of the United Kingdom, *Report on the Arbitration Bill* (Final Report, February 1996) [194]–[196] ('*DAC Report*') where the committee stated they were 'not disturbed' by the prospect of offers of compromise being placed before the tribunal. They said '[i]t seems to us that a tribunal, properly performing its duty under Clause 33, could and should not be influenced by such matters, if the case proceeds to a hearing on the merits, nor do we accept that the disclosure of such information could somehow disqualify the tribunal from acting'.

127 See *Model Law* art 17D; Ali Yeşilirmak, 'Provisional Measures' in Loukas A Mistelis and Julian DM Lew (eds), *Pervasive Problems in International Arbitration* (Kluwer, 2006) 191 [9–19] ('*Provisional Measures*').

128 Born (n 16) 2659 [17.02][G][3][b][iii].

129 (n 110) 453 [28.27].

130 Redfern and O'Leary (n 121) 401.

131 Yeşilirmak (n 127) 177–8 [5.28]–[5.29].

132 Klaus Peter Berger and J Ole Jensen, 'Due Process Paranoia and the Procedural Judgment Rule: A Safe Harbour for Procedural Management Decisions by International Arbitrators' (2016) 32 *Arbitration International* 415; Robin Oldenstam, 'Chapter 8: Due Process Paranoia or Prudence?' in Axel Calissendorff and Patrik Schöldstrom (eds), *Stockholm Arbitration Yearbook* (Kluwer Law International, 2019) 122; IBA, 'Review of National Case Law with Respect to the Conduct of the Arbitral Process' (Report, October 2018) <https://www. ibanet.org/Document/Default.aspx?DocumentUid=B4B532BB-90E1-40AB-AB3D-F730C19984FB>.

133 Menon, *Due process paranoia* (n 112) [37].

categories of arguments and they are considered in the diminishing order of their perceived strength.

(3) Contrary to the international nature of international commercial arbitration

8.38. Four arguments to restrict security for costs in international commercial arbitration can be seen to be underpinned by the contention that security for costs is inimical to the international nature of international arbitration. They are that the facility:

(a) Inhibits international trade;[134]
(b) Runs counter to the transnationalisation of international arbitration. It is said to be desirable for international arbitration to transcend the civil and common law divide, and the peculiar procedures of domestic courts;[135]
(c) Is out of place in [an ICC] arbitration; and
(d) Is an English idiosyncrasy that should be excluded from the cosmopolitan world of institutional arbitration.

Possible responses to those arguments are given as follows.

(3a) Inhibits international trade

8.39. An argument raised against security for costs in its infancy in litigation in the 18th century was that it would inhibit international trade.[136] There is no evidence to support this contention, and the contrary could be expected to be true. Security for costs reduces the risks associated with international trade by providing security when a party is sued by an impecunious claimant. The risks of trade are reduced if the chances of not recovering costs from an unsuccessful claimant are eliminated or reduced through an order for security. Without security, impecunious companies with weak claims can indulge in 'fail-safe' proceedings with impunity, secure in the knowledge that they will not pay any adverse costs order. Proceedings can be used as instruments of oppression by smaller companies with few assets against larger or more prosperous companies,[137] resulting in the not-uncommon outcome of respondents paying an amount by way of settlement to underserving claimants based on the costs the respondent would not recover even if it defeated the claim.[138] There is also no evidence to suggest parties negotiating and entering international transactions are aware of the security for costs facility nor base any of their decisions or negotiations on its presence or absence.[139]

---

134 *Fitzgerald v Whitmore* (1786) 1 TR 362 ('*Fitzgerald v Whitmore*'); *Han v Cho* 2008 BCSC 1229 [15] (Dillon J) ('*Han v Cho*').

135 Berger (n 132).

136 *Fitzgerald v Whitmore* (n 134); *Han v Cho* (n 134).

137 *Flender Werft AG v Aegean Maritime Ltd* [1990] 2 Lloyd's Rep 27, 30–1 ('*Flender Werft*'); *Pearson v Naydler* [1977] 1 WLR 906G–907A).

138 A respondent facing an impecunious claimant loses either way – ignoring the claim will likely result in an award against it, and defending the claim will result in an unsatisfied costs award: Marc D Veit, 'Note: Procedural Order No. 14 of 27 November 2002: Security for Costs in International Arbitration: Some Comments to Procedural Order No. 14 of 27 November 2002' (2005) 23(1) *ASA Bulletin* 116, 117.

139 See *Ferris v Plaister* (1994) 34 NSWLR 474, 491G, agreeing with Black J in *Prima Paint Corp v Flood & Conklin Mfg Co* 388 US 395 (1967); Waincymer (n 16) 645 [8.3.2]; Born (n 16) 2632 [17.02][A][6]; David D Caron in Barry E. Carter et al. (eds), 'Comparative Analysis of International Dispute Resolution Institutions' (1991) 85 *American Society of International Law* 64, 66.

(3b) Counter to the transnationalisation of international arbitration

8.40. Transnationalisation was a movement, or an ethos,[140] that maintained international commercial arbitration is a self-contained juridical system, separate from and antithetical to national systems of law.[141] It held that, ideally, national courts will not be involved in international commercial arbitration and differences between national laws will become irrelevant.[142]

8.41. Leaving aside the currency of the ethos,[143] the fact that a measure is borrowed from national courts does not detract from transnationalism. Arbitration can adopt a measure and make it its own while staying true to the notion of being autonomous of national courts. Arguably, the more procedures arbitration incorporates from courts, the more independent from them and less reliant on them it becomes, just as it has been with the gradual transfer of interim measure powers from courts to tribunals.[144]

8.42. Allied to this argument but not raised directly against security for costs is the complaint of the judicialisation or 'industrialisation' of arbitration.[145] Arbitration has taken on a variety of procedures traditionally available in Anglo-American litigation such as pleadings, requests for further and better particulars, document discovery, injunctions, and aggressive tactics.[146] Redfern views this as a function of the professionalisation of arbitration and its emergence as the international dispute resolution method of choice.[147] He notes the corporate concern that arbitration has the expense of litigation without all the procedural safeguards and appellate rights available in litigation.[148] To counter these concerns, security for costs may be seen as a procedural safeguard against unnecessary steps or obstructive tactics and a useful check on the industrialisation of arbitration.[149] Rejection of security for costs on the basis it is judicialising the process may be seen as arbitrary and inconsistent with the introduction of many other procedures from litigation.

(3c) A misplaced English idiosyncrasy

8.43. While it is true that the modern form of security for costs developed from the English version (ironically, said to be a reaction to an earlier requirement by Continental courts),[150] its utility in international commercial arbitration is attested by its increasing

140 *Coppée–Lavalin v Ken–Ren* (n 1) 50F–G.

141 Hayward (n 16) 50 [2.03], saying that 'claims that arbitration can be completely detached from State laws no longer find support' and that 'delocalization is considered a particular feature of French law rather than a general principle'. See also Waincymer (n 16) 27 [1.3].

142 *Coppée–Lavalin v Ken–Ren* (n 1) 52A-C.

143 Lord Mustill doubted its currency in 1994, ibid, and Lord Mance denounced it in a speech published as Jonathan Mance, 'Arbitration: A Law Unto Itself?' (2016) 32(2) *Arbitration International* 223.

144 Born (n 16) 2606 [17.02].

145 James Allsop, 'Commercial and Investor–State Arbitration: The Importance of Recognising Their Differences' [2018] *Federal Judicial Scholarship* 3 [26]. He prefers 'industrialisation' so as to avoid the pejorative implications of 'judicialisation'.

146 Alan Redfern, 'The Changing World of International Arbitration' in David D Caron et al. (eds) *Practising Virtue: Inside International Arbitration* (Oxford University Press, 2015) 45–51.

147 Ibid 51.

148 Ibid 49.

149 Günther J Horvath, Stephan Wilske and Niamh Leinwather, 'Countering Guerilla Tactics' and 'Conclusion and Outlook' in Günther J Horvath and Stephan Wilske (eds), *Guerilla Tactics in International Arbitration* (Kluwer, 2013) 43 [2.01][A][3][a], 351 [6.06]; Reed (n 113) 99 [2.04][A][2][b].

150 *Fitzgerald v Whitmore* (n 134); *Han v Cho* (n 134).

express adoption in institutional rules, its regular application in LCIA arbitrations,[151] and the advocacy for its wider adoption.[152]

(3d) Security for costs is out of place in an ICC arbitration

8.44. ICC arbitrations are considered by some to be different in some respects from ad hoc arbitrations and arbitrations administered by other institutions, due to the nature and purpose of the ICC itself. Internationalism could be said to be the feature of the ICC Court of Arbitration differentiating it from institutions formed elsewhere such as the LCIA, SCC, SIAC, and HKIAC. Naturally, those other institutions are intended to appeal to an international audience, but they are essentially national institutions, drawing disputes and the dispute ecosystem to their home country. The ICC was formed in 1920 by national chambers of commerce endeavouring to achieve together internationally what each could not achieve alone, and was intended from the beginning to have a function of resolving international commercial disputes.[153] Steingruber says that the ICC generally has been and remains the voice of the international business community.[154]

8.45. A result of the ICC being such an international institution is that parties choosing ICC arbitrations in their contracts have, by definition, no connection with the home jurisdiction of the ICC, as there is none. Other institutions make something of the increasing use of their rules and administration by parties with no connection to the institutions' home jurisdiction.

8.46. This absence of a home jurisdiction is said to have the consequence that, by the choice of ICC arbitration, the parties have given an 'unmistakable signal of their intentions' for a relationship with particular national courts and diverse national laws which is less closely coupled than would otherwise be the case.[155] This is not borne out by the results of *QMUL 2018* as to the reasons parties choose institutions and seats. On analysis, the reasons for choosing institutions do not include the degree of connection with the local legal system, and the choice of seats and the reasons for choosing them are contrary to that suggestion. These are both considered next.

Reasons for choosing institutions

8.47. Responses to the 2018 Queen Mary University of London survey do not support the contention that its international nature is a reason for selecting a particular institution to administer an arbitration. The survey gave respondents the ability to nominate their four most important reasons for choosing an institution, and gave 15 reasons to choose from, together with 'other'.[156] The five most common reasons, and the total percentage of respondents who gave those reasons as their first, second, third, or fourth reason, were:

General reputation and recognition of the institution	18%
High level of administration (including efficiency, pro-activeness, facilities, quality of staff)	15%

151 See [4.39] et seq.

152 Redfern and O'Leary, (n 121) 397, 412; John Beechey, 'International Arbitrations and the Award of Security for Costs' (1994) 12 *ASA Bulletin* 179, 190.

153 *Coppée–Lavalin v Ken–Ren* (n 1) 50C-D.

154 Steingruber (n 16) 19 [2.31].

155 *Coppée–Lavalin v Ken–Ren* (n 1) 63D-E.

156 QMUL, *2018 International Arbitration Survey: The Evolution of International Arbitration* (Report, 2018) 14, Chart 13 ('QMUL 2018').

Previous experience of the institution	12%
Neutrality/'internationalism'	10.5%
Access to wide pool of high quality arbitrators	10%

8.48. When asked their first reason for choosing an institution, only 1.5% gave 'neutrality/"internationalism"' as the reason.

Reasons for choosing seats

8.49. Three of the four seats most popular with participants[157] in the 2018 Queen Mary University of London survey have express provision for security for costs in their arbitration laws – London (64%),[158] Singapore (39%),[159] and Hong Kong (28%).[160] Only Paris, the second most preferred seat,[161] has no provision for security for costs in its *lex arbitri*.[162] Contrary to the predictions of some,[163] parties did not desert London as a seat due to the House of Lord's decision in *Coppée–Lavalin v Ken–Ren*,[164] suggesting that they are not aware of, or concerned by, such minutiae when negotiating contracts.

8.50. Reasons given for preferring these seats also suggest party ignorance of or indifference to arbitration's independence from the local legal or judicial system. The top four reasons participants gave for choosing seats were 'general reputation and recognition of the seat' (14%), 'neutrality and impartiality of the local legal system' (13%), 'national arbitration law' (12%), and 'track record in enforcing agreements to arbitrate and arbitral awards' (11%).[165] Those second and third reasons indicate that parties choose a seat, not because they want to be separate from its laws and courts, but because they anticipate the possibility of some interaction and prefer to have it with the laws and courts of that seat.[166] If parties choose seats based on the level of interaction, a reason for choosing a seat would have been the local courts' disinclination to be involved in arbitral proceedings.

Conclusion – security for costs is not out of place in ICC arbitration

8.51. The empirical evidence does not support the judicial assumption that parties make a conscious choice of ICC based on its relative autonomy from courts and legal systems. That may be a sound legal reason for them to do so yet it does not appear to resound in reality. Even if it did, it would not translate into an intention to be free from interim measures in general and security for costs in particular. Interim measures are now

157 With the indicated percentage of participants including the seat in their answer.

158 *Arbitration Act 1996* (UK) s 38.

159 *International Arbitration Act* (Singapore, cap 143A, 2002 rev ed) s 12.

160 *Arbitration Ordinance* (Hong Kong) cap 609 s 56.

161 With 53% of participants including it in their answer: *QMUL 2018* 9 Chart 6 (n 156).

162 *Code of Civil Procedure*, Book IV. Note that in *QMUL 2021*, Paris dropped to the fourth preferred seat, with Singapore and London as equal first and Hong Kong next: *QMUL 2021* 6 Chart 2.

163 David Branson, 'The Ken-Ren Case: It Is an Ado Where More Aid Is Less Help' (1994) 10(3) *Arbitration International* 313, 315, 316; Beechey (n 152) 188–9, 191; Brian Davenport, 'The Ken-Ren Case: Much Ado About Nothing Very Much' (1994) *Arbitration International* 303, 310.

164 *Coppée–Lavalin v Ken–Ren* (n 1).

165 *QMUL 2018* 10 (n 156).

166 Croft notes that sophisticated corporations take heed of the relative merits of arbitration jurisdictions, creating a level of competition among them. He says that legislatures must do all they can to facilitate laws that create a favourable arbitral environment, and courts should understand and support arbitration by being impartial, efficient, knowledgeable, and relevantly experienced: Clyde Croft, 'How the Judiciary Can Support Domestic and International Arbitration' (2014) *XVII Hors Serie, Victoria University of Wellington* 115, 116.

an established, accepted component of arbitration, all the more so since the 2006 amendments to the *Model Law* significantly expanded the provisions on interim measures. Those amendments were enacted in the UNCITRAL Arbitration Rules 2010, by far the most commonly used rules in ad hoc arbitrations.[167] Attribution to the parties of an intention to have access to arbitral interim measures is consistent with an attribution of an intention to be untethered from local courts and laws.

(4) Enforcement issues

8.52. Two arguments against security for costs in international commercial arbitration may be grouped under the headings of enforcement issues. They are that security for costs is:

(a) Unnecessary because enforcement of costs awards is sufficiently effective in international arbitration that security is not needed. This is said to be due to the apparent ease of enforcement under the *New York Convention*; and
(b) Pointless as the tribunal lacks the power to stay the arbitration if it is not provided, the usual remedy for failure to give security.

(4a) Enforcement is adequate without security for costs

8.53. It has been argued that security for costs is unnecessary because enforcement of costs awards is sufficiently effective in international arbitration under the *New York Convention* that security is not needed.[168] Three responses may be given to this contention, namely:

(i) The modern basis of security for costs is not enforceability;
(ii) The law should not withhold an additional remedy; and
(iii) Enforceability is not guaranteed even in *New York Convention* and *Model Law* jurisdictions.

(i) The modern basis of security for costs is not enforceability

8.54. Enforceability of an order for costs was once the prime criterion for granting security for costs, often resulting in the claimant's foreign residence being the sole or determinative factor.[169] That is no longer the case, with the focus being on the claimant's ability and willingness to pay an adverse costs order.[170] Particularly is this so in international arbitration where a number of jurisdictions have enacted legislation expressly forbidding it being the sole basis of an order.[171]

---

167 84% of parties reported using the UNCITRAL Arbitration Rules in ad hoc arbitrations: *QMUL 2018* 15 Chart 14.

168 *Coppée–Lavalin v Ken–Ren* (n 1) 61E–F, noted and rejected by Lord Mustill; Michael Hwang and Rajesh C Muttath, 'The Role of Courts in the Course of Arbitral Proceedings: Singapore and Other Asian Perspectives' (2002) 68 *Arbitration* 3; Born (n 16).

169 *DSQ Property Co Ltd v Lotus Cars Ltd* [1987] 1 WLR 127, 129. See [2.6].

170 In the words of Lord Mustill, '[t]he network of national laws for the mutual enforcement of awards will not help [the respondent] if there are no assets against which to enforce': *Coppée–Lavalin v Ken–Ren* (n 1) 65D.

171 *International Arbitration Act* (Singapore, cap 143A, 2002 rev ed) s 12(4); *Arbitration Ordinance* (Hong Kong) cap 609 s 56(2); *International Arbitration Act 1974* (Cth) s 23K(2).

(ii) The law should not withhold an additional remedy

8.55. If the ability to enforce an award of costs remains relevant to the exercise of the discretion to award security, the law should not 'abstain from adding a further means to ensure that a party in default does not escape from its obligations simply because an existing procedure may, in the event, serve the purpose'.[172]

(iii) Enforceability is not guaranteed

8.56. Enforceability of awards is not guaranteed despite the wide accession to the *New York Convention*. The convention does not prescribe the manner in which states recognise and enforce arbitral awards, stating only that states will enforce awards 'in accordance with the rules of procedure of the territory where the award is relied upon'.[173] With some countries, there can be doubt that the local procedures will be adequate. As a first point, what is conveniently referred to by the shorthand of 'enforcement' of awards is recognition and enforcement of the award, followed by repatriation of the proceeds. There are three distinct phases of 'enforcement',[174] with the potential of each to frustrate, delay, or increase the cost of, recovery of the proceeds of the award.[175]

8.57. One issue that has arisen in that process is in some national courts breaching 'an almost sacrosanct principle of international arbitration' by scrutinising the merits of awards under the guise of the public policy exception to recognition and enforcement. This often involves 'illegitimate re-litigation of the substance of the parties' dispute in violation of the Convention'[176] and undermines the efficacy of recognition and enforcement.

8.58. An irony of international commercial arbitration is that the second most important reason parties gave for choosing that mechanism is to avoid national courts,[177] yet when it comes to enforcement – the stage that gives meaning to every previous stage and expense – the parties are at the mercy of the national system they wished to avoid by agreeing to arbitration. This reinforces the utility of security for costs to allow for the vagaries of local enforcement.

(4b) Tribunal's power to stay arbitration

8.59. A temporary stay of proceedings until security for costs is provided is usually ordered when security is granted.[178] It has been said that '[a] stay of proceedings is an integral part of an order for security for costs'.[179] The stay may be made permanent if it becomes clear after some time that the claimant will not be able to provide security.[180]

---

172 *Coppée–Lavalin v Ken–Ren* (n 1) 61H-62A.

173 *New York Convention* art III; Joseph E Neuhaus, 'Current Issues in the Enforcement of International Arbitration Awards' (2004) 36(1) *University of Miami Inter-American Law Review* 23, 27.

174 Blackaby and Partasides (n 2) 610–11 [11.19]–[11.22].

175 Cameron Ford, 'The Enforcement Chimera' *Kluwer Arbitration Blog* (Blog Post, 10 May 2018) <http://arbitrationblog.kluwerarbitration.com/2018/05/10/the-enforcement-chimera/>.

176 Born (n 16) 388–9 [23].

177 *QMUL 2018* 7 Chart 3 (n 156), with 60% giving 'avoiding specific legal systems/national courts' as one of international arbitration's most valuable characteristics, and with 64% giving 'enforceability of awards'. The next most valuable characteristics were 'flexibility' (40%), 'ability of parties to select arbitrators' (39%), and 'confidentiality and privacy' (36%).

178 *Coppée–Lavalin v Ken–Ren* (n 1) 48C; *Flender Werft* (n 137) 32; *Petromin* (n 125) 609–11; *Hudson Strumpffabrik GMBH v Bentley Engineering Co Ltd* [1962] 2 QB 587, 593.

179 *The Argenpuma* [1984] 2 Lloyd's Rep 563, 565 (CA).

180 *Petromin* (n 125) 611.

8.60. It is a serious matter to stay an arbitration pending the claimant's provision of security for costs, and naturally more serious to stay the arbitration permanently.[181] In their arbitration agreement, parties have agreed that they should have access to justice through arbitration. Courts of states who have acceded to the *New York Convention* are required to recognise and enforce the arbitration agreement,[182] not to frustrate it by a stay. Unlike a plaintiff whose litigation has been permanently stayed, a claimant in a similar position in an arbitration cannot commence a fresh arbitration as the contractual entitlement to arbitrate has been exhausted, and there is no entitlement to commence litigation as that would be liable to be stayed as being contrary to the arbitration agreement.[183]

8.61. Support for stays may be found in similar arbitral powers such as suspension or termination of proceedings. Despite the obligation to recognise and enforce the arbitration agreement, and the obligation to afford the parties equal treatment and an appropriate opportunity of presenting their case,[184] arbitral institutions acknowledge that some circumstances justify suspension or termination of the arbitration other than on the merits, for example for non-payment of the filing fee,[185] or of the advance to cover the costs of the arbitration,[186] or of an increase in fees relating to an emergency arbitrator.[187] It is clear that the concept of a stay of proceedings for non-payment of financial obligations is accepted in international commercial arbitration.[188]

8.62. The Departmental Advisory Committee considering the draft Bill that became the *Arbitration Act 1996* (UK), under the chairmanship of Saville LJ, was of the view that agreement to arbitration did not necessitate a determination on the merits but that it was an agreement to have the dispute resolved by the arbitral process, of which security for costs and stays are a part.[189] To the contrary, it has been held in England by an Official Referee that an arbitrator does not have power to stay the arbitration for non-payment of security for costs.[190]

8.63. A stay of the arbitration is the logical sanction for non-payment of security for costs. Necessarily inherent in an order for security for costs is a finding that it is unfair for the respondent to continue to incur costs at the instance of the claimant without having security for those costs.[191] To allow the claimant to continue with the arbitration and force the respondent to incur costs is contrary to that finding.

---

181 Ibid.

182 Article II(1) of the *New York Convention*, and *Coppée–Lavalin v Ken–Ren* (n 1) 64H.

183 *Petromin* (n 125) 611; art II(3) of the *New York Convention*, and art 8(1) of the *Model Law*.

184 Article 18 of the *Model Law*. 'Appropriate' opportunity of presenting the case is referred to here as, although the *Model Law* states that each party shall be given 'full' opportunity, some state enactments require only a 'reasonable' opportunity, e.g., the *International Arbitration Act 1974* (Cth) s 18.

185 ICC Rules 2021 Article 4(4).

186 Ibid Article 37(6).

187 Ibid Appendix X, Article 7(2).

188 Davenport (n 163) 308.

189 *DAC Report* (n 126) [192].

190 *Guaranteed Asphalt (London) Ltd (in Administrative Receivership) v Taylor Woodrow Construction Ltd* [1998] EWHC Technology 317 [78]–[80]. But see Richard Chesterman, 'Security for Costs – A Cautionary Tale' (June 2021) *The Arbitrator and Mediator* 33–9, 35–6 for a critique of that decision.

191 As an example of the many statements as to fairness being at the root of the facility, see *Coppée–Lavalin v Ken–Ren* (n 1) 67A-B.

8.64. A stay is also the only realistically available sanction.[192] A claimant cannot be forced to provide funds it does not have or does not wish to pay, and it is not in the respondent's interests nor consistent with an order for security for costs for the claimant to be forced to continue proceedings without security that has been ordered. Tribunals do not have a power to punish disobedience of their orders by committal for 'contempt of tribunal'.[193]

8.65. An order for security of costs without a corresponding stay would be in reality no order at all for no sanction would attach to non-compliance.[194] 'One without the other would be a futility'.[195]

8.66. The grant of an express power necessarily implies the conferral of powers to do everything necessary for the exercise of the express power to ensure that the exercise of the express power is not a futility.[196] This principle applies equally to statutory and contractual grants of power.[197]

8.67. Power to grant a stay may also be found in the width of the conferral of power to order security. If the grant is to make orders '*with respect to* security for costs' rather than '*for* security for costs', that 'phrase means "relating to", and denotes the widest connection between subject matters'.[198] Given the 'intimate'[199] connection between an order for security and a stay of proceedings, a stay would be 'with respect to' security for costs.[200]

8.68. Staying the arbitration pending provision of security is not as drastic a measure as some powers the tribunal is considered to have under plenary powers of case management, such as an implied power to determine a claim expeditiously[201] under an express general power to conduct proceedings efficiently.[202] An expeditious determination, if granted, results in a partial or final award finally disposing of that part of the claim the subject of the determination, a more drastic result than a stay of proceedings. It must have been considered by the ICC Secretariat in drafting the ICC Note, and the ICC Court of Arbitration in approving it, under art 5(2) of the ICC Internal Rules of

192 Davenport (n 163) 308.

193 A possible course is to register the tribunal's order with the appropriate court to 'convert' it to an order of the court, and then for the court to commit the claimant for contempt of court if that order is not obeyed: Blackaby and Partasides (n 2) 319 [5.42]. This is not in the interests of the respondent who is more content with the arbitration being stayed than in punishing the claimant, or coercing it into providing security.

194 *James v Australia and New Zealand Banking Group Ltd* (1985) 9 FCR 422, 446; *Matthews v SPI Electricity Pty Ltd & Ors* (No 9) [2013] VSC 671 [116].

195 Chesterman (n 190) 36.

196 Ibid 37, citing *Pelechowski v Registrar, Court of Appeal* (1999) 198 CLR 435, 451 [50].

197 Chesterman (n 190) 38, noting that an implied power to grant a stay would easily satisfy the five requirements for implication of contractual terms: *BP Refinery (Westernport) Pty Ltd v Hastings Shire* (1977) 180 CLR 266, 282–3.

198 Chesterman (n 190) 39.

199 Ibid 38.

200 Ibid 39.

201 Constantine Partasides and Ben Prewett, 'Rediscovering the Lost Promise of International Arbitration' in Lurent Levy and Michael Polkinghorne (eds), *Expedited Procedures in International Arbitration* (Kluwer; ICC, 2017) 110, 112–13; Menon, *Due process paranoia* (n 112) [58]; Charlie Caher and Jonathan Lim, 'Summary Disposition Procedures in International Arbitration' in *The International Comparative Legal Guide to: International Arbitration 2018* (Global Legal Group, 2018) [43], citing *Travis Coal Restructuring Holdings LLC v Essar Global Fund Limited* [2014] EWHC 2510 (Comm) [47]; ICC *Note to Parties and Arbitral Tribunals on the Conduct of the Arbitration 01-01-2021* (ICC Note) [92]–[93].

202 For example, Article 22(1) of the ICC Rules 2021, requiring the tribunal to conduct proceedings in an expeditious and cost effective manner, having regard to the complexity and value of the dispute.

the Court of Arbitration that the power expeditiously to determine a claim resided in art 22 of the ICC Rules 2021, as art 5(2) of the ICC Internal Rules does not confer on the Secretariat a rule-making power. To be a valid exercise of power, the ICC Note must be explanatory of existing powers – whether derived from the procedural rules, inhering in the tribunal, from the *lex arbitri*, conferred by the parties or otherwise – and of procedures to exercise those powers. It is said that the ICC Note is intended to give substance to provisions in the Rules.[203]

8.69. If art 22(1) of the ICC Rules 2021 contains a power finally to determine a claim expeditiously (that is, summarily), it is logical that it would also contain a lesser power to stay an arbitration pending provision of security for costs that a tribunal has ordered in the exercise of a recognised power. Especially is this the case since a stay leaves open the possibility of the claimant's obtaining funds and continuing the arbitration and, as an interim measure, it is open for either party to apply to vary the order if circumstances change.[204] Further, an order should only be made where the stifling principle is satisfied with the result that the sum ordered as security and the consequential stay are proportionate in all the circumstances.[205] A tribunal would not be *functus officio* where a proceeding is stayed and would retain power to lift the stay or to terminate the arbitration in appropriate circumstances.

8.70. If a stay is not appropriate, or further means of enforcement are required, art 17H of the *Model Law*, added in 2006, states:

> An interim measure issued by an arbitral tribunal shall be recognized as binding and, unless otherwise provided by the arbitral tribunal, enforced upon application to the competent court, irrespective of the country in which it was issued, subject to the provisions of article 17I.

8.71. States that have enacted the *Model Law* in this or analogous form permit enforcement of orders or awards for interim measures. Other states may not be so generous and may require requests from parties, tribunals, or both, or may only recognise orders for interim measures made by tribunals seated in their jurisdiction.[206]

(5) Basis of security for costs

8.72. The final arguments are related to the basis of security for costs – that it is (a) unfair to creditors in a corporate liquidation and that it is (b) inappropriate where costs do not shift – and are dealt with next.

(5a) Unfair to creditors

8.73. The existence of a liquidator claimant should be a factor relevant to the exercise of the discretion rather than its precluding security for costs in international commercial arbitration. Considerations should be that the liquidator is performing a public function on behalf of all creditors which should not be stifled by one debtor (or potential debtor),

---

203 Webster and Bühler (n 110) 349 [22–4].

204 See, for example, Procedural Order, ICC, Case No 2020–225, 2014 [6.3] reported in Haridi (n 122) 100.

205 See [5.5] et seq.

206 James E Castello and Rami Chahine, 'Enforcement of Interim Measures' in J William Rowley, Emmanuel Gaillard and Gordon E Kaiser (eds), *Guide to Challenging and Enforcing Arbitral Awards* (Law Business Research, 2019) 105.

against which may be balanced the amount of assets the company has, the number and value of debtors and creditors, the size of the particular claim, whether those standing behind the company are able to provide security, and any other factors relevant to the individual case.[207]

(5b) Inappropriate where no costs shift

8.74. It is axiomatic that there is no basis for security for costs if there is no possible liability for costs, as there is nothing for which to give security. An absence of possible liability for costs in a particular case will mean that security for costs is not appropriate, but it is to be decided as a factor in each case, not as a barrier against all security for costs in international commercial arbitration.

207 *Green v CGU Insurance Ltd* [2008] NSWCA 148 [27], [45]; *Bell Wholesale P/L v Gates Export Corporation (No 2)* (1984) 8 ACLR 588; *Forest Pty Ltd v Keen Bay Pty Ltd* (1991) 4 ACSR 107, 123; *Australian Battery Distributors Pty Ltd v Robert Bosch (Australia) Pty Ltd* [2015] FCA 1164 [54].

CHAPTER 9

Utility of security for costs in international commercial arbitration

Introduction

9.1. Security for costs may have utility in international commercial arbitration by adopting a multifactorial approach without the need for exceptional circumstances and without a predisposition for or against granting security. Benefits may flow to the parties to arbitration and to the institution of arbitration.

A. For the parties

(1) To foster enforcement of costs awards;
(2) As a control mechanism against unmeritorious claims, improper conduct, and excessive cost and delay;
(3) To enhance procedural fairness and access to justice for both parties;
(4) To enable tribunals to correct injustices;
(5) To counter-balance the judicialisation of arbitration; and
(6) Assist settlement.

B. For the institution of arbitration

(7) To provide a rich source of jurisprudence and guidance;
(8) To bring uniformity to the application of the facility in international commercial arbitration;
(9) To maintain the attraction and competitiveness of international commercial arbitration; and
(10) To contribute to the harmonisation of international commercial arbitration and common law litigation.

A. For the immediate benefit of the parties

(1) Enforcement of costs awards

9.2. An obvious benefit of security for costs is that it enhances enforcement of costs awards. The provisions of the New York Convention are not always sufficient to ensure awards are enforced, concentrating as it does on the state's mechanisms for recognition

DOI: 10.4324/9781003479628-9

and enforcement of awards.[1] Security for costs, on the other hand, looks to the ability of the award debtor to pay.[2]

9.3. Tribunals conducting proceedings under some arbitral rules are required to 'make every effort' to ensure that the award is enforceable,[3] interpreted as an obligation to make best endeavours in following the appropriate procedure and giving each party a fair hearing.[4] It could be argued that such an obligation, emphasising enforcement as the ultimate goal of the proceedings, reinforces the position of security for costs in international commercial arbitration, not as a duty of the tribunal to grant, but as a legitimate procedural tool to be considered and deployed appropriately.[5]

9.4. The practical ability to enforce an award benefits not only an award creditor but also the institution of arbitration as a whole, including parties who depend upon it for the success of their international transactions.

9.5. The cost of international commercial arbitration is already said to be threatening its legitimacy.[6] That threat is increased if wealthy claimants, particularly if they have poor cases, can force less wealthy respondents to incur significant cost, safe in the knowledge that they can avoid payment of an adverse costs order. Genn says that '[o]ne of the most important elements of power is insulation from legal costs'.[7] Security for costs removes that insulation and exposes those benefitting from the proceedings to costs consequences (or stays the proceedings).[8]

9.6. Statistics are not available for the proportion of costs awards in international *commercial* arbitration that are not enforced due to the debtor's inability or unwillingness to pay. The Queen Mary Survey 2008 reported that 92% of international commercial arbitration disputes are resolved by agreement, but that 11% result in recognition and enforcement proceedings.[9] This suggests that around 3% of settlement agreements are not performed and require enforcement proceedings.[10] No distinction was made in those

---

1 Nigel Blackaby and Constantine Partasides with Alan Redfern and Martin Hunter, *Redfern and Hunter on International Arbitration* (Oxford University Press, 6th ed, 2015) 613 [11.27].

2 *Carter v Mehmet* [2021] NSWCA 32 [31].

3 For example, ICC 2017 art 41; LCIA Rules 2021 art 32(2); SIAC Rules 2016 r 41.2.

4 Blackaby and Partasides (n 1) 608 [11.11].

5 For example, to deal with guerilla tactics by one of the parties: Günther J Horvath, Stephan Wilske and Niamh Leinwather, 'Countering Guerilla Tactics' and 'Conclusion and Outlook' in Günther J Horvath and Stephan Wilske (eds), *Guerilla Tactics in International Arbitration* (Kluwer, 2013) 43 [2.01][A][3][a], 351 [6.06]; Lucy Ferguson Reed, 'Sanctions Available for Arbitrators to Curtail Guerilla Tactics' in Horvath and Wilske (eds) (n 5) 99 [2.04][A][2][b].

6 Menon, 'Arbitration's Blade: International Arbitration and the Rule of Law' (2021) 38(1), *Journal of International Arbitration* 1 [45] ('*Arbitration's Blade*'). See also James Allsop, 'Commercial and Investor-State Arbitration: The Importance of Recognising Their Differences' [2018] *Federal Judicial Scholarship* 3 [26] ('Commercial and investor-state arbitration') [26]; Klaus Sachs, 'Time and Money: Cost Control and Effective Case Management' in Loukas Mistelis and Julian Lew (eds), *Pervasive Problems in International Arbitration* (Kluwer, 2006) 103 [5.45] who expresses the hope that parties, particularly mid-sized companies, would not avoid arbitration for fear they cannot afford it. No distinction appears to be made in the literature between claimants and respondents in the discussion of costs affecting arbitration's legitimacy.

7 Hazel Genn, 'Understanding Civil Justice' (1997) 50 *Current Legal Problems* 155, 179.

8 *Flender Werft AG v Aegean Maritime Ltd* [1990] 2 Lloyd's Rep 27, 30–1 ('*Flender Werft*'); *Pearson v Naydler* [1977] 1 WLR 906G–907A.

9 Queen Mary University – PwC, *International Arbitration: Corporate attitudes and practice 2006* 2, 5 ('*QMUL 2006*').

10 The difference between the percentage of cases not settled (8%) and the percentage requiring enforcement (11%). According to those statistics, only 8% of cases proceed to an award, but 11% require enforcement.

figures between substantive awards and others such as costs awards. Settlement agreements might be presumed to make provision for costs, but this is not always the case in arbitration[11] or litigation.[12]

9.7. A 2015 study of the rate of satisfaction of international *investment* arbitration costs awards found that a much lower proportion of respondents were paid without enforcement than claimants – 46% of respondents compared to 71% of claimants were paid without enforcement, voluntarily or through settlement. Similarly, twice the percentage of respondents were paid nothing at all compared to claimants – 37% of respondents and 19% of claimants received no payment on their costs award.[13]

9.8. Such a marked difference may not be wholly representative of international *commercial* arbitration as it may partly reflect the prevalence of claimants in international investment arbitration who are special purpose vehicles with no significant assets,[14] and the lack of a need or ability to preserve a business relationship (a reason given for voluntary compliance in international commercial arbitration).[15]

9.9. Critically for security for costs, the usual reason for non-payment of an award in international commercial arbitration was not the lack of legal means of enforcement in the foreign jurisdiction, but the lack of assets or ability to identify assets of the debtor.[16] This speaks directly to the problem security for costs is designed to address – a debtor's inability or unwillingness to pay – as opposed to the systemic issues addressed by the *New York Convention.*

(2) Control mechanism against unmeritorious claims, improper conduct, and excessive cost and delay

9.10. International commercial arbitration has few summary or other procedures to deal effectively with (a) unmeritorious claims, (b) improper conduct, and (c) excessive cost and delay. The few procedures it has are extreme in their consequences, such as the claim or defence being dismissed, causing hesitation in tribunals for fear of the award being set aside for not giving the vanquished the proper opportunity of presenting its case.[17] Most of the summary disposition procedures are of relatively recent origin and are largely untested in the courts.[18]

---

11 Judith Gill and Matthew Hodgson, 'Costs Awards – Who Pays?' (2015) 10(4) *Global Arbitration Review* 2 <https://www.allenovery.com/en-gb/global/news-and-insights/publications/costs-awards-who-pays-judith-gill-qc-and-matthew-hodgson>.

12 *Re the Minister for Immigration and Ethnic Affairs of the Commonwealth of Australia; Ex parte Lai Qin* (1997) 186 CLR 622, 625.

13 Gill and Hodgson (n 11) 20, Charts 5 and 6.

14 Producing an asymmetry between the parties: ibid 18.

15 Queen Mary University – PwC, *International Arbitration: Corporate Attitudes and Practice 2008* 5, 6.

16 *QMUL 2006* (n 9) 3. Only 17% of participants reported state hostility to recognition and enforcement, although this did not always result in non-enforcement.

17 Contrary to art 18, and in pursuance of art 34(2)(a)(ii) of the *Model Law*. English courts have indicated, obiter, that the use of summary judgment procedures can be consistent with giving each party a fair opportunity to present its case: Charlie Caher and Jonathan Lim, 'Summary Disposition Procedures in International Arbitration' in *The International Comparative Legal Guide to: International Arbitration 2018* (Global Legal Group, 2018) [43] (citing *Travis Coal Restructuring Holdings LLC v Essar Global Fund Limited* [2014] EWHC 2510 (Comm) [47]).

18 Ibid [41]. Note the power of summary disposition in s 7 of the *Arbitration Bill 2023* (UK) introducing s 39A into the *Arbitration Act 1996* (UK).

(2a) Unmeritorious claims

9.11. Participants in the Queen Mary Surveys in 2018[19] and 2019[20] expressed an increasing desire for summary disposal methods and expedited procedures to deal with claims perceived to be unmeritorious.

9.12. When asked in the 2021 Queen Mary Survey what adaptations would make other institutions or rules more attractive to users, 25% named provision of expedited procedures, 21% said rules giving extensive case management powers to arbitrators including robust sanctions in relation to the behaviour of parties and counsel, and 18% selected provision for summary determination/dismissal of unmeritorious claims.[21]

9.13. Applicants for summary disposal must meet the very high threshold of showing that a claim or defence is manifestly devoid of merit or falls manifestly outside the arbitral tribunal's jurisdiction.[22] Tribunals hesitate to use summary disposal powers due to the absence of express powers in institutional rules, concerns about due process and the enforceability of resulting awards, and cultural prejudices against such procedures.[23] Support appears to be growing in the arbitral community for summary disposition powers,[24] and more institutions are empowering tribunals to dispose of cases summarily,[25] suggesting that a less drastic, less final form of disposal with a lower threshold of satisfaction may be attractive to parties, counsel, and tribunals.

9.14. Security for costs may be seen as a less drastic form of control than summary disposal with a lower threshold for satisfaction. Poor merits may be taken into account to order the claimant to provide security and in fixing the amount of security, rather than the only options under summary disposal methods being dismissal or not.[26] If security is

19 Queen Mary University of London and White & Case, 2018 International Arbitration Survey: The Evolution of International Arbitration 27 ('QMUL 2018').

20 Queen Mary University and Pinset Masons, International Arbitration Survey: Driving Efficiency in International Construction Disputes 6, 27 ('QMUL 2019').

21 Queen Mary University of London and White & Case, 2021 International Arbitration Survey: Adapting arbitration to a changing world 12, Chart 8 ('QMUL 2021').

22 For example, under art 22 of the ICC 2021 Rules and the *Note to Parties and Arbitral Tribunals on the Conduct of the Arbitration under the ICC Rules of Arbitration* (ICC, 2021) [110]. See also Gary Born and Kenneth Beale, 'Party Autonomy and Default Rules: Reframing the Debate Over Summary Judgment Disposition in International Arbitration' (2010) 21(2) *ICC International Court of Arbitration Bulletin* 19, 24–6.

23 Born and Beale (n 22) 21.

24 Ibid 22; Judith Gill, 'Applications for the Early Disposition of Claims in Arbitration Proceedings' in Albert van den Berg (ed), *50 Years of the New York Convention: ICCA International Arbitration Conference* (ICCA, 2009) 521–2; Lauran San Roman Guijarro, 'Summary Disposition – The Only Way Out Is Through' (2012) 66 *University of Miami Law Review* 879, 896; Robert Dawes, 'Dispositive Motions – A Step Change?' *Kluwer Arbitration Blog* (Blog Post, 12 August 2020) <http://arbitrationblog.kluwerarbitration.com/2020/08/12/dispositive-motions-a-step-change/>; Charlie Caher and Jonathan Lim, 'Summary Disposition Procedures in International Arbitration' *The International Comparative Legal Guide to International Arbitration 2018* (Global Legal Group, 15th ed, 2018) 1 [1]–[3]; David Ryan and Kanaga Dharmananda, 'Summary Disposal in Arbitration: Still Fair or Agreed to Be Fair' (2018) 35(1) *Journal of International Arbitration* 31; Michael M Collins, 'Summary Disposition in International Arbitration' in Albert Jan Van den Berg (ed), *50 Years of the New York Convention: ICCA International Arbitration Conference*, ICCA Conference Series, Volume 14 (Kluwer, 2009) 532; James P Duffy, 'Chapter 13: Dispositive Motions and the Summary Disposition of Claims in International Arbitration' in Laurence Shore et al. (eds), *International Arbitration in the United States* (Kluwer, 2018) 275; David L Wallach, 'The Emergence of Early Disposition Procedures in International Arbitration' (2021) 37 *Arbitration International* 835.

25 By at least 2010, JAMS Rules 2010 r 18; in 2011, ICDR 'Guidelines on Early Disposition of Issues in Arbitration; in 2016, SIAC Rules 2016 r 29; in 2017 SCC Rules 2017 art 39 and the ICC 'Note to parties and Arbitral Tribunals on the Conduct of the Arbitration Under the Rules of Arbitration' asserting a power of expeditious determination under ICC Rules art 22; in 2018, HKIAC Rules 2018 art 43; in 2020, LCIA Rules 2020 art 22.1.

26 Born and Beale (n 22) 24–6.

ordered, the claimant has the opportunity of obtaining funds and providing security including through third party funding or otherwise. Funders take the merits and size of the case into account in deciding whether or not to fund claims.[27] Unavailability of finance may be a further indicator of poor prospects of success but will only result, in the short term, in the arbitration being stayed rather than dismissed.[28] If the perception of the merits improves, for example through new evidence or arguments, funds may become available and the stay lifted.

(2b) Improper conduct

9.15. There are few mechanisms in international commercial arbitration to deal with improper conduct by party and counsel, with the tribunal not having the coercive power of a court nor the reach into international lawyers' regulating bodies.[29] Guerilla tactics are said to be 'quickly becoming a global epidemic in international arbitration', ranging from having nuisance effect to completely derailing the proceedings.[30] The problem is seen as growing with the 'tremendous increase in the number and diversity of new entrants to the global arbitration . . . from myriad legal traditions and their own conceptions of what constitutes ethically acceptable conduct'.[31] Ethical standards have been developed after much debate but are still difficult to enforce.[32]

9.16. Four leading authors suggest security for costs may be used as a tool for tribunals to control guerilla tactics and other improper conduct,[33] three of them lamenting that the facility is only available in exceptional circumstances.[34] Improper conduct of the parties or counsel is a proper consideration in allocating costs between the parties,[35] and in the imposition of security for costs as a sanction and to compensate, potentially, the respondent for costs incurred as a result.[36]

(2c) Cost and delay

9.17. It has been suggested that unrestricted costs-shifting encourages parties to take excessive steps to ensure the other party pays them.[37] Whether that is true or not, costs can quickly escalate with counsel feeling the obligation to take all available steps.[38]

---

27 See [7.26].

28 See [8.59] et seq.

29 VV Veeder, 'The 2001 Goff Lecture – The Lawyer's Duty to Arbitrate in Good Faith' (2002) 18(4) *Arbitration International* 431.

30 Günther J Horvath and Stephan Wilske, 'Conclusion and Outlook' in Günther J Horvath and Stephan Wilske (eds), *Guerilla Tactics in International Arbitration* (Kluwer, 2013) 341, 342 [6.01].

31 Sundaresh Menon, 'Adjudicator, Advocate, or Something in Between? Coming to Terms with the Role of the Party-Appointed Arbitrator' (2017) 34 *Journal of International Arbitration* 347, 354 ('Adjudicator, Advocate or Something in Between?').

32 For example, the IBA Guidelines on Party Representation (2013); Doak Bishop and Margrete Stevens, 'The Compelling Need for a Code of Ethics in International Arbitration: Transparency, Integrity and Legitimacy' 5 <https://www.josemigueljudice-arbitration.com/xms/files/02_TEXTOS_ARBITRAGEM/01_Doutrina_ScolarsTexts/ethics/ethics_in_int_arb_-_icca_2010_-_bishop.pdf>.

33 Horvath, Wilske and Leinwather (n 5) 43 [2.01][A][3][a]; Reed (n 5) 99 [2.04][A][2][b]; Horvath and Wilske (n 5) 351 [6.06].

34 Horvath, Wilske and Leinwather (n 5).

35 ICC Arbitration Commission, *Report on Techniques for Controlling Time and Costs in Arbitration* (Report, 2018) ('*Techniques for Controlling Time and Costs*') 15[82].

36 *Hong Kong Company v Vendor Company* (Award, SIAC, 21 October 2011) reported in [2012] 1 Singapore Arbitration Awards 127 ('*Hong Kong Company v Vendor Company*').

37 Neil Kaplan, 'Winter of Discontent' (2017) 34 *Journal of International Arbitration* 384.

38 Alan Redfern, 'The Changing World of International Arbitration' in David D Caron et al. (eds), *Practising Virtue: Inside International Arbitration* (Oxford University Press, 2015) 45–51.

9.18. Security for costs may be used to encourage a measure of proportionality in the claimant's conduct and the steps it effectively forces the respondent to take,[39] within the bounds of tribunal propriety.[40] Costs are often disproportionate.[41] For example, if a claimant increases the quantification of its claim, with an intention or effect of causing financial distress to the respondent in having to increase its advance on tribunal fees, a requirement that the claimant provide an amount of security equivalent to the increase in the advance would assist in ensuring re-quantifications are genuine.[42] A tribunal could determine whether there was sufficient substance to the revaluation not to require security. Likewise, if the claimant has proposed or takes excessive interlocutory steps,[43] the respondent could seek security to cover its increased costs of responding to them.[44]

9.19. One of the techniques for reducing time and cost suggested by ICC and writers is for tribunals to address both expressly early in the proceeding and to exert more control over the proceeding.[45] An application for security for costs provides that opportunity, being required to be made without inexplicable delay[46] and with the applicant evidencing the costs it expects to incur, with a justification for their expenditure.[47] Having that material before it enables the tribunal to express views on the necessity for proposed steps and evidence, their extent and cost, and, in appropriate cases, to direct they not be taken,[48] or to exclude the costs of unnecessary or excessive steps from the quantum of security ordered.[49]

9.20. Delay has been a perennial problem in international commercial arbitration[50] with users complaining regularly[51] and guides published on how to reduce the time of arbitrations.[52] Time in arbitration has been suggested as one of the twin causes of all international commercial arbitration's ills and is intertwined with costs.[53] Security for

39 There should be proportionality between the amount in dispute and the costs to be incurred for which security is sought: *Hercules Carparking Systems 2004 Pty Ltd v Gennie Holdings Pty Ltd* [2021] NSWDC 50 [39].

40 The extent to which tribunals should be concerned that the time and cost of a case are proportionate to its value and difficulty is contentious in its balancing of fairness and efficiency: Jeffrey Waincymer, *Procedure and Evidence in International Arbitration* (Kluwer, 2012) 22 [1.2.11].

41 Sachs (n 6) [5.31].

42 See [5.42].

43 For example, the fierce battles on procedural issues such as challenging the jurisdiction of the tribunal, the extension of the arbitration clause to a non-signatory, challenges against an arbitrator, requests for various forms of interim relief, voluminous document requests and provision, and challenges to claims for privilege: Sachs (n 6) [5.37]; *Nasser v United Bank of Kuwait* [2002] 1 WLR 1868 [60] ('*Nasser*'). [30]; Sam Luttrell, *Bias Challengers in International Commercial Arbitration* (Kluwer, 2009) 3–5.

44 *Hong Kong Company v Vendor Company* (n 36).

45 *Techniques for Controlling Time and Costs* (n 35) 15 [82]; Kaplan (n 37) 375, 383; Sachs (n 6) [5.40]–[5.41]; David W Brown, 'What Steps Should Arbitrators Take to Limit the Cost of Arbitration?' (2014) 31(4) *Journal of International Arbitration* 499, 500–1.

46 See [5.42].

47 Stephen Colbran, *Security for Costs* (Longman, 1993) 277–8 [15.13].

48 *CBS v CBP* [2021] SGCA 4 [61]–[62] where the Singapore Court of Appeal said that tribunals may limit evidence and other steps as part of the broad, general case management power to ensure the just, expeditious, economical, and final determination of the dispute, subject to the fundamental rules of natural justice.

49 Kaplan (n 37) 385; *Al-Koronky v Time-Life Entertainment Group Ltd* [2006] EWCA Civ 1123 [28] ('*Al-Koronky*').

50 Sachs (n 6) [5.38]

51 For example, Quen Mary University of London – White & Case, *2018 International Arbitration Survey: The Evolution of International Arbitration* 5.

52 For example, *Techniques for Controlling Time and Costs* (n 35).

53 Kaplan (n 37) 375.

costs may be used to curb unnecessary or inefficient procedural steps that serve mainly to delay the proceedings.

(3) Procedural fairness and access to justice

9.21. Security for costs may enhance procedural fairness by assisting to recalibrate the imbalance between the parties created by a claimant's effective immunity from costs orders. It can help ensure respondents have more adequate access to *justice* as opposed to mere access to the *tribunal*.

9.22. Concerns that security for costs will undermine procedural fairness or access to justice are typically viewed from the perspective of the claimant only,[54] arguing, for example, that being required to provide security will place an unfair burden only on the claimant.[55] It can be overlooked that the respondent is also entitled to procedural fairness and access to justice. The requirement of fairness is bilateral[56] including where article 6 of the *European Convention on Human Rights* applies.[57]

9.23. Two components of procedural fairness in international arbitration under art 18 of the *Model Law* are (a) equality of treatment and (b) an adequate opportunity to present a case.[58]

(3a) Equality of treatment

9.24. At one time it was suggested a consequence of the requirement of equality of treatment demanded that, if the claimant be ordered to provide security, the respondent should also.[59] This misunderstands both the duty to treat the parties with equality and the circumstances in which security for costs will be granted.

9.25. Treating the parties 'with equality' is not the same as affording them 'equal treatment', the common, misleading, shorthand for the duty. Aristotle asserted that identical treatment of unequal people is not equality.[60] Being treated with equality entails treating comparable situations equally and dealing appropriately with differences, and aspires to substantive rather than formalistic equality.[61] Equality of treatment may also be achieved by some reciprocity or mutuality other than by identical treatment.[62]

9.26. To treat the parties with equality, 'it is necessary to consider in detail the *circumstances of the parties' respective positions*, claims and evidence, and the arbitral process

54 *Al-Koronky* (n 49); *Rowe v Ingenious Media Holdings plcs* [2021] EWCA Civ 29 [82] ('*Rowe v Ingenious*').

55 Waincymer (n 40) 643 [8.3.1].

56 James Allsop, 'National Courts and Arbitration: Collaboration or Competition?' (2015) 81(4) *Arbitration: The International Journal of Arbitration, Mediation and Dispute Management* 434, 436 ('Allsop, National Courts and Arbitration').

57 *Rowe v Ingenious* (n 54) [56], citing *Al-Koronky* (n 49).

58 Emanating from art 18 of the *Model Law* and the grounds under it and the *New York Convention* for refusing to recognize and enforce awards: Waincymer (n 40) 16 [1.2.5]; Blackaby and Partasides (n 1) 586–7 [10.53]; Ryan and Dharmananda (n 24) 35, 55.

59 Otto Sandrock, 'The Cautio Judicatum Solvi in Arbitration Proceedings or the Duty of an Alien Claimant to Provide Security for the Costs of the Defendant' (1997) 14 *Journal of International Arbitration* 17, 34.

60 Waincymer (n 40) 16 [1.2.6], citing Aristotle, *Nichomacheon Ethics*, trans Martin Ostwald (Prentice Hall, 1999) 1131a22–25.

61 Waincymer (n 40) 16–17, 82, citing Tina Wüstermann and Cesare Jermini, 'Minimal Procedural Requirements (Part 1)' in Tobias Zuberhühler, Christoph Müller and Phillip Habegger (eds), *Swiss Rules of International Arbitration Commentary* (Kluwer, 2007) 64; Gary Born, *International Commercial Arbitration* (Kluwer, 3rd ed, 2021) 2174 [15.04[B]].

62 For example, as in the experience related in Gill and Hodgson (n 11) 21; Born (n 61) 2174.

as a whole'.[63] It is not limited to mere mechanical aspects such as the number of submissions or time in hearings. A test to ensure the parties are being treated with equality is to ask whether the same procedural decision would be made if the parties' positions were reversed.[64] The 'circumstances of the parties' respective positions'[65] would include their financial and other positions relative to each other and relevant to the claimant's ability and willingness to satisfy a costs award.

9.27. When a security for costs order is made, taking into account all of the discretionary factors relevant in that case, it necessarily implies that the parties' positions are not equal. The claimant is found, in effect, to be unwilling or unable to pay the respondent's costs, leaving the claimant free to force the respondent into arbitration or fierce procedural battles[66] and to incur costs in response to steps taken by the claimant, with the claimant secure in the knowledge that it will never pay the respondent's costs. Waincymer suggests this is an extreme example justifying security for costs.[67]

9.28. The playing field is not level, and it should be.[68] There is an asymmetry of resources, power, liability, and choice. The claimant has the choice of whether to sue or not, a decision it makes after considering the likelihood of success, the costs involved, and the chances of the respondent satisfying any award. That last assessment will sensibly be made after researching the respondent's finances and assets, its attitudes to payment, and the enforcement regime. It has the choice of when to sue before any limitation period expires, and the amount of preparation it wishes to undertake before launching proceedings.[69] It may bring frivolous or exaggerated claims for their nuisance value or for strategic reasons.[70] Costs-shifting is said to deter a number of those claims, indicating that they are costs-sensitive.[71] A freedom from liability to costs removes that deterrence, requiring something more than the potential for costs to shift. Security for costs provides the additional deterrent.

9.29. On the other hand, the respondent's choice is simply to defend or surrender; as Veit says, where the claimant is impecunious, the respondent loses either way – ignoring the claim will likely result in an award against it, and defending the claim will result in an unsatisfied costs award. He suggests that, '[t]o re-establish the balance in such a situation, security for costs should not be the exception but the rule'.[72] Redfern and O'Leary, speaking of the same invidious choice facing a respondent, say that usually 'the safer option is for the defending party to take arms against a sea of troubles rather than to quietly suffer the slings and arrows of outrageous fortune'.[73] Compounding the

63 Ibid 2174–5 [emphasis added].

64 Ibid.

65 Ibid.

66 (n 43).

67 Waincymer (n 40) 643 [8.3.1].

68 Alan Redfern and Sam O'Leary, 'Why It Is Time for International Arbitration to Embrace Security for Costs' (2016) 32 *Arbitration International* 412; Born (n 61) 2173.

69 The length of pre-commencement preparation is acknowledged to tip the scales in favour of the claimant: Born (n 61) 2174.

70 Micha Bühler, 'Awarding Costs in International Commercial Arbitration' (2004) 22(2) *ASA Bulletin* 249, 268.

71 Ibid.

72 Marc D Veit, 'Note: Procedural Order No. 14 of 27 November 2002: Security for Costs in International Arbitration: Some Comments to Procedural Order No. 14 of 27 November 2002' (2005) 23(1) *ASA Bulletin* 116, 117.

73 Redfern and O'Leary (n 68) 397, 398.

respondent's dilemma, rarely do respondents have access to third party funding,[74] and must prepare their defence in a much shorter time than that available to the claimant who has bided its time.[75]

9.30. Security for costs has the potential to rebalance the field to compensate the respondent for its lack of options and, above all, the claimant's decision to sue combined with its inability to pay costs, or its intention not to pay,[76] or its access to third party funding[77] or contingency based representation.[78] Commencing a claim knowing that an adverse costs order cannot or will not be paid is arguably a breach of the duty implied in arbitration agreements to arbitrate in good faith.[79]

9.31. This form of equality is achieved by the *Model Law* in art 17G which renders an applicant for interim measures liable for any costs and damages caused to the claimant, if the tribunal later determines that the measure should not have been granted. Article 17G provides a means to redress any imbalance inadvertently caused by an order for security for costs where no costs order is ultimately made in the respondent's favour.[80] The combined mechanism of security for costs and liability for costs and damages operates, first, by overcoming the imbalance in favour of the claimant to more of a balanced position, and, secondly, to recalibrate the balance back towards the claimant if that rebalancing overcompensated the respondent or if the order was wrongly made.

(3b) Opportunity to present case

9.32. The second component of procedural fairness under art 18 of the *Model Law* is that 'each party shall be given a full opportunity of presenting his case'. Respondents are entitled to the same level of procedural fairness as claimants.[81] A claimant unconstrained by potential liability for costs is able to indulge in guerilla tactics and excessive interlocutory steps, subject only to the tribunal's procedural control tempered by due process concerns. Forcing the respondent to respond to those steps and expend time and funds on them has the real potential of depriving a respondent who is concerned with costs of an opportunity of presenting its case. Resources intended to be expended on defending the claim must be diverted to unproductive procedural maneuvres. Tribunals can redress this imbalance by requiring security either of the whole claim or as a condition of permitting the requesting party to take the desired step.[82]

9.33. Imposing security for costs in those circumstances is not an encroachment on the injunction to give each party a full opportunity of presenting his case. That obligation is not absolute and is discharged by giving the parties a reasonable and fair opportunity.[83]

---

74 ICCA–Queen Mary Task Force, *Report on Third-Party Funding in International Arbitration* (Report, ICCA and QMUL, April 2018) 166 ('*ICCA Report on Third-Party Funding*') 20–1, 23–4.

75 Waincymer (n 40) 82 [2.7.6]; Born (n 61) 2174.

76 Redfern and O'Leary (n 68) 412; Gill and Hodgson (n 11) 21; John Beechey, 'International Arbitrations and the Award of Security for Costs in England' (1994) 12 *ASA Bulletin* 179, 190.

77 *Nasser* (n 43) [60].

78 Waincymer (n 40) 643 [8.3.1].

79 Born (n 61) 1009–10; Waincymer (n 40) 753 [10.3.3].

80 *Rowe v Ingenious* (n 54) [64].

81 Ibid; Allsop, 'National Courts and Arbitration' (n 56) 436.

82 See [5.46].

83 Sundaresh Menon, 'Dispelling Due Process Paranoia: Fairness, Efficiency and the Rule of Law' (2021) 17(1) *Asian International Arbitration Journal* 1 [24] ('*Due process paranoia*'), citing Blackaby and Partasides (n 1) 357 [6.14], *China Machine New Energy Corp v Jaguar Energy Guatemala LLC* [2020] SGCA 12, *Terna*

(3c) Access to justice

9.34. Respondents are as equally entitled to access to justice as claimants, and have an entitlement to have claimants' access limited by relevant and proportionate conditions.[84] Access to justice does not merely mean access to arbitration or the courts, but to justice through those mechanisms. Respondents' ability to achieve justice, in the form of satisfaction of an award of costs duly made after an agreed process of adjudication, is denied if they are unable to obtain that satisfaction. Security for costs has been developed to mitigate that risk where it appears during the proceedings that the claimant will be unable or unwilling to pay. In that way, it provides access to justice, as opposed merely to access to arbitration.

(4) Enabling tribunals to correct injustices

9.35. Lord Mustill said in 1994 that parties choose arbitration for better or for worse and that, when the worst happens, there is a limit to when they can run to the courts for help. Sometimes, he said, the courts should not intervene to correct an injustice even though 'on a narrower view it appears to answer the justice of the case'.[85] He declined to grant security for costs in that case, not because it was not justified, but because he believed the court should not intervene in an ICC arbitration with no connection to England other than its being the seat.[86]

9.36. Now that it is clear that tribunals have the power to order security for costs,[87] the facility would enable them to correct potential injustices such as a claimant, or someone standing behind a claimant, prosecuting a weak claim where it is effectively immune from an adverse costs order.[88]

(5) Counter-balancing the judicialisation of arbitration

9.37. Interlocutory procedures and tactics have multiplied in international commercial arbitration over the decades so that it now resembles 'offshore litigation'[89] following the dominance of Anglo-American law firms in the system, seen as 'the defining feature affecting the industry today'.[90] A result is that arbitration has become judicialised,[91] or

Bahrain Holding Co v Ali Marzook Ali Bin Kamil Al Shamsi [2012] EWHC 3283 (Comm), *ASM Shipping Ltd of India v TTMI Ltd of England* [2005] EWHC 2238 (Comm), *ALS & Assocs v AGM Marine Constructors Inc* 557 F Supp 2d 180 (D Mass 2008), *T Reasuransi Umum Indonesia v Evanston Ins Co*, XIX YB Comm Arb 788, 790 (US District Court, SDNY 1992), *Trustees of Rotoaira Forest Trust v Attorney-General* [1999] 2 NZLR 452 and cases from Spain and the People's Republic of China.

84 Article 6 of the *European Convention on Human Rights*; *Rowe v Ingenious* (n 54) [56], citing *Al-Koronky* (n 49).

85 *Coppée–Lavalin v Ken–Ren Chemicals and Fertilizers Ltd (in liquidation in Kenya)* [1995] 1 AC38, 65D ('*Coppée–Lavalin v Ken–Ren*') 65E–F.

86 See [4.26] – [4.28].

87 See Chapter 4.

88 The 'classic example' given by Redfern and O'Leary (n 68) 399, and the 'Heads I win, and Tails I do not lose' 'gambler's nirvana' envisaged by Gavan Griffith QC in his Assenting Reasons in *RSM Production Corporation v Saint Lucia* (Decision, ICSID, Case No ARB/12/10, 13 August 2014) [13].

89 Roger P Alford, 'The American Influence on International Arbitration' (2003) 19(1) *Ohio State Journal on Dispute Resolution* 69, 80, 83, 88.

90 Ibid 88.

91 Sundaresh Menon, *International Commercial Courts: Towards a Transnational System of Dispute Resolution* (Speech, Dubai International Financial Centre Courts Lecture Series 2015, 22 January 2015) [13], [47] ('Towards a Transnational System'); Alan Redfern, 'The Changing World of International Arbitration' in David D Caron et al. (eds), *Practising Virtue: Inside International Arbitration* (Oxford University Press, 2015) 45, 49.

'industrialised',[92] 'relentlessly professional',[93] and has taken on more of the characteristics of adversarial common law litigation.[94] These include not only the general adversarial style but procedures such as party witnesses, cross-examination and document production,[95] depositions, evidentiary principles and practices,[96] and, in its extreme form, repeated demands for the tribunal to resolve discovery or other pre-arbitration disputes, and lack of cooperation and frequent objections.[97] Due process paranoia is perceived to allow some offending parties to engage in that conduct, with little meaningful compensation to the other party.[98] An order for costs thrown away by the conduct is not a panacea.[99] The lack of effective sanctions during the arbitral process was the second cause for dissatisfaction of users reported in the 2015 Queen Mary University survey, following closely behind costs, said to indicate tribunal inaction.[100] Users complained that, while the system and its costs have approximated or exceeded those of litigation, it does not have all of the latter's procedural safeguards and appellate rights.[101]

9.38. Security for costs can provide a procedural safeguard and counter-balance to such developments by providing an option for a condition on indulgences to and requests by parties, particularly where a denial of the request might amount to a denial of procedural fairness, but where granting the request would prejudice the other party. In those circumstances, an order for security for costs may balance the competing interests of the parties.[102] It is anomalous to import many of the interlocutory processes from litigation but to exclude a very useful facility such as security for costs which has its own self-contained controls and limitors and which often acts in combination with those imported processes to temper their operation.

9.39. It may appear paradoxical to attempt to meet judicialisation with another judicial facility, yet this facility may be useful as described if the circumstances of its exercise are clear and consistent, with the result that applications become routine (not meaning common) and are determined speedily and cheaply on well-understood principles.[103]

(6) Facilitate settlement

9.40. Respondents to the 2019 Queen Mary University of London – Pinsent Masons International Arbitration Survey – Driving Efficiency in International Construction

---

92 Allsop, 'Commercial and Investor-State Arbitration' (n 6) [38].

93 Redfern (n 38) 46.

94 Ibid 83.

95 Susan L Karamanian, 'Overstating the "Americanization" of International Arbitration: Lessons from ICSID' (2003) 19(1) *Ohio State Journal on Dispute Resolution* 5, 10–14.

96 Ibid 14–17.

97 Ibid 17–19.

98 Menon, 'Due Process Paranoia' (n 83).

99 *Queensland v JL Holdings Pty Ltd* (1997) 189 CLR 146, 155, 170–1.

100 Doug Jones, 'Using Costs Orders to Control the Expense of International Commercial Arbitration' (2016) 82(3) *International Journal of Arbitration, Mediation and Dispute Management* 291, 292.

101 Redfern (n 38) 49.

102 For example, Jones cites two instances of using costs orders to balance the rights of the parties where late adjournments were granted: (n 100) 300–1. In both of those situations, security for costs would have been an effective and proper condition to impose on granting the adjournments: *Michael Wilson & Partners, Limited v Emmott* [2020] NSWCA 245 [4]; *Goldus Pty Ltd (Subject to a Deed of Company Arrangement) v Cummins* [2020] FCA 959 [22].

103 See [4.31] and *K/S A/S Bani v Korea Shipbuiding and Engineering Corporation* [1987] 2 Lloyd's Rep 445, 448, quoted in *Coppée–Lavalin v Ken–Ren* (n 85) 69G–70B.

Disputes gave using case management conferences to help reach settlement and facilitating settling as characteristics of an efficient international construction arbitration. A security for costs application and ruling directs attention to the merits, even if superficially, and provides an opportunity for the parties and the tribunal to assess costs against the prospects of recovery. Comments by the tribunal in its reasons for decision – even if heavily caveated – may reveal strengths or weaknesses in a party's case and facilitate settlement.

B. For the institution of arbitration

9.41. Section A considered the possible benefits of security for costs to the parties to an arbitration. This section considers potential benefits the facility may bring to the institution of arbitration.

(7) A rich source of jurisprudence and guidance

9.42. The dearth of published decisions on security for costs in international commercial arbitration has hindered the growth of jurisprudence on the topic and has deprived tribunals and practitioners of useful references in applications for security. The Departmental Advisory Committee drafting what became the *Arbitration Act 1996* (UK) received a number of responses expressing concern that there were no principles or guidelines for the exercise of the security for costs power in the draft of s 38.[104] While acknowledging this, the committee felt that codification of all the relevant case law and principles 'carefully worked out over many years' would be extremely difficult, and would result in very lengthy and complicated provisions.[105] Haridi noted in 2021 that there were relatively few resources available to guide counsel and tribunals.[106]

9.43. Adopting the multifactorial approach to security for costs would immediately make available over 200 years of jurisprudence and guidance from numerous, established jurisdictions – UK, Australia, Singapore, New Zealand, Hong Kong, and Canada, to name the more obvious – where the principles have been 'carefully worked out over many years'.[107]

(8) Uniformity within international commercial arbitration

9.44. It is evident from the decisions and statistics examined in Chapter 4 that there is a lack of uniformity in the approaches taken within international commercial arbitration to security for costs. Adopting one approach would naturally bring greater uniformity.

(9) Attraction and competitiveness of international commercial arbitration

9.45. With questions being raised of international commercial arbitration's legitimacy, including the universal concerns over time and cost, there is a need to improve the attraction of international commercial arbitration and to enhance its competitiveness, not only with state courts, but with the new international commercial courts being created in

104 Departmental Advisory Committee, Parliament of the United Kingdom, *Report on the Arbitration Bill* (Final Report, February 1996) [364] ('*DAC Report*').

105 Ibid [365].

106 Samaa AF Haridi, 'Security for Costs and Claim under the ICC Rules of Arbitration – Rare, But Possible' (2020) 2 *ICC Dispute Resolution Bulletin* 77, 78.

107 *DAC Report* (n 104) [365].

respected jurisdictions. While international commercial courts are promoted as being complementary to, and not in competition with, international commercial arbitration,[108] they are partly (if not largely)[109] created to respond to the perceived deficiencies of international commercial arbitration.[110] International commercial arbitration will suffer if the courts do this well and international commercial arbitration fails to improve. In the words of then Chief Justice Allsop of the Australian Federal Court, 'if arbitration cannot exist as an efficient and cost effective means of dispute resolution then it will simply not find favour with commercial parties'.[111]

9.46. Security for costs is not proffered here as a panacea, but in its less restricted form it may provide a tool to deal with the issues and may assist in maintaining international commercial arbitration's position, particularly when considering a respondent's concern to protect itself from impecunious claimants with weak claims, and in the absence of clear methods of summary disposition.

(10) Harmonisation of arbitration and litigation

9.47. Harmonisation of the international commercial arbitration and common law litigation systems is not necessarily desirable for its own sake but creates a 'useful symmetry in the law'[112] and has attractions of enhancing dispute resolution options for parties, reducing transaction costs at the time of the agreement[113] and at the time of the dispute[114] by having fewer differences between systems, by having a wealth of authority available for practitioners in international commercial arbitration, by having clearer, more readily accessible standards,[115] and, over time, enabling the systems to learn and develop from each other to refine the facility further.[116] Allsop suggests that the approach to the issue of litigation vs arbitration should be to recognise and harness the best of procedures of arbitration and courts in dispute resolution generally.[117] Transaction costs are directly related to the volume of economic activity and over-all economic well-being.[118]

108 For example, Allsop, 'National Courts and Arbitration' (n 56) 438.
109 Menon, 'Towards a Transnational System' (n 91) [13]–[15], [56].
110 Ibid [10]; Allsop, 'National Courts and Arbitration' (n 56) 438.
111 Allsop, 'Commercial and Investor-State Arbitration' (n 6) 14.
112 Penny Tridimas, 'The Long and the Short of It: Introducing a Summary Procedure for the Dismissal of Unmeritorious Claims in the Arbitration Act 1996' (Essay, Bar Council, 2019) 8 <https://www.barcouncil.org.uk/uploads/assets/46c948b3-f7aa-4c23-b8bb0917a5feb99f/firstprizeessay.pdf>.
113 Benjamin Hayward, *Conflict of Laws and Arbitral Discretion* (Oxford University Press, 2017) 158–60 [4.34]–4.38].
114 Ibid 151–5 [4.14]–[4.22].
115 Ibid.
116 Allsop, 'National Courts and Arbitration' (n 56) 437.
117 Ibid.
118 Hayward (n 113) 150 [4.11], citing the Coase Theorem.

CHAPTER 10

Security for costs in international investment arbitration

Introduction

10.1. Security for costs has traditionally been restricted to proof of exceptional circumstances in international investment arbitration (IAA), perhaps to a greater extent than in international commercial arbitration (ICA).[1]

10.2. Reasons given for the narrow approach have been the origins of IAA in state-to-state dispute settlement, the public international law elements of IAA, states having designed the system of IAA and negotiated the terms of the relevant treaty, a history of no costs-shifting in IAA, states having assumed the risk of dealing with investors, maintaining access to justice, and the exceptionality of provisional measures.[2]

10.3. Orders for security for costs have been made in the 2014 ICSID case of *RSM v Sant Lucia*,[3] the 2018 UNCITRAL case of *Amas v Venezuela*,[4] the 2020 ICSID case of *Unionmatex v Turkmenistan*,[5] and the 2020 ICSID case of *Kazmin v Latvia*.[6]

The need

10.4. A 2015 study of the rate of satisfaction of IAA costs awards found that a much lower proportion of respondent states were paid without enforcement than claimant investors – 46% of states compared to 71% of investors were paid without enforcement, voluntarily or through settlement. Twice the number of states were paid nothing at all compared to investors – 37% of states and 19% of investors received no payment on their costs award.[7]

---

1 See Chapter 4.

2 Christine Sim, 'Security for Costs in Investor-State Arbitration' (2017) (33) *Arbitration International* 427. See also for a detailed analysis of IAA decisions on security for costs and a discussion of the policies engaged.

3 *RSM v St Lucia* (ICSID ARB/12/10) Decision on St Lucia's Request for Security for Costs (13 August 2014), Decision on St Lucia's Request for Suspension or Discontinuation of Proceedings (8 April 2015) ('*RSM v St Lucia*').

4 *Manuel García Armas et al. v Bolivarian Republic of Venezuela*, PCA Case No. 2016–08, Procedural Order 9, Decision on Respondent's Request for Provisional Measures (20 June 2018) ('*Amas v Venezuela*').

5 *Dirk Kerzig as Insolvency Administrator over the assets of Unionmatex Industrieanlagen GmbH v Turkmenistan* (UCSID Case No. ARB/18/35 Decision on Security for Costs on (27 January 2020) ('*Unionmatex*').

6 *Eugene Kazmin v Republic of Latvia*, ICSID Case No. ARB/17/5, Procedural Order No. 6 (Decision on the Respondent's Application for Security for Costs), 13 April 2020 ('*Kazmin v Latvia*').

7 Judith Gill and Matthew Hodgson, 'Costs Awards – Who Pays?' (2015) 10(4) *Global Arbitration Review* 2 <https://www.allenovery.com/en-gb/global/news-and-insights/publications/costs-awards-who-pays-judith-gill-qc-and-matthew-hodgson> 20, Charts 5 and 6.

DOI: 10.4324/9781003479628-10

10.5. These figures strongly suggest the need for a facility to increase the rate of payment of states' costs, particularly given the perception of tribunals' bias in favour of investors.[8]

Juridical basis

10.6. The judicial basis of security for costs in IAA has been given as the protection of the integrity of the arbitral process, which can be seen to be another expression of the basis in ICA and in litigation of prevention of abuse of process.[9]

Power

10.7. Power to order security for costs in IAA is contained in:

(1) Rarely, treaties;
(2) *ICSID Convention*,[10] Article 47 and *ICSID Arbitration Rules*,[11] rule 53;
(3) *UNCITRAL Rules*,[12] Articles 26(2)(c) and 42(1);
(4) Institutional rules;
(5) Inherent powers;
(6) Court rules.

(1) Treaties

10.8. Treaties could include provision for security for costs if states wished to descend to such level of detail in negotiations.[13] A provision for security in the 2016 draft of the Vietnam-EU Free Trade Agreement does not appear to have been included in the final version.

(2) ICSID

10.9. ICSID tribunals have power to award costs,[14] the *sine qua non* of security for costs.[15] Rule 53 of the *ICSID Arbitration Rules* expressly empowers tribunals to order security for costs considering all relevant circumstances including the party's ability and willingness to comply with an adverse decision on costs, the effect that providing security for costs may have on that party's ability to pursue its claim or counterclaim,

---

8 David Riesenberg, 'Fee Shifting in Investor-State Arbitration: Doctrine and Policy, Justifying Application of the English Rule' (2011) 60 *Duke Law Journal* 977, 980.

9 See 2.3, 2.12–2.17.

10 International Centre for the Settlement of Investment Disputes (ICSID), *Convention on the Settlement of Investment Disputes between States and Nationals of other States 1965* ('*ICSID Convention*').

11 *ICSID Arbitration Rules 2022*.

12 *UNCITRAL Arbitration Rules 2021*.

13 See [3.2] as to the unlikelihood of such considerations in commercial negotiations.

14 *Togo Electricité v Togo* (ICSID Case No. ARB/06/07) (ARB/06/07), Decision on Annulment (6 September 2011) [257].

15 See [8.74].

and the conduct of the parties. The tribunal may suspend the arbitration if security is ordered and not provided.

10.10. This rule is similar in effect to the multifactorial, total circumstances approach of common law courts[16] and apparently by LCIA tribunals in ICA, particularly when combined with IAA tribunals' overriding concern of access to justice[17] which equates to the operation of the common law stifling principle – that is, security will not be ordered if to do so would stifle the claim and prevent access to justice.[18]

10.11. ICSID tribunals also have inherent powers to preserve the integrity of the process[19] and may grant provisional measures *proprio motu*.[20]

(3) UNCITRAL

10.12. Costs-shifting to the successful party is the default position under Article 42(1) of the *UNCITRAL Rules*, laying the foundation for security for costs.[21] The power under Article 26(2)(c) to grant interim measures as a means of preserving assets to satisfy an award encompasses security for costs.[22]

(4) Institutional rules

10.13. Rules of institutions are occasionally used for IAA and contain express or implied provision for security for costs.[23]

(5) Inherent powers

10.14. Tribunals are accepted to have inherent powers to order security for costs as part of their ability to protect the integrity of the process.[24]

(6) Court rules

10.15. Parties to ICSID[25] or UNCITRAL[26] arbitrations may seek security for costs from a court with a connection to the dispute.[27] Security for costs is theoretically available from

---

16 See [2.11].

17 *RSM v St Lucia* (n 3) [5.19]; *Unionmatex* (n 3) [64].

18 See [2.47], [5.56]–[5.59], [7.24].

19 Karin Oellers-Frahm, 'Article 41' in Andreas Zimmermann, and others (eds), *The Statute of the International Court of Justice: A Commentary* (OUP, 2006) 923, 945.

20 Régis Bismuth, 'Anatomy of the Law and Practice of Interim Protective Measures in International Investment Arbitration' (2009) 26(6) *Journal of International Arbitration* 773, 782.

21 See [8.74].

22 See [3.5] as to the identical wording in Article 17(2)(c) of the *UNCITRAL Model Law*, and Gabrielle Kaufmann-Kohler and Aurélia Antonietti, 'Interim Relief in International Investment Agreements' in Katia Yannaca-Small (ed), *Arbitration Under International Investment Agreements: A Guide to the Key Issues* (OUP, 2010) 507, 528.

23 See [3.8]. For example, *SIAC Investment Rules* (1st ed, 2017), r 27(1) as to interim relief generally.

24 (n 13); see [3.9] as to the inherent power of tribunals acting under institutional rules.

25 *Atlantic Triton Company Limited v People's Revolutionary Republic of Guinea* (ICSID Case No ARB/84/1) unreported decision (1984) [106].

26 UNCITRAL Model Law, Article 9.

27 *Bank Mellat v Helliniki Techniki SA* [1984] QB 308.

common law courts where the arbitration is under institutional rules but legislation in a number of jurisdictions empowers the tribunal to grant security, encouraging the parties and the court to defer to the tribunal.[28]

Burden and standard of proof

10.16. As with any interim measure, the burden is on the party applying to prove its entitlement. *Kazmin v Latvia* held that the standard of proof is not so strict as for a final decision or a criminal conviction, but 'it is sufficient that the evidence before it makes it more plausible than not that the right of the Respondent to be able to enforce a costs award is at risk'.[29]

10.17. An evidential burden was placed on the investor in *Kazmin v Latvia* in the same manner as in the common law's multifactorial approach.[30] The tribunal said it could not but note the investor's continued insistence on the state's burden of proof without himself producing a single document to dissipate concerns and suspicions[31] or provided any counter-balancing evidence.[32] They said that the investor could have avoided the order by producing convincing and reliable evidence of his assets.[33]

Standard

UNCITRAL

10.18. The *UNCITRAL Rules* mirror the *UNCITRAL Model Law* in requiring an applicant to 'satisfy' the tribunal that:

(a) Harm not adequately reparable by an award of damages is likely to result if the measure is not ordered, and such harm substantially outweighs the harm that is likely to result to the party against whom the measure is directed if the measure is granted; and
(b) There is a reasonable possibility that the requesting party will succeed on the merits of the claim. The determination on this possibility shall not affect the discretion of the arbitral tribunal in making any subsequent determination.

10.19. 'Harm not adequately reparable by an award of damages' is a lower threshold than 'irreparable harm'.[34] The relevant harm suffered to a respondent is the incurrence of costs that will not be repaid by the claimant. That is usually ongoing in an arbitration and satisfies any condition of immediacy or urgency. By definition, the harm will not be reparable if the claimant is unable to pay damages.

---

28 For example, Arbitration Act 1996 (UK) s 38; *International Arbitration Act* (Singapore, cap 143A, rev ed 2007) s 12(1); *Arbitration Ordinance* (Hong Kong) cap 609 ss 56(1)(a); *International Arbitration Act 1974* (Cth) (Australia) s 23K.

29 (n 6) [48].

30 See [3.10], [4.14], [5.57], [6.7], [6.10].

31 (n 6) [48]–[49].

32 Ibid [51].

33 Ibid [61].

34 Howard M Holtzmann et al., *A Guide to the 2006 Amendments to the UNCITRAL Model Law on International Commercial Arbitration* (Kluwer, 2015) 170.

10.20. 'Likely to result' in par (a) directs attention to two aspects – the likelihood of a costs order being made, and the likelihood of the costs order being paid. The first of those raises the merits of the proceeding on the 'loser pays' basis of costs-shifting and is dealt with later when considering par (b). The likelihood of the costs order being paid raises the ability and willingness of the claimant to pay a costs order, and anything logically probative of those predictions.[35]

10.21. The respondent's harm substantially outweighing the claimant's harm requires consideration of proportionality[36] similar to the balance of convenience,[37] or fairness in terms of the touchstone of the multifactorial, total circumstances approach.[38]

10.22. As to par (b) and the reasonable possibility of success, tribunals in ICA and IAA are reluctant to intrude into consideration of the merits for fear of jeopardising the award, but merits are said only to be relevant at the extremes of success or failure, and are otherwise treated as neutral.[39] Consideration of the merits is a preliminary evaluation only and is not to be a mini trial.[40] It has been suggested in ICA that such a preliminary evaluation need not be seen as a prejudgment of the merits[41] and that concerns are not borne out by the results of challenges.[42]

10.23. The determination referred to in the second sentence of par (b) has been interpreted to mean that the tribunal should be careful not to prejudge the merits.[43] Avoidance of prejudgment is axiomatic without that sentence, and it is open to at least two other interpretations. It could be read as an injunction to the tribunal not to allow its determination to affect the final outcome, or as a declaration that the determination is not to be taken as having affected the outcome. The first of those alternatives is more consistent with an earlier draft that the determination not 'prejudice' later findings.[44]

10.24. An holistic, pragmatic approach to the standard of proof is usually taken, having regard to likelihood, degree and character of harm, the perceived prospects of success, and the fairness of who should bear the risks of granting and not granting the measure.[45] With security for costs, these considerations are engaged twice – first in the determination of whether or not to grant security, and then in the assessment of quantum.[46] Arguably they can arise a third time in fixing the form of security.[47]

---

35 See [5.1].

36 Sergei Paushok, *CJSC Golden East Co. and CJSC Vostokneftegaz Co. v Mongolia, Order on Interim Measures* (UNCITRAL, 2 September 2008) [36].

37 Holtzmann et al (n 24).

38 See [2.11], [5.1].

39 See [5.30].

40 See [5.31].

41 See [8.31]–[8.36]; Alan Redfern and Sam O'Leary, 'Why It Is Time for International Arbitration to Embrace Security for Costs' (2016) 32 *Arbitration International* 397.

42 See [8.27], [8.36].

43 *South American Silver Ltd (Bermudas) v Bolivia* (PCA Case no 2013–15), Procedural Order No 10 (11 January 2016) [55].

44 Holtzmann et al. (n 24) 171.

45 Adrian Fourie, 'Unionmatex v Turkmenistan: The Emerging Jurisprudence of Security for Costs in Investor-State Arbitration' (2020) 37(5) *Journal of International Arbitration* 649, 652.

46 See [6.24].

47 See [6.30]–[6.40].

ICSID

10.25. ICSID tribunals have traditionally considered five elements in determining applications for interim measures:

(1) The tribunal must have *prima facie* jurisdiction;
(2) There must be a *prima facie* basis to the claim;
(3) The measures must be necessary to protect the applicant's rights (or protect the status quo and avoid aggravating the dispute);
(4) The measures must be urgent;
(5) The measures must be proportional or necessary in the circumstances.[48]

10.26. To order security for costs in the 2020 decision of *Unionmatex v Turkmenistan*,[49] the tribunal required only that the state (1) specify a right to be preserved, (2) outline the measures necessary to protect the right, and (3) demonstrate circumstances that move the tribunal to order the measure. Jurisdiction was not an issue and urgency was not an issue as the arbitration was at an early stage.[50]

10.27. In *Kazmin v Latvia*, the tribunal considered necessity, urgency, exceptional circumstances, and proportionality as the matters justifying provisional measures.[51]

10.28. A majority of the tribunal in *Unionmatex* found that it was practically impossible for the state to enforce a costs order because the investor was insolvent and was funded by a third party funder under an agreement that expressly absolved the funder of liability for an adverse costs order.[52] The tribunal were prepared to look at all of the circumstances, with the majority finding that the arbitration would not be stifled by granting security because the investor would be able to obtain a bank guarantee.[53] It was on this last point that the dissenting arbitrator disagreed.[54]

10.29. The majority held that a party's impecuniosity and reliance on third party funding were each, in and of itself, not enough to warrant security.[55] They also held, contrary to the dissenter,[56] that the tribunal should ignore the allegation that the state had caused the investor's impecuniosity.[57]

10.30. *Unionmatex* was decided before the introduction of rule 53 of the ICSID Arbitration Rules, but the tribunal were referred to it in submissions.[58] Their approach was consistent with that rule and with the multifactorial, total circumstances approach where impecuniosity[59] and third party funding[60] are insufficient on their own to attract an order,

48 Sam Luttrell, 'ICSID Provisional Measures "In the Round"' (2015) (31) *Arbitration International* 393, 397.
49 *Unionmatex* (n 3).
50 Fourie (n 35).
51 *Kazmin v Latvia* (n 6) [28], [29], [31], [61].
52 *Unionmatex* (n 3) [54]–[63].
53 Ibid [65].
54 Ibid [79]–[83].
55 Ibid [54]–[55].
56 Ibid [77].
57 Ibid [66], *cf* the statement at [55] that impecuniosity alone is insufficient because the investor may be able to prove on the merits that the state caused that condition.
58 Fourie (n 35) 661.
59 See [5.56].
60 See [5.23].

the application is considered without predisposition, with fairness as the touchstone and where security is not ordered if it would stifle the claim.[61] Before engaging, or as part of, the stifling principle, the claimant must show that it is unable to raise funds from any other source including lenders, third party funders, shareholders or investors, or even directors, and not merely that they are unwilling to provide funds.[62]

10.31. *Kazmin v Latvia* took a similar approach, saying that the claimant's repeated denials of impecuniosity indicated it would not be difficult for him to obtain a bank guarantee at reasonable cost, and that he would not be denied access to justice.[63]

Exceptional circumstances

10.32. Exceptional circumstances have been required in most, if not all, of IAA decisions on security for costs. Situations sufficiently exceptional to justify ordering security were:

(1) *RSM v St Lucia*, where the investor had consistently disregarded costs orders, lacked assets, and relied on third party funding;[64]
(2) *Amas v Venezuela*, where the investor's third party funder was not obliged to pay an adverse costs order;[65]
(3) *Unionmatex*, where the investor was insolvent, was able to raise a guarantee, and its third party funder was not obliged by the terms of its agreement to pay an adverse costs order; and
(4) *Kazmin v Latvia*, where the investor had not paid previous counsel, had engaged in business conduct the subject of criminal investigations, had used creative ways to avoid paying debts, and had diverted assets from creditors. These later facts gave the tribunal serious doubts that the investor would comply with an adverse costs order.[66]

10.33. It is noteworthy that IAA tribunals do not appear to consider the claimant's being a natural person as an additional barrier to security for costs, as does the common law,[67] with the investors in *Amas v Venezuela* and *Kazmin v Latvia* both being natural persons. Otherwise, the modern approach of IAA tribunals is similar to the common law's multifactorial, total circumstances approach, including in the effective imposition of an evidential burden on the investor when the state has established a *prima facie* case.[68]

10.34. Historical reasons for requiring exceptional circumstances set out at [10.2] may be seen no longer to support that high threshold. IAA has become more commercial between investor and state than its state-to-state origins;[69] the public international law elements of IAA, where they exist, can be a factor taken into account in a particular arbitration rather than a blanket increase in the threshold;[70] states, by definition, do not act unilaterally in

61 See [1.13], [2.11], (n 17).
62 See [5.58].
63 (n 6) [61].
64 Sim (n 2) 438 [2.4.1.12].
65 Fourie (n 35) 654.
66 (n 6) [59].
67 See [5.6].
68 *Kazmin v Latvia* (n 6) [61].
69 Sim (n 2) 432.
70 See [5.62].

negotiating treaties and are limited by consensus; costs-shifting is becoming more common in IAA[71] and is the default position in UNCITRAL arbitrations;[72] maintaining access to justice in individual cases can be ensured by application of the stifling principle;[73] and requiring exceptional circumstances because interim measures are exceptional is circular and self-fulfilling (or -defeating) reasoning, nor is it supported by the data. The number of publicly available decisions on provisional measures has steadily grown from one in 2001 to a high of 18 in 2016 and seven and eight in 2021 and 2022 respectively.[74]

10.35. A state's assumption of the risk of dealing with a shell corporate investor is not a sound ground to require exceptional circumstances before granting security. Even where states create that risk by insisting on a local corporate entity as the investor, they are entitled to admit the investor on the expectation that it is appropriately funded to complete the investment by a parent, affiliate, or others such as partners standing behind it. The investor in that case is effectively a nominal claimant and the multifactorial, total circumstances approach would require those behind a nominal claimant to fund an arbitration, including being responsible for providing security for the state's costs.[75]

10.36. An animating but unspoken sentiment underlying the requirement of exceptional circumstances before granting security for costs may be the perceived disparity between the resources of the state and the investor. This concern could be allayed without requiring exceptional circumstances by adopting the multifactorial approach of acknowledging any imbalance in the power or finances of the parties but only taking it into account in the exercise of the discretion if it appears that the application is being brought to stifle the claim rather than to protect the state's interests.[76]

10.37. One difference between applications in IAA from those in ICA is that in the latter, the public importance of the claim or an issue would rarely be a relevant factor given that many ICA awards are not published and do not have precedential effect.[77] There could well be an important principle of public international law in an IAA that would justify refusal of security if ordering security would prevent a ruling on the issue.[78]

10.38. The factors discussed in Chapter 5 would be relevant to security for costs in IAA, and others might be, whether under rule 53, UNCITRAL Rules, the multifactorial approach, or otherwise:

- The length of time the investor has been active in the state;
- The investor's type and level of activity;
- Whether the investment was negotiated at ministerial level or was admitted administratively through the normal regulatory process;
- Whether the investment is regulated by a separate investment agreement or simply the usual regulations;
- The amount of taxes paid by the investor to the state;

71 Sim (n 2) 459.
72 *UNCITRAL Rules* Article 42(1).
73 See [10.10].
74 David Goldberg, Yarik Kryvoi and Ivan Philippov, *Provisional Measures in Investor-State Arbitration* (BICL/White & Case, 2023) 4 Chart 1.
75 See [5.11].
76 See [5.57].
77 See [5.63].
78 See [5.62].

- The incentives and allowances given to the investor by the state;
- The investment's contribution to the economy or public interest of the state;
- The profits made by the investor from the investment;
- The proportion of profits the investor has repatriated or reinvested; and
- The future of the investment.

10.39. These and other matters go to the fairness or justice of an order, or its proportionality or the balance of convenience, and to the state's ability to protect itself against unmeritorious claims.

Quantum, form, orders, and costs

10.40. The principles guiding assessment of quantum, form, and orders for security should be similar to those in ICA.[79] In *Kazmin v Latvia*, the tribunal based the quantum of security on the median average of respondents' costs claimed in other arbitrations,[80] rather than on an estimate of the costs incurred and to be incurred in the instant arbitration.[81] Costs notionally incurred at the date of the application were included in the amount of security by virtue of the tribunal's assessment on the basis of respondents' total costs. They made no comment on Latvia's inclusion of costs incurred in the amount of security.[82] No discount was made for contingencies.[83]

10.41. Security should be in a form least burdensome to the providing party. In *Kazmin v Latvia* this was an irrevocable guarantee from a first-class international bank.[84]

10.42. Costs of applications might be dealt with as in ICA[85] although IAA tribunals tend to be reluctant to make any costs awards before the end of proceedings.[86] Costs orders have been made in favour of the winning party where the request was granted in full,[87] including in *Kazmin v Latvia*.[88]

79 See chapter 6.

80 (n 6) [65], citing M. Hodgson and A. Campbell, 'Damages and Costs in Investment Treaty Arbitration' *Global Arbitration Review Online News*, 14 December 2017, pp. 2 et seq. (Table 1).

81 *Cf* [6.4].

82 See [6.26].

83 *Cf* [6.25].

84 (n 6) [66].

85 See [6.13]–[6.16].

86 Goldberg, Kryvoi and Philippov (n 64) 14–15.

87 *SL Mining Limited v Republic of Sierra Leone*, ICC Case No. 24708/TO, Order of the Emergency Arbitrator, 8 September 2019, [124]–[125]; *Kazmin v Latvia* (n 6) [68].

88 (n 6) [68].

INDEX

Abuse of process
prevention of as basis of security 2.12, 2.13, 2.3
Access to justice
cf access to the tribunal 9.21
bilateral 2.46
limitations on 2.14, 2.46
maintaining 2.46
public interest in 2.14
security for costs to enhance 9.34
stifling principle 2.47
tension with finality 2.14–2.17
American costs rule
bear own costs 2.4
history and purpose 2.5
Appeal in arbitration
usually none 2.16, 5.33
Applications for security for costs
costs of 6.13–6.16
determining *see* Orders
making and responding to 6.1–6.10
not a mini trial 5.31
promptly made 6.1
Arbitration agreements
consent marginalised 7.5
pre-dispute agrements the norm 7.5
Arbitration's expansionism 7.4
Arbitrator appointment
constraints on 8.22
arguments against security for costs
English idiosyncrasy 8.43
creditors, unfair to 8.73
denies procedural fairness 8.26–8.37
inappropriate to ICC arbitration 8.44–8.51
inhibits trade 8.39
nature of arbitration, contrary to 8.38–8.51
party autonomy, contrary to 8.2–8.25
party consent, contrary to 7.1–7.8
prejudges substantive merits 8.30–8.36
respondent assumed the risk 7.9–7.46
summarised 1.14
transnationalisation, contrary to 8.40–8.42
tribunals' power to stay arbitration 8.59–8.71
unnecessary 8.52–8.38
aristotle
equal, not identical, treatment 9.25
assumption of risk
as a factor 5.53–5.54
assumes unlikely knowledge 7.21
presents binary choice 7.45–7.46
consent to transaction vs risk 7.19–7.20
contrary to good faith 7.29
freedom of choice 7.32–7.33
freedom of contract 7.14–7.18
ICC approach to 4.10
ignores subtleties 7.44
international trade risks 7.30–7.31
involves non-sequitur 7.22–7.26
proposition and responses 7.9–7.46
third party funding and 7.27–7.28
undermines security for costs 7.42–7.43
unevenly applied 7.40–7.41
awards, review of
improper merits review 8.59
public policy ground 8.59

Burden of proof
evidential burden 3.10, 4.14, 5.57, 6.7, 6.10
on applicant for security 3.10

Cautio judicatum solvi
disappearance in France 2.1
Clausula rebus sic stantibus
as basis of facility 2.12, 2.24–2.36
Competitive institutionalisation 7.4
consequences of security
Applications and orders 2.41–2.45
Coppée–Lavalin v Ken–Ren
true ruling 4.27–4.35
UK arbitration survived 8.49
corporate responsibility
changes to 7.11

corporations
emergence 2.9
security as protection against 2.9
cost and delay
security for costs to control 9.17–9.20
costs
American rule 2.5
applications for security, of 6.13–6.16
courts' ability to award 2.2
enforcement of awards 9.6
English rule 2.5
general rule 6.21
interest on costs 6.21
internal costs 6.21
need for proportionality 9.18
pre-commencement costs 6.21
reason for non-payment 9.9
tribunals' concern for 9.18 n 40
costs follow the event
meaning 2.5
costs shifting
late development 4.9
meaning 2.5
sine qua non of security for costs 8.74
Creditor protection
alternative juridical basis of security 2.18–2.23
cross-undertakings
rare 6.17

Departmental Advisory Committee
report on Arbitration Bill 4.23, 4.37–4.29
discretion to grant security
instinctive synthesis 2.38
multifactorial 1.11, 1.13, 2.11, 2.49, 3.18, 4.11, 4.14, 7.24, 9.1, 9.43, 10.10, 10.17, 10.21, 10.30, 10.33, 10.35–10.38
nature 2.37
due process paranoia
effect 9.37
meaning 8.27
unwarranted 8.27, 8.36

enforcement of awards
history and relevance 2.7
enforcement issues
is security unnecessary? 8.52–8.58
tribunals' power to stay arbitration 8.59–8.71
English costs rule
purpose 2.5
equal treatment
liability for costs and damages 9.31
Model Law Art 17G 9.31
not identical treatment 9.24–9.31
security for costs to enhance 9.24–9.31
ethics
difficulty of enforcement 9.15
guerilla tactics *see* Guerilla tactics
standards 9.15
European Convention for the Protection of Human Rights and Fundamental Freedoms
applies to both parties 2.48
French approach 8.8
Evolution of security for costs
1750, 1755, 1786 2.6
decline in Europe 2.1
England 2.2
English response to European security 2.7
residence abroad 2.6
Roman law 2.1
exceptional circumstances
doubted in Swiss arbitrations 4.16–4.19
for natural persons 2.49
fraudulent, abusive, extravagant claim 4.13
fundamental financial deterioration 4.13
ICC approach 4.2, 4.8–4.14
more than financial weakness 4.13
not required in LCIA arbitrations 4.45
third party funding 4.13
unpaid costs *see*
expeditious determination
compared to security for costs 8.68

factors in discretion
ability and willingness to pay costs 5.1
abuse of process etc 5.34–5.38
against security 5.47–5.68
agreement as to costs 5.26
categories - financial, liability, conduct and fairness 5.2
claimant in fact respondent 5.47–5.48
condition of indulgence 5.46
conduct factors 5.39–5.46
corporate claimant 5.9
corporate liquidation 5.10
counterclaim 5.13–5.17
delay 5.41–5.45
dissipation of assets 5.21–5.22
enforcement difficulties 5.24
fairness 5.1
financial factors 5.5–5.24
impecuniosity 5.6
intrinsic persuasiveness of 2.38
liability factors 5.25–5.38
means to pay 5.8
mixed natural and corporate claimants 5.66
no costs shifting 5.27–5.28
nominal claimant 5.11
non-compliance with orders 5.20
not closed 5.1

offers or admissions 5.64
oppression 5.55–5.61
outstanding costs or debts 5.19
poor substantive merits 5.29–5.33
prejudice from delay 5.41–5.45
public importance 5.62–5.63
quantum of costs 5.12
residence abroad 5.5
respondent assumed the risk 5.53–5.54
respondent caused claimant's impecuniosity 5.49–5.22
respondent has security 5.67
small vs large company 5.61
special relationship 5.65
subject to source of power 5.3
third party funding 5.23
unclean hands 5.68
unreasonable conduct 5.39–5.40
weight of factors 2.38
fairness
touchstone of security 2.11
creditors, to 8.73
finality
in arbitration 2.16
principle 2.14–2.17
tension with access to justice 2.14
form of security
after the event insurance 6.40
all circumstances relevant 6.36
least disadvantageous form 6.33
onus on claimant to show adequacy 6.34
preserving from creditors 6.31
preserving from security registration legislation 6.32
undertaking from third party funder 6.30
usual forms 6.30
Freeman, R Edward
stakeholder model 7.17
Friedman, Milton
shareholder model 7.17
fundamental change in circumstances
assumption of risk basis 4.10
common deminator in ICC arbitrations 4.10
sole basis of *cautio* 2.1

Guerrilla tactics
security for costs to control 1.5, 9.15–9.16

Hague Conventions 1905,1954 4.18

ICC approach to security
assumption of the risk 4.2, 4.8–4.14
exceptional circumstances 4.2, 4.8–4.14
financial weakness insufficient 4.13
fundamental change 4.2, 4.8–4.14
more restrictive 1.8
substantial deterioration 4.2, 4.8–4.14
improper conduct *see* Guerilla tactics
institutions
reasons for choosing 8.47–8.48
International investment arbitration
access to justice 10.34
assumption of the risk 10.35
costs of applications for security 10.42
costs shifting 10.34
court rules, relevance of 10.15
exceptional circumstances, history of 10.2
exceptional circumstances, relevance of 10.32
factors 10.38
form of security 10.41
ICSID approach 10.9, 10.25
institutional rules 10.13
interim measures, increase of 10.34
international commercial arbitration, *cf* 10.37
juridical basis 10.6
natural person claimants 10.33
need for security 10.4
orders, form of 10.40
power to order security 10.7–10.15
public international law elements 10.34
quantum of security 10.40
stifling principle 10.34
UNCITRAL approach 10.12, 10.18
interim measures
liability for costs and damages 9.31
International commercial courts
effect on arbitration 7.4

Judicialisation of arbitration 8.42, 9.37–9.39
Juridical basis of security for costs
abuse of process, prevention of 2.3, 2.12–2.17
clausula rebus sic stantibus 2.24–2.36
creditor protection 2.18–2.23

LCIA tribunals
approach to security 4.40–4.53
exceptional circumstances not required 4.45
non-publication of decisions 4.40, 4.53
number of applications and orders 1.9, 4.40–4.45
legal profession
emergence of paid 2.2
legislation Annexure 1A
legitimacy of international commercial arbitration
threatened 7.11–7.13, 9.5, 9.45

merits of claim
neutral in discretion unless extreme 5.30
not a mini trial 5.31
preliminary evaluation of only 5.31

New York Convention
bedrock of arbitration 8.3
enforcement under 4.19
ineffective if no assets 9.2
party autonomy recognised 8.2

opportunity to present case
security for costs to enhance 9.32–9.33
Orders
cross-undertakings rare 6.17
form of 6.11–6.12
lump sum or staged 5.59–5.60
security for costs of enforcement 6.39
staged security 6.29

party autonomy
arguments based in 8.2–8.25
inner and outer limits 8.21–8.24
role of 8.1–8.4
summary 8.25
party consent
arguments based in 7.1 et seq
evolution of 7.4
marginalisation of 7.4
role of 7.4
poverty of claimant
insufficent alone as factor 2.8
power to order security
case management powers 3.9
institutional rules 3.8
lex arbitri 3.3
party agreement 3.2
court's inherent power 2.8
procedural fairness
equal treatment 8.26–8.29
Model Law requirements 8.33
prejudging substantive merits 8.30–8.37
security for costs to enhance 9.21–9.33
purpose of security for costs
funds available to pay costs 5.25
prevent abuse of process 2.12, 2.13, 2.3

quantum of security
broad brush estimate 6.19
discounting - settlement and vicissitudes 6.25
for costs of enforcement 6.39
including instiution and tribunal fees 6.32
just and reasonable 6.20
liability factors relevant 6.24
no discounting where staged 6.25
pre-commencement costs included 6.26–6.27
protection vs oppression 6.20

residence abroad
forbidden as basis of *cautio* 2.1
formerly determinative 2.6, 2.8, 8.54
insufficient alone in arbitration 2.11
Rules Annexure 1B

seats
reasons for choosing 8.49–8.50
security for costs
controversy over 1.6
definition 1.1
significance 1.3
settlement facilitation
parties' desire for assistance 9.40
standard of proof for security
balance of probabilities 3.12
low threshold 3.15
no established standard 3.11
past vs future events, estanlishment of 3.15
possible standards 3.11
pragmatic approach 3.16
prima facie plausibility 3.12
'reasonable possibility' of success 3.14
'reasonable probability' of harm 3.12
'satisfy' the tribunal 3.14
'some likelihood' of no risk 3.12
UNCITRAL Model Law 3.13
stay of arbitration
tribunals' power 8.59–8.71
stifling principle
all factors weighed 5.56
meaning and importance 2.47
no funding available 5.58
on balance of probabilities 5.58
operation of 7.24
staged security to avoid 5.59
summary disposition 9.10–9.14
Arbitration Bill 2023 (UK) 9.13
high threshold 9.13
'no real prospect of succeeding' 9.13
security for costs as less drastic form of 9.14
support growing for 9.13
Swiss approach
exceptional circumstances doubted 4.16–4.19
less exceptional circumstances 4.15–4.20

tests for security
exceptional, special and total circumstances 1.11
Treaty of Rome
article 6 2.1
tribunals
duty to ensure awards enforceable 9.3
power to order security for costs 3.1–3.9
power to stay arbitration 8.59

UK courts 1934–1997
  exceptional circumstances not required 4.26–4.36
  security in arbitration 4.21–4.36
UNCITRAL *Model Law*
  2006 amendment 1.2
  articles 17, 17A 3.3–3.7
  interim measures 3.3–3.7
  party autonomy recognised 8.4
unmeritorious claims
  security for costs to control 9.11–9.14
utility of security
  attractiveness and competitiveness 9.45–9.46
  control mechanism 9.10
  control mechanism - cost and delay 9.18–9.20
  control mechanism - improper conduct 9.15–9.16
  control mechanism - unmeritorius claims 9.11–9.14
  correct injustice 9.35–9.36
  counterbalance judicialisation 9.37–9.39
  enforcement 9.2–9.9
  enhance access to justice 9.34
  enhance equal treatment 9.24–9.31
  enhance opportunity to present case 9.32–9.33
  enhance procedural fairness 9.21–9.33
  facilitate settlement 9.40
  for instution of arbitration 9.41–9.47
  for parties 9.2–9.40
  harmonisation arbitration and litigation 9.47
  jurisprudence and guidance 9.42–9.43
  reduce transaction costs 9.47
  uniformity 9.44

For Product Safety Concerns and Information please contact our EU
representative GPSR@taylorandfrancis.com
Taylor & Francis Verlag GmbH, Kaufingerstraße 24, 80331 München, Germany

www.ingramcontent.com/pod-product-compliance
Lightning Source LLC
LaVergne TN
LVHW082342011026
849160LV00025B/1589
* 9 7 8 1 0 3 2 7 6 6 8 8 1 *